T.S. ELIOT'S
INTELLECTUAL DEVELOPMENT
1922-1939

T.S. ELIOT'S
INTELLECTUAL DEVELOPMENT
1922-1939

JOHN D. MARGOLIS

THE UNIVERSITY OF CHICAGO PRESS
CHICAGO AND LONDON

The University of Chicago Press, Chicago 60637
The University of Chicago Press, Ltd., London
© 1972 by The University of Chicago

International Standard Book Number: 0-226-50518-9
Library of Congress Catalog Card Number: 71-171071

The epigraph, from "East Coker," is reprinted
from *Four Quartets,* copyright 1943 by T. S.
Eliot, by permission of Harcourt Brace Jovanovich,
Inc., and Faber and Faber, Ltd.

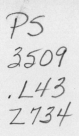

To My Mother and Father

So here I am, in the middle way, having had twenty years—
Twenty years largely wasted, the years of
   l'entre deux guerres—
Trying to learn to use words, and every attempt
Is a wholly new start, and a different kind of failure
Because one has only learnt to get the better of words
For the thing one no longer has to say, or the way in which
One is no longer disposed to say it. And so each venture
Is a new beginning, a raid on the inarticulate
With shabby equipment always deteriorating
In the general mess of imprecision of feeling,
Undisciplined squads of emotion. And what there is to
   conquer
By strength and submission, has already been discovered
Once or twice, or several times, by men whom one cannot
   hope
To emulate—but there is no competition—
There is only the fight to recover what has been lost
And found and lost again and again: and now, under
   conditions
That seem unpropitious. But perhaps neither gain nor loss.
For us, there is only the trying. The rest is not our business.

"EAST COKER," V

CONTENTS

PREFACE

As he himself well understood, T. S. Eliot's literary criticism was largely a consequence of his creative activity. "Both in my general affirmations about poetry and in writing about authors who had influenced me," he once said, "I was implicitly defending the sort of poetry that I and my friends wrote."[1] In his negative judgments on other writers he pointed to qualities he himself wished to avoid, and in his appreciative remarks he called attention to achievements that he doubtless hoped would be noticed by later critics of his own works. It is richly significant, then, that in memorializing the careers of three famous writers, his contemporaries, Eliot should have commented especially on a characteristic they and he shared in common: a capacity for intellectual and artistic development.

In a 1918 essay on Henry James, he remarked that "James's greatness is apparent both in his capacity for development as an artist and his capacity for keeping his mind alive to the changes in the world. . . ."[2] Twenty-two years later, in a memorial lecture on Yeats, Eliot again pointed approvingly to the capacity for development as an important quality in a great writer: "To have accomplished what Yeats did in the middle and later years is a great and permanent example—which poets-to-come should study with reverence—of what I have called Character of the Artist: a kind of moral, as well as intellectual, excellence." Eliot himself was fifty-two at the time, and he now spoke

1. "To Criticize the Critic," in *To Criticize the Critic and Other Writings* (New York: Farrar, Straus and Giroux, 1965), p. 16. Some twenty years before he remarked similarly that "the poet, at the back of his mind, if not as his ostensible purpose, is always trying to defend the kind of poetry he is writing, or to formulate the kind that he wants to write" ("The Music of Poetry," in *On Poetry and Poets* [New York: Farrar, Straus and Cudahy, 1957], p. 17).
2. "The Hawthorne Aspect," *Little Review*, August 1918, p. 52.

with authority in describing the significance of those years:

It is difficult and unwise to generalize about ways of composition —so many men, so many ways—but it is my experience that towards middle age a man has three choices: to stop writing altogether, to repeat himself with perhaps an increasing skill of virtuosity, or by taking thought to adapt himself to middle age and find a different way of working. . . . Most men either cling to the experiences of youth, so that their writing becomes an insincere mimicry of their earlier work, or they leave their passion behind, and write only from the head, with a hollow and wasted virtuosity. There is another and even worse temptation: that of becoming dignified, of becoming public figures with only a public existence—coat-racks hung with decorations and distinctions, doing, saying, and even thinking and feeling only what they believe the public expects of them.

"But in fact," Eliot said, "very few poets have shown this capacity of adaptation to the years. It requires, indeed, an exceptional honesty and courage to face the change."[3] Yeats, of course, possessed that honesty and courage; so too, Eliot felt, did Joyce.

In his remarks on Joyce, written nine years later, Eliot reaffirmed his conviction that "one of the greatest capacities of genius is the power of development." And he noted a regrettable tendency in many readers to see that gradual and continuous *development* as an abrupt and discontinuous *change*. "While an artist is still living and working," he said, "we see his development rather as change." But when the author is dead and his work, complete, his career can be seen more nearly for what it was. Joyce's was a case in point:

Joyce's writings form a whole; we can neither reject the early work as stages, of no intrinsic interest, of his progress towards the latter, nor reject the later work as the outcome of decline. As

3. "Yeats," in *On Poetry and Poets,* pp. 301, 297, 301–2.

with Shakespeare, his later work must be understood through the earlier, and the first through the last; it is the whole journey, not any one stage of it, that assures him his place among the great.[4]

While Eliot himself was still living and working, his career—like Joyce's—seemed to many people to be one of frequent changes. On closer scrutiny, however, one discovers development, rather than change; and as Eliot appreciatively remarked on "development" in the careers of James, Yeats, and Joyce, so he would surely have us note it in his own.

This book explores the years of Eliot's most profound intellectual development. Through an examination of his prose, it endeavors to trace that development, to suggest its causes, and to insist, in Eliot's terms, that it was development, not change.

II

There is hardly need for a scholarly study to demonstrate that Eliot underwent several major conversions during the half-century of his literary career. Few readers need be reminded that he announced one of them in 1928, when he described his attitudes as those of an "anglo-catholic in religion." Around the same time, another conversion—Eliot spoke of it as a "mutation"—became apparent as his critical interests turned from largely literary to social, political, and religious matters. Yet another major redirection of his efforts occurred in the 1930s as he began trying his hand at poetic drama as well as poems; a decade later nearly all his creative energies went into the writing of plays.

Though the fact of these conversions is now a commonplace in discussions of Eliot, few critics have inquired as to why his career unfolded as it did; fewer still have been able to generate much sympathy for its course. Even so informed a critic as Herbert Howarth could call Eliot's

4. In *James Joyce: Sa Vie, Son Œuvre, Son Rayonnement,* ed. Bernard Gheerbrant (Paris: La Hune, 1949), n. pag.

religious writing—an enterprise in which he was engaged for more than three decades—his "besetting temptation."[5] Missing in his later career what they see as the distinctive greatness of his earlier work, some readers surmise that his religious conversion and the subsequent redirection of his literary efforts represent a radical discontinuity in his work —even, perhaps, a premature senescence. As early as 1917, Eliot curiously anticipated this response to his development in some remarks on Ezra Pound.

When a poet alters or develops, many of his admirers are sure to drop off. Any poet, if he is to survive as a writer beyond his twenty-fifth year, must alter; he must seek new literary influences; he will have different emotions to express. This is disconcerting to that public which likes a poet to spin his whole work out of the feelings of his youth; which likes to be able to open a new volume of his poems with the assurance that they will be able to approach it exactly as they approached the preceding.[6]

As they did during his career, so today some of Eliot's readers have "dropped off" during their explorations of his career. For many such readers, the unwillingness to follow Eliot appreciatively to the end has been a result of informed critical judgment; there can be little quarrel with them. Other readers, however, have simply been unable to discern the vital connections between his early and later poetry, between his poems and his plays, between his literary "modernism" and his religious traditionalism, and between his criticisms of literature and of society. To this second group of readers, Eliot's career has seemed largely without unity; and, twentieth-century attitudes and tastes being what they are, these readers have generally studied his early work eagerly while largely ignoring the apparently inexplicable departures of his later career.

5. "T. S. Eliot's *Criterion:* The Editor and His Contributors," *Comparative Literature* 11 (1959), 98.

6. *Ezra Pound: His Metric and Poetry* (New York: Knopf, 1917), p. 23.

There is double reason to regret such a situation. First, the popular conception of Eliot has been distorted as a consequence of many readers'—and especially students'—knowing only his early work. But no less regrettable is the fact that those who have failed to follow Eliot beyond his work of the mid-1920s have missed one of the distinctive rewards of an extended study of his career: the understanding of that quality that Eliot found so notable in the careers of his contemporaries, the writer's continuous effort of development.

III

To an extent, Eliot himself is responsible for the general incomprehension of his intellectual development. Having so successfully urged in his early essays the purification of literary study, he contributed to the modern suspicion of criticism that relates a writer's work to his life and considers his excursions into fields other than literature. Though they frequently make use of his literary essays, critics have generally concentrated their attention on his poems and plays. Those works, of course, justify Eliot's claim on our interest; but a narrow concentration on them is inadequate in illuminating the development of Eliot's ideas. Eliot's poetic product was relatively slight in volume, and the handful of poems for which he is best known were published over a period of nearly three decades. However, in the years that elapsed between the appearances of such works Eliot was experiencing significant adjustments in his interests and attitudes. The two volumes of collected poems and plays are not the collected *works* of Eliot; his prose—and not only his properly literary prose, at that—constitutes a major part of his labor as a man of letters. If, then, on the evidence of merely a few of his more famous poems and plays, Eliot's development appears to have been a matter of sudden and erratic change, the essays—often, to be sure, of ephemeral intrinsic interest—suggest the gradual, almost inevitable, unfolding of his attitudes and interests.

Among the most important of Eliot's nonpoetic works is the eighteen-volume file of the *Criterion,* the literary review he edited from 1922 until 1939. The disciplined framework of regular periodical publication offered him a way to approach systematically issues important to him. In his selection of works that would appear there; in his editorial direction of symposia on such issues as classicism and romanticism, the Action Française, and the New Humanism; and not least of all in his own contributions and his regular "Commentaries," Eliot left a valuable chronicle of the evolution of his interests.

There is, besides, the considerable lode of fugitive writings that Eliot published throughout his career and that have yet to receive the serious attention they deserve. Like the file of the *Criterion,* these hundreds of periodical essays, book reviews, contributions to symposia, prefaces and introductions, published letters, and texts of radio talks provide abundant evidence of his continuous intellectual development. While the poetic works appeared infrequently, hardly a month passed in which Eliot did not publish some essay or review. The volume of such publication is apparent to anyone who looks beyond my footnotes to Donald Gallup's bibliography; since much of this material remains difficult of access, I have quoted from it generously here. It may be—though I hope not—that my study bears out W. H. Auden's observation, "In general, when reading a scholarly critic, one profits more from his quotations than from his comments."[7]

IV

It is perhaps well at the outset to make clear what this study does not attempt. First, this is not a study of Eliot's

7. "Prologue," in *The Dyer's Hand and Other Essays* (New York: Random House, 1962), p. 9.

art, nor even of his theories of art. Though his artistic development and his intellectual development were hardly distinct, I have chosen to focus on the latter since the former has already been well treated by others. I am concerned here with the ideas that lay behind his literary career rather than the art that transmuted those ideas into poetry.

Just as this is not a study of Eliot's art, so it is not a full, critical analysis of his ideas on such matters as education, politics, religion—or literature. Though he had many penetrating observations on these topics, he was not a systematic thinker with comprehensive theories.[8] His remarks —and especially those on literature—are often more valuable for the light they cast on Eliot's own thinking at the time than for the contribution they make to the fields they concern. It is largely in that spirit that I approach them.

Nor is this a biography of Eliot, except in the sense that it is a study of what is surely a central part of any biography: the evolution of his interests and ideas. Materials for a biography are sketchy, at best. The forthcoming edition of his letters by Mrs. T. S. Eliot will offer valuable material for our fuller understanding of his life. Currently, however, biographical discussion of Eliot tends rapidly towards gossip or speculation, both of which I have endeavored to avoid. My treatment here of Eliot's relations with various of his contemporaries is offered less as a contribution to our understanding of his life-story than as an attempt to present in terms of personal relationships various stages of his intellectual development.

I recognize that a topical study of Eliot's intellectual development might seem fully as useful as the chronological

8. Eliot made this point in a letter to Paul Elmer More: "I am not a systematic thinker, if indeed I am a thinker at all. I depend upon intuitions and perceptions; and although I may have some skill in the barren game of controversy, [I] have little capacity for sustained, exact, and closely knit argument and reasoning" (20 June 1934, Princeton University Library).

approach I have adopted here. I have preferred the latter not only because I believe that Eliot's interests—literary, religious, political, and others—are inextricably connected one to another but also because I want to stress their continuous evolution. Much of the misunderstanding of his ideas has been caused by the wrenching of isolated statements from their contexts—both rhetorical and chronological. "I find myself constantly irritated," he said in 1961, "by having my words, perhaps written thirty or forty years ago, quoted as if I had uttered them yesterday. . . . When I publish a collection of essays, or whenever I allow an essay to be republished elsewhere, I make a point of indicating the original date of publication, as a reminder to the reader of the distance of time that separates the author when he wrote it from the author as he is today."[9] As it surveys Eliot's ideas over a period of some seventeen years, this study attempts to take account of that distance of time.

Finally, a word about the chronological limits I have imposed upon this study. Though the first chapter concerns Eliot's activities prior to 1922, and though throughout the book I draw, where relevant, on material from the forties, fifties and sixties, I concentrate on the years 1922–1939. I might, of course, have written an intellectual biography of Eliot's entire life. It would have been at least twice as long a book—though not, I think, necessarily twice as useful. But since my interest is in his development, I have chosen to dwell on the years in which that development is most pronounced.

The year 1922 is a convenient one at which to begin: it was the year in which his early career was crowned with the publication of *The Waste Land* and in which his middle phase—the period that Eliot spoke of as "middle age"— began with his editorship of the *Criterion*. Eliot then was

9. "To Criticize the Critic," p. 14. See also Eliot's remarks in his introduction to *Literary Essays of Ezra Pound* (London: Faber and Faber, 1954), p. xi.

thirty-four years old. During the following several years he experienced the most important (and perhaps the least understood) of his conversions, that to Anglo-Catholicism. Were this merely a study of his religious development, it might well have concluded with that famous 1928 announcement. But I am anxious to insist that the conversion to Anglo-Catholicism was not so much an arrival at a resting place as an event from which other important conversions radiated. To stop at 1928 would be to ignore the important way in which his new faith affected him as a man of letters.

The year 1939—his fifty-first—was one of unusual fruitfulness for him; it offers an ideal point at which to close. By then the most dramatic period of Eliot's development had come to an end. With the termination of the *Criterion* in January of that year he ended his editorship of one of the most distinguished literary periodicals of the century; with the production of *The Family Reunion* in March he demonstrated his dedication to revitalizing a popular, English verse-drama as part of his Christian witness; with the publication in October of his first book-length study of Christian sociology, *The Idea of a Christian Society,* he offered his first comprehensive statement of the plight of contemporary civilization and the hope of Christian renewal; and with the death of Yeats that year, he became indisputably the greatest living English poet.

ACKNOWLEDGMENTS

It is a pleasure to acknowledge the many kindnesses that have contributed to the making of this book.

I began this study some years ago as a dissertation for Princeton University. Since the inception of the project I have benefited from the advice and encouragement not only of my Princeton advisers, A. Walton Litz and Willard Thorp, but also of two Eliot scholars from other universities, Donald Gallup of Yale University and Herbert Howarth of the University of Pennsylvania. It is a particular source of joy that I now think of each of them primarily as a friend.

My colleagues at Northwestern have been especially generous in their willingness to read and criticize my manuscript. I especially want to thank Wallace Douglas, Gerald Graff, Christopher Herbert, and Samuel Hynes for their help.

Richard Lehan, my former colleague at the University of California, Los Angeles, extended not only his advice but also the hospitality of his family during the summer of 1970 when I returned to UCLA to complete my work on the book. The kindness of the Lehans and my other friends in Los Angeles helped make that summer no less pleasant than it was productive.

Northwestern University and the University of California at Los Angeles both made available funds to support my work on this study. Tara English and Randy Warniers typed various drafts of the manuscript. Barry Qualls and Tony Wieczorek helped in proofreading. I am, of course, grateful to all of them for their assistance.

Finally, without the generous permission of Mrs. T. S. Eliot I would have been unable to use the previously unpublished letters by her late husband that appear in this book. 25 June 1971

T. S. ELIOT'S

INTELLECTUAL DEVELOPMENT

1922-1939

1916-1922

I

"TO DISTURB AND ALARM THE PUBLIC"

The plaque in the parish church at East Coker where his ashes are buried reads "Thomas Stearns Eliot, Poet"; and of course it is as a poet that one first thinks of him. But during his remarkably various career he was also a critic, playwright, social commentator, churchman, editor, publisher, even banker. And it is significant that after completing his formal graduate study and settling in London, it was as a schoolteacher that he first eked out a living while revising the poetry that would soon bring him fame. Eliot's five terms as a schoolmaster were apparently not very pleasant; he preferred unemployment to continuing at Highgate School and was out of work for several months before finding a job in the Colonial and Foreign Department of Lloyds Bank. Unpleasant though it may have been, however, Eliot's first job as a schoolteacher suggests an impulse that from the beginning directed his career.

Even after he abandoned the classroom, Eliot remained an educator. Much of his writing after his religious conversion—especially in essays and plays—was inspired by his calling, to teach an increasingly secularized world the moral and religious values he felt it had forgotten. Similarly, the voice of Eliot the teacher was evident in the book reviewing and extension lecturing he undertook early on to supplement his meager income from the bank. In many of those earliest publications one discerns the voice of a self-assured young writer using his critical forum as a teacher might a classroom. He seems often to have written with the hope of creating an audience for the kind of poetry he was himself composing and a world in which the kind of civilization he valued might flourish. Both in the certainty of

3

principle and the pedagogical tone which he brought to many of those essays, one recognizes the impact of the most influential of Eliot's own teachers: his Harvard professor, Irving Babbitt.

Few modern literary figures have been so open to the influence of other men as was Eliot; fewer still have been able to assimilate and transform those influences so thoroughly. The literary influences on Eliot's early verse have been much rehearsed; but the impact of Babbitt upon his thought remains largely unexplored.[1] "The magnitude of the debt some of us owe to him should be more obvious to posterity than to our contemporaries," Eliot said of Babbitt in 1941.[2] Clearly the debt was immense, and it is proper to recognize it at the outset. As Babbitt's student Eliot acquired a set of attitudes and concerns—even, perhaps, a rhetoric—that informed him throughout his career.

As with most significant student-teacher relationships, Eliot's with Babbitt began in the classroom, but was not limited to it. When Eliot was working for his master's degree in English literature at Harvard during 1909–10, Babbitt did not yet enjoy his later fame; his French 17, "Literary Criticism in France with Special Reference to the Nineteenth Century," had but a sparse enrollment.[3] As a student in that seminar, Eliot deepened his already considerable knowledge of the French. But the course with Babbitt was still more important for the opportunity it afforded Eliot to study under one of Harvard's most incisive critics of modern life and thought. Babbitt was a man of definite preferences—occasionally, in fact, of narrow

1. A notable exception is Herbert Howarth's discussion in *Notes on Some Figures behind T. S. Eliot* (Boston: Houghton Mifflin, 1964), pp. 127–35. Howarth's book is an essential source for an understanding of Eliot's intellectual development.

2. In *Irving Babbitt: Man and Teacher*, ed. Frederick Manchester and Odell Shepard (New York: Putnam's, 1941), p. 104.

3. The content of this seminar almost certainly found its way into Babbitt's *Masters of Modern French Criticism*, published in 1912.

dogmatism. But Eliot was apparently won over by the authority of Babbitt's pronouncements; he quickly embraced his teacher's attitudes as his own. "Babbitt had been my teacher," he said in 1946. "And by 'teacher' I do not mean merely a tutor, or a man whose lectures I attended, but a man who directed my interests, at a particular moment, in such a way that the marks of that direction are still evident."[4]

I do not believe that any pupil who was ever deeply impressed by Babbitt, can ever speak of him with that mild tenderness one feels towards something one has outgrown or grown out of. If one has once had that relationship with Babbitt, he remains permanently an active influence; his ideas are permanently with one, as a measurement and test of one's own.

A slavish disciple of no man, Eliot would eventually quarrel with some of Babbitt's ideas, but it was always a lover's quarrel: "Even in the convictions one may feel, the views one may hold, that seem to contradict most important convictions of Babbitt's own, one is aware that he himself was very largely the cause of them."[5]

Perhaps the greatest of Babbitt's excellences was his exemplification of the excitement of the life of the mind. An acute, often iconoclastic, observer of modern culture, he ranged freely through contemporary philosophy and literature and zealously diagnosed their malaise. As a critic, he did not scruple to judge; as a teacher, he doubtless urged the same venturesomeness in his students. More given to diagnosis than prescription, Babbitt offered no ready-made philosophy; he was, as Eliot said, "too extreme an individualist to be a system-builder or the founder of a school." But implicit throughout his writing was a constellation of attitudes that obviously made its impression on the young Eliot. Looking back on Babbitt's career, Eliot remarked

4. "Ezra Pound," *Poetry* 68 (1946), 329.
5. In *Irving Babbitt: Man and Teacher*, p. 104.

that "the point at which Babbitt's ideas converged with
the greatest force was the subject of Education. . . ."[6] The
book most centrally concerned with that topic was, in fact,
his first, *Literature and the American College*. In that collection of essays, published in 1908, he presented themes
that he reasserted with remarkable (even tedious) consistency for the next twenty-five years. It provides a convenient exposition of Babbitt's thought.

In all American colleges, and especially in the Harvard
of President Eliot, Babbitt detected a bankruptcy of principles that he felt left education a parody of its proper self.
Lacking either intellectual discipline or an appreciation of
the authority of a cultural tradition, students lapsed into
"the pedantry of individualism."[7] The "intellectual and
moral impressionism" that Babbitt discerned throughout
popular culture had, he thought, infected the college as well
(99). "The firmness of the American's faith in the blessings
of education is equalled only by the vagueness of his ideas
as to the kind of education to which these blessings are
annexed" (2). Thus, as a corrective to the "democratic
inclusiveness of our modern sympathies," Babbitt proposed
"the aristocratic aloofness of the ancient humanist" (11).

Professing himself a member of this humanist tradition, Babbitt insisted upon the inadequacy of the current
"educational *laissez-faire*" and the necessity of reinstitut-
ing a rigorous, principled authoritarianism. "The function
of the college . . . should be to insist on the idea of quality,"
he said. "It should hold all the faster to its humane standards now that the world is threatened with a universal
impressionism" (81). Like Eliot later, Babbitt wrote that
he found those standards nowhere so clearly expressed as

6. "Commentary," *Criterion* 13 (1933), 118, 116.
7. *Literature and the American College: Essays in Defense of the
Humanities* (Boston: Houghton Mifflin, 1908), p. 94. Subsequent
references, inserted in the text, are to this edition.

in the classics. "Links in that unbroken chain of literary and intellectual tradition which extends from the ancient to the modern world," the classics, Babbitt said, appeal "to our higher reason and imagination—to those faculties which afford us an avenue of escape from ourselves, and enable us to become participants in the universal life" (166, 173). "The classical spirit feels itself consecrated to the service of a high, impersonal reason. Hence its sentiment of restraint and discipline, its sense of proportion and pervading law" (174).

Drawing on that classical spirit, Babbitt's humanism insisted upon the importance of reason, restraint, discipline, proportion, and law. The humanist, he said, "believes that the man of to-day, if he does not, like the man of the past, take on the yoke of a definite doctrine and discipline, must at least do inner obeisance to something higher than his ordinary self, whether he calls this something God, or, like the man of the Far East, calls it his higher self, or simply the Law." Eliot's entire career was, in a sense, built upon this humanist faith as he sought to discover "something higher than his ordinary self"—first, when his interests were primarily literary, in the "tradition"; ultimately, as his interests became religious, in Christian dogma. He shared Babbitt's conviction that "without this inner principle of restraint man can only oscillate violently between extreme opposites, like Rousseau" (60).

Even in his earliest writings, Babbitt had given Rousseau a central role in his plentifully stocked demonology. "The direct and demonstrable influence of Rousseau is . . . enormous," Babbitt wrote. "His influence so far transcends that of the mere man of letters as to put him almost on a level with the founders of religions" (36). "In the name of feeling Rousseau headed the most powerful insurrection the world has ever seen against every kind of authority" (184). As early as 1910, nine years before its publication, Babbitt was promising his "book to be entitled 'Rousseau and Romanticism' ";[8] it is little wonder that he could have been so certain of the title. Both the man and the movement were obsessions with him; in Rousseau he saw the source and in romanticism, the codification, of nearly everything he found diseased in modern thought: for example, the lack of discipline, the individualism, the emphasis on sensation, the infatuation with primitivism, and the glorification of spontaneity. No less than education, contemporary literature and criticism had, Babbitt thought, been corrupted by the influence of romanticism. To Rousseau's "warfare in the name of feeling against everything formal and traditional," he traced the "impressionism" of contemporary thought. "With the spread of impressionism," he wrote, "literature has lost standards and discipline, and at the same time virility and seriousness; it has fallen into the hands of aesthetes and dilettantes, the last effete representatives of romanticism. . . ."[9]

In romanticism, then, Babbitt discerned the dangerous excesses of modern thought; in humanism, the beneficent corrective. Throughout his career, Eliot shared both of his teacher's preferences: Though at times his reactions to the romantic seem nearly as passionately instinctive—and perhaps irrational—as his master's, much of Eliot's early career was given over to criticizing the heirs of Rousseau. Likewise, though he became critical of the secular foundations of Babbitt's humanism, Eliot never doubted that man must "do inner obeisance to something higher than his ordinary self."

In his *Masters of Modern French Criticism* Babbitt described pointedly the kind of critic necessary if contemporary thought were to pass beyond its muddled romanticism:

8. *The New Laokoon: An Essay on the Confusion of the Arts* (Boston: Houghton Mifflin, 1910), p. xiv.
9. Ibid., pp. 15, xiii.

What we are seeking is a critic who rests his discipline and selection upon the past without being a mere traditionalist; whose holding of tradition involves a constant process of hard and clear thinking, a constant adjustment, in other words, of the experience of the past to the changing needs of the present. . . . The chief problem of criticism, namely, the search for standards to oppose to individual caprice, is also the chief problem of contemporary thought in general: so that any solution which does not get back to first principles will be worthless.[10]

In defining the impulses behind Eliot's early critical career one could hardly do better than refer to Babbitt's call. From the beginning Eliot aspired to be a critic of the type Babbitt desired; Babbitt's understanding of "the chief problem of criticism" became Eliot's own. Through his Harvard teacher he discovered concerns that would engage him throughout his career.

II

His debt to Babbitt echoes throughout Eliot's early work, but the influence is nowhere clearer than in an Oxford University Extension Course that he offered in 1916. The very topic, "Modern French Literature," recalls what he studied under Babbitt at Harvard. Even in the reading list, Babbitt's presence was obvious; his *Masters of Modern French Criticism* was among the secondary sources recommended for a study of "the leading ideas of the nineteenth century." Though no notes or drafts remain of those six lectures given at Ilkley, Yorkshire, the twelve-page descriptive syllabus, preserved in the Houghton Library of Harvard University, offers a remarkably full account of Eliot's intentions for the course. This syllabus is surely one of the most fugitive of Eliot's known prose works. It is also one of the most valuable both in reflecting Babbitt's impact on the early Eliot and in offering a remarkably concise summary of Eliot's concerns during the next dec-

10. (Boston: Houghton Mifflin, 1912), pp. 362, 368.

ade. Significantly, the literature Eliot treated in those lectures was not the imaginative literature of modern France that had so influenced his early verse. Instead, he declared that he would "consider men of letters only as they represent political, religious, or philosophical tendencies," and concentrated, like Babbitt, on intellectual prose.[11]

"During the nineteenth century several conflicting tendencies were manifested," Eliot explained in his first lecture, "but they may all be traced to a common source. The germs of all these tendencies are found in Rousseau." Babbitt's influence was clear as Eliot then offered a "Short sketch of Rousseau's life," which he outlined as follows:

His public career consisted in a struggle against
   (1) *Authority* in matters of religion.
   (2) *Aristocracy* and *privilege* in government.
His main tendencies were
   (1) Exaltation of the *personal* and the *individual* above the *typical.*
   (2) Emphasis upon *feeling* rather than *thought.*
   (3) Humanitarianism: belief in the fundamental goodness of human nature.
   (4) Depreciation of *form* in art, and glorification of *spontaneity.*
His great faults were
   (1) Intense egotism.
   (2) Insincerity.

"Romanticism," he said, "stands for *excess* in any direction. It splits up into two directions: escape from the world of fact, and devotion to brute fact. The two great currents of the nineteenth century—vague emotionality and

11. *Syllabus of a Course of Six Lectures on Modern French Literature,* Oxford University Extension Lectures (Oxford: Oxford University Press, 1916), n. pag.

the apotheosis of science (realism) alike spring from Rousseau."[12]

Eliot's italics provide a catalogue of concepts that he would be working with long after the completion of his lectures. The values that Rousseau scorned were precisely those that lay at the center of Babbitt's humanism and for which Eliot would soon become a vocal advocate: authority, aristocracy, privilege, the typical, thought, and form. Likewise, the exaltation of the personal and the individual, of feeling and spontaneity that Eliot attributed to Rousseau had, he thought, created the climate of thought so disturbing to Babbitt and his student.

The general character of Eliot's subsequent response was clearly suggested in the description of his second lecture, "The Reaction against Romanticism." Here, too, his terms echo Babbitt's; and while speaking about French thought Eliot was also describing the course of his own career. For their remarkable anticipation of Eliot's own development, these paragraphs from the syllabus deserve to be quoted at length:

The beginning of the twentieth century has witnessed a return to the ideals of classicism. These may roughly be characterized as *form* and *restraint* in art, *discipline* and *authority* in religion, *centralization* in government. . . . The classicist point of view has been defined as essentially a belief in Original Sin—the necessity for austere discipline.

It must be remembered that the French mind is highly theoretic—directed by theories—and that no theory ever remains merely a theory of art, or a theory of religion, or a theory of

12. In another statement that same year Eliot wrote: "Rousseau is not a classic, nor was he a wise man; he has proved an eternal source of mischief and inspiration" ("Leibniz's Monads and Bradley's Finite Centers," *Monist* 26 [1916], 566). The student had appropriated not only the ideas of his Harvard teacher but also something of his polemical style.

politics. Any theory which commences in one of these spheres inevitably extends to the others. . . .

The present-day movement is partly a return to the ideals of the seventeenth century. A classicist in art and literature will therefore be likely to adhere to a monarchical form of government, and to the Catholic Church. But there are many cross-currents. Our best procedure is to sketch briefly the relation of politics, literature and religion, and then consider the work of a few representatives of these three interests.

The four subsequent lectures went on to describe the reactions to romanticism in politics (stemming from a "general feeling of dissatisfaction with the Third Republic, crystallizing since the Dreyfus trial"); in religion (taking the form of Neo-Catholicism, "partly a political movement, associated with monarchism, and partly a reaction against the sceptical scientific view of the nineteenth century"); and in literature (with a "movement away from both realism and purely personal expression of emotion" and a "growing devotion to form"). That Eliot himself was involved in such a "reaction" was already apparent in his early poetry. Before long, he would be following similar courses in politics and religion.

III

The lectures on "Modern French Literature" represent only a small, albeit fascinating, part of Eliot's activity during his first years in London. While working at Lloyds Bank and writing a number of the poems, including four in French, that would appear in 1920 in *Ara Vos Prec*, Eliot was busy with still other pursuits. He gave two additional series of extension lectures and by 1922 he had written nearly a hundred book reviews and occasional essays for various periodicals. Such prodigious activity as a lecturer and reviewer was hardly a labor of love. Above all Eliot thought of himself as a poet; and in an early letter to Ezra Pound he described reviewing as "one of the most corrupting, degrading and badly-paid means of live-lihood that a writing man can ply."[13] As that statement suggests, Eliot himself recognized the rather tenuous con-nection between his poetic aspirations and the many other activities in which he was engaged early in his career; the poems in *Ara Vos Prec,* for example, offer little evidence of being the work of Eliot the schoolmaster, banker, lecturer, or reviewer. But if these activities represented a distrac-tion from his primary interest, poetry, they were necessary in order for him to support himself and his new wife.

His early poetry—where he sought scrupulously to separate "the man who suffers and the mind which cre-ates"—is of limited value in illuminating the intellectual concerns that were exercising Eliot during the first years of his career; his many articles, like his lectures, are con-siderably more revealing. Among those publications were a number of the literary essays that, reprinted in *The Sacred Wood,* contributed so much to Eliot's reputation as a critic. Hardly less interesting, however, are many of the dozens of nonliterary pieces written for general circu-lation periodicals like the *New Statesman,* the *Athenaeum,* and the *Dial,* or for philosophical journals such as the *Monist* and the *International Journal of Ethics.* This latter group included discussions of a number of writers and issues that Eliot's early critical principles disallowed from his properly literary essays. Among those remarks on phi-losophy, religion, and society one discovers valuable evi-dence of his early attitudes—and of interests that he would subsequently be exploring in his own periodical, the *Criterion.*

13. Quoted by Donald Gallup in "T. S. Eliot and Ezra Pound: Collaborators in Letters," *Atlantic Monthly,* January 1970, p. 54. Eliot's activity as banker, lecturer, poet, and reviewer took its toll on his health during these years, and Pound wrote that after a brief illness in 1918 Eliot was ordered by his doctor "not to write any prose for six months" (p. 53). Eliot appears not to have heeded the advice.

Especially in the reviews for the philosophical journals one sees the hand of the recent graduate student in philosophy who had just completed a distinguished dissertation on F. H. Bradley.[14] But equally evident in much that he wrote during those early years was the influence of Babbitt: the alertness to symptoms of romanticism, in whatever form; the concern for the disciplined reason of the humanist tradition; the pursuit of issues to first principles; and, not least of all, the readiness to pass judgment on what he took to be inferior thinking and writing. Nietzsche, for example, he dismissed as "one of those writers whose philosophy evaporates when detached from its literary qualities. . . . Such authors," he noted dourly, "have always a peculiar influence over the large semi-philosophical public. . . ."[15] Of Shaw he said, "There is evidence that Mr. Shaw has many thoughts by the way; as a rule he welcomes them and seldom dismisses them as irrelevant." Such Shavian ideas as "creative evolution" may once have had a stimulant or sedative virtue, Eliot acknowledged. But no longer. And, having rejected the comfort of Shaw's empty philosophy, Eliot could only hope "that an

14. There is hardly need here once again to examine Eliot's dissertation, published in 1964 as *Knowledge and Experience in the Philosophy of F. H. Bradley* (London: Faber and Faber). Despite Eliot's (possibly disingenuous) suggestion in the 1964 preface that the book's primary value lay in the insight it offered into the development of his prose style, a number of critics have fruitfully considered the impact of his study of Bradley. See especially: Anne C. Bolgan, "What the Thunder Said: Mr. Eliot's Philosophical Writings," Diss. Toronto 1960; E. P. Bollier, "T. S. Eliot and F. H. Bradley: A Question of Influence," *Tulane Studies in English* 12 (1962), 87–111; Hugh Kenner, *The Invisible Poet* (New York: McDowell, Obolensky, 1959), pp. 40–69; J. Hillis Miller, *Poets of Reality* (Cambridge: Belknap Press of Harvard University Press, 1965), pp. 131–89; Kristian Smidt, *Poetry and Belief in the Work of T. S. Eliot* (London: Routledge and Kegan Paul, 1961), pp. 158–63; and George Whiteside, "T. S. Eliot's Dissertation," *ELH* 34 (1967), 400–424.

15. Review of *The Philosophy of Nietzsche* by A. Wolf, *International Journal of Ethics* 26 (1916), 426. This journal will hereafter be cited as "*IJE*."

exasperated generation may find comfort in admiring, even if without understanding, mathematics, may suspect that precision and profundity are not incompatible, may find maturity as interesting as adolescence, and permanence more interesting than change. It must," he concluded, "at all events be either much more demoralized intellectually than the last age, or very much more disciplined."[16]

Theology was one form of such discipline, and a number of the books Eliot reviewed were theological. Suggesting that his own religious ideas were still rather inchoate, his statements here were curiously inconsistent. At one point he could suggest "that religion, however poor our lives would be without it, is only one form of satisfaction among others, rather than the culminating satisfaction of all satisfactions,"[17] while elsewhere he maintained that "the struggle of 'liberal' against 'orthodox' faith is out of date. The present conflict is far more momentous than that."[18] Apart from any personal religious belief, Eliot's intellectual sympathies seemed to lie with orthodoxy. Welcoming a new book that "represents the resistance of the orthodoxy, the brains, and the scholarship of Oxford to a new heresy in religion," he approvingly noted that its author, Clement C. J. Webb, "stands for the humane tradition; his opponents, for the novelties of science."[19]

The rigorous pursuit of ideas to first principles that distinguished Eliot throughout his career made him uneasy with facile compromises in religion, as elsewhere. He scorned the efforts of such writers as the famous historian and theologian Hastings Rashdall whom he found "arbitrating between the claims of theology and ethics, not without exacting considerable sacrifices from both sides."

16. "London Letter," *Dial* 71 (1921), 455.

17. Review of *Mens Creatrix* by William Temple, *IJE* 27 (1917), 542–43.

18. Review of *Group Theories of Religion and the Religion of the Individual* by Clement C. J. Webb, *IJE* 27 (1916), 117.

19. *New Statesman*, 29 July 1916, p. 405.

Reviewing Rashdall's published lectures *Conscience and Christ,* Eliot wrote:

If one holds a theory of conscience similar to Dr. Rashdall's, that conscience will consist in the usual structure of prejudices of the enlightened middle class. To this middle-class conscience the teaching of Jesus is gradually assimilated. . . . All that is anarchic, or unsafe or disconcerting in what Jesus said and did is either denied, or boiled away by the "principle of development."

In a tone worthy of a student of Babbitt, Eliot concluded, "Certain saints found the following of Christ very hard, but modern methods have facilitated everything. Yet I am not sure, after reading modern theology, that the pale Galilaean has conquered."[20]

His philosophical training and his intellectual kinship with Babbitt doubtless combined to make Eliot impatient with liberalism's erosion of the theological tradition. At the same time, he was also gradually recognizing the intrinsic appeal of religious orthodoxy. After a lengthy summary of the neoscholastic theology underlying a book he was reviewing, Eliot added a highly significant, personal statement:

The non-catholic reader will be unable to avoid a tribute of grave respect to the only Church which can even pretend to maintain a philosophy of its own, a philosophy, as we are increasingly aware, which is succeeding in establishing a claim to be taken quite seriously. . . .[21]

Similarly, in one of his regular "London Letters" for the *Dial,* he spoke of the beauty of church buildings, then threatened with demolition, which "give to the business quarter of London a beauty which its hideous banks and commercial houses have not quite defaced. Some are by

20. *IJE* 27 (1916), 111–12.
21. Review of *Epistemology* by P. Coffey, *New Statesman,* 29 December 1917, p. 312. Eliot's own background was, of course, Unitarian. See Howarth, pp. 1–35.

Christopher Wren himself, others by his school; the least precious redeems some vulgar street. . . ." In addition to the attraction of its theology, the church offered havens of beauty, rest, and comfort.

To one who, like the present writer, passes his days in this City of London . . . the loss of these towers, to meet the eye down a grimy lane, and of these empty naves, to receive the solitary visitor at noon from the dust and tumult of Lombard Street, will be irreparable and unforgotten.[22]

In their anticipation of Eliot's later discussions of the intellectual and aesthetic appeal of Christianity, these early remarks offer interesting suggestions of forces long working toward his religious conversion.

His early essays also provide evidence regarding the motives that led Eliot to follow the path of expatriation so current among American writers at the time. Even as early as 1909, in a *Harvard Advocate* review of Van Wyck Brooks's *Wine of the Puritans,* he was speaking of "the failure of American life (at present)—social, political, in education and in art." Already, settling abroad must have seemed a real possibility to Eliot. "This is a book," he remarked, "which probably will chiefly interest one class of Americans (a class, however, of some importance): the Americans retained to their native country by business relations or socialities or by a sense of duty—the last reason implying a real sacrifice—while their hearts are always in Europe."[23] "We Americans," one of the characters in Brooks's book had said, "have no bonds with a remote antiquity, no traditions of the soil old enough as yet to have become instincts."[24] Early on, Eliot recognized the importance to the poet of such bonds and traditions.

22. *Dial* 70 (1921), 690, 691. Eliot's note to the Magnus Martyr passage in *The Waste Land* echoes this concern.
23. *Harvard Advocate,* 7 May 1909, p. 80.
24. *The Wine of the Puritans: A Study of Present-Day America* (London: Sisley's, 1908), p. 31.

For Eliot the deracination that he took to be characteristic of America was exaggerated in his own personal history. Recalling his youth, he wrote to a friend:

Some day I want to write an essay about the point of view of an American who wasn't an American, because he was born in the South and went to school in New England as a small boy with a nigger drawl, but who wasn't a southerner in the South because his people were northerners in a border state and looked down on all southerners and Virginians, and who so was never anything anywhere and who therefore felt himself to be more a Frenchman than an American and more an Englishman than a Frenchman and yet felt that the U.S.A. up to a hundred years ago was a family extension. It is almost too difficult even for H. J. who for that matter wasn't an American at all, in that sense.[25]

Basically, Eliot had never felt himself truly to be an American; and one can hardly imagine his expatriation to have been painful. His dissatisfaction with life in the United States led him to fancy the possibility of a better life in England; he hoped that the characteristics of American life so alien to artistic creation were not present across the Atlantic. His remaining in England beyond the expiration of his graduate fellowship was only in part a function of the wartime difficulty of securing passage home; in fact, he was eager to settle there.

But if he had been too sanguine about the congeniality of England's intellectual climate to writing, he soon found that contemporary British culture was not without its deficiencies; in fact, it in many ways resembed the America he had recently left. Reviewing Stephen Leacock's *Essays and Literary Studies,* he found "some hard, important, and unpopular truths." Summarizing Leacock's views, Eliot wrote:

25. Quoted by Sir Herbert Read in "T. S. E.—A Memoir." *Sewanee Review* 74 (1966), 35. See also Eliot's remarks in his preface to Edgar Ansel Mowrer, *This American World* (London: Faber and Gwyer, 1928), pp. xiii–xiv.

He upholds the classical, the Oxford education: Latin and Greek "as the starting-point for a general knowledge of the literature, the history, and the philosophy of all ages." His attitude is austere, pessimistic, almost mediaevalist. He believes in discipline, form, restraint; in a real contrast of good and evil not to be obscured by talk about "social evolution"; he believes furthermore in the importance of imagination. *And he sees in the chaos of American life only an advanced stage of a disease which menaces Europe;* the philosophy of comfort without ideals, the cheap and easy utilitarianism of popular education, and the dead level.

Doubtless with Babbitt in mind, he added: "There are a few writers in America who share Mr. Leacock's views."[26] Eliot also shared those views: the words he used in his description of Leacock's book—*classical, austere, discipline, imagination*—also describe Eliot's concerns. To an observer with such a perspective, British culture seemed inauspicious for art.

That England, as Leacock suggested, should share many of the cultural weaknesses of America was no doubt especially disappointing to the Eliot who planned to settle there. He reflected this recognition in a review of the letters of John Butler Yeats:

There are [Eliot said of the elder Yeats's letters] many criticisms of America, and at the present time . . . when England seems drifting toward Americanization, it is well to hear what Mr. Yeats has to say: ". . . No American, of those I have met or heard, has ever felt the inward and innermost essence of poetry, because it is not among the American opportunities to

26. "Mr. Leacock Serious," *New Statesman,* 29 July 1916, pp. 404–5. My emphasis. In Leacock's book Eliot also found "a truthful picture of the American graduate student, the prospective Doctor of Philosophy: his specialisation in knowledge, his expansion in ignorance, his laborious dulness, his years of labour and his crowning achievement—the Thesis. . . . This labor," continued one who spoke with the authority of having recently completed *his* thesis, "is fatal to the development of intellectual powers."

live the solitary life. . . . In America they make war on solitude."[27]

In England, too, Eliot found an atmosphere unconducive to art. The arbiters of taste were the philistine middle class, and, Eliot noted, "At the very moment when the middle class appears to be on the point of perdition—beleaguered by a Coalition Government, the Three Trades-Union, and the Income Tax—at this very moment it enjoys the triumph, in intellectual matters, of being able to respect no other standards than its own. . . ."[28] A similar disappointment over the slight attendance at a revival of *Marriage-à-la-Mode* prompted Eliot to write a letter to the editor of the *Athenaeum:* ". . . Dryden is a great poet and a great dramatist, and the Civilized Class has not supported the people who would support him, the Civilized Class has not supported Dryden against Archer. If, at the next performance of the Phoenix, the Civilized Class has not taken advantage of the reduced rates, I shall no longer be able to stifle my suspicion that the Civilized Class is a myth."[29]

Three years later he wrote in a "London Letter" to the *Dial,*

There is certainly, in the atmosphere of literary London, something which may provisionally be called a moral cowardice. It is not simply cowardice, but a caution, a sort of worldly prudence which believes implicitly that English literature is so good as it is that adventure and experiment involve only unjustified risk; lack of ambition, laziness, and refusal to recognize foreign competition; a tolerance which is no better than torpid indifference; not cowardice merely, but still a composition of inertias which is usually to be found in general cowardice.

His catalogue of the causes of the situation recalled Bab-

27. "The Letters of J. B. Yeats," *Egoist* 4 (1917), 89.
28. "London Letter," *Dial* 70 (1921), 451.
29. *Athenaeum,* 27 February 1920, p. 285.

bitt's: newspapers, the quest for economic security, democracy. The conditions were not unique to England. "But in London," he said, "these poisons are either more pernicious, or their effects more manifest, than elsewhere. Other cities decay, and extend a rich odour of putrefaction; London merely shrivels, like a little bookkeeper grown old."[30]

Remarking on the "dulness" of the most recent volume of *Georgian Poetry,* Eliot noted "the extreme lack of culture on the part of a number of writers in prose and verse. . . . It is certain that culture does not reside solely in a university education, or in extensive reading. . . . Culture is traditional and loves novelty; the General Reading Public knows no tradition, and loves staleness."[31] The prospects for a vital literature in such a society were, Eliot felt, slight; the health of literature depends upon the health of society, and because he was devoted to the one, he was concerned for the other. England needed a prophetic voice to call it from its torpor, and Eliot, as we have seen, was already beginning to fill that role.

What we want is to disturb and alarm the public. . . . To point out that every generation, every turn of time when the work of four or five men who count has reached middle age, is a *crisis.* Also that the intelligence of a nation must go on developing, or it will deteriorate. . . . That the forces of deterioration are a large crawling mass, and the forces of development half a dozen men.[32]

Eliot's goal was no less than that of re-educating his society. In those numerous, scattered reviews he offered the first evidence of his qualifications for being numbered among those half-dozen men. When he collected a number of his more important essays and published them in 1920 as *The Sacred Wood,* his credentials were assured.

30. *Dial* 72 (1922), 510.
31. "London Letter," *Dial* 70 (1921), 451.
32. "Observations," *Egoist* 5 (1918), 69.

IV

As we have seen, Eliot had lectured and written widely on nonliterary matters before the publication of *The Sacred Wood;* however, in that first volume of his essays, he scrupulously avoided such matters and insisted on their exclusion from literary criticism. "Most critics," he had acknowledged in 1919, "have some creative interest—it may be, instead of an interest in any art, an interest (like Mr. Paul More's) in morals; but an interest in morals will not produce sound criticism of art. Consequently, we may say that the only valuable criticism is that of the workman."[33]

Of course, Eliot himself shared More's "creative interest" in "morals"; but he held such nonliterary concerns to be irrelevant to his work as a literary man. Though he had a genuine interest in the various topics treated in his lectures and occasional essays, his primary concern was literature. To his mind, those other matters represented a distraction from his literary career, and in his criticism he sought strenuously to avoid them. In fact, even the enterprise of literary criticism seemed peripheral to his poetizing. Though he recognized the need for a renewed and purified literary criticism, he must—at this early stage of his career—often have doubted the propriety of his engagement in this activity. He remarked somewhat ill-temperedly in *The Sacred Wood* that "the creative artist in England finds himself compelled, or at least tempted, to spend much of his time and energy in criticism that he might reserve for the perfecting of his proper work: simply because there is no one else to do it."[34] But as his many early essays testify, he accepted the responsibility. Both out of financial necessity—a consideration not to be over-

33. "The Local Flavour," *Athenaeum*, 12 December 1919, p. 1333.
34. *The Sacred Wood: Essays on Poetry and Criticism*, 2d ed. (London: Methuen, 1928), p. 46. Subsequent references, inserted in the text, are to this edition.

looked—and out of a recognition of the need for such social and literary criticism, he devoted much of his energy to such writing. And though the criticism of *The Sacred Wood* was, as he had said valuable criticism should be, that of the workman, he brought to these "Essays on Poetry and Criticism," as to his other writing, his characteristic concern for "standards to oppose to individual caprice" and "first principles."

Eliot's eagerness to repress his nonliterary interests was apparent in the introduction to the volume where he insisted on the necessity of a purely *literary* criticism. Significantly, it was Matthew Arnold—a writer whose career Eliot's own would so closely resemble—whom he singled out for especial comment:

To anyone who is at all capable of experiencing the pleasures of justice, it is gratifying to be able to make amends to a writer whom one has vaguely depreciated for some years. The faults and foibles of Matthew Arnold are no less evident to me now than twelve years ago, after my first admiration for him; but I hope that now, on re-reading some of his prose with more care, I can better appreciate his position. And what makes Arnold seem all the more remarkable is, that if he were our exact contemporary, he would find all his labour to perform again (xi).

The labor to which Eliot pointed specifically was Arnold's criticism of the "prematureness" of English Romantic poetry of the early nineteenth century which had " 'plenty of energy, plenty of creative force, [but] did not know enough'. . . . This judgment of the Romantic Generation has not, so far as I know," he said, "ever been successfully controverted; and it has not, so far as I know, ever made very much impression on popular opinion" (xii). Arnold's reservations were, of course, shared by Babbitt and Eliot himself. But, to Eliot's mind, Arnold's critical activity fell short of its proper end. Where he should have confined his attention to literature and gone beyond his diagnosis of romanticism to establish positive criteria of poetic maturity, Arnold in his criticism was merely negative—and not always literary:

In *Culture and Anarchy,* in *Literature and Dogma,* Arnold was not occupied so much in establishing a criticism as in attacking the uncritical. The difference is that while in constructive work something can be done, destructive work must incessantly be repeated; and furthermore Arnold, in his destruction, went for game outside of the literary preserve altogether, much of it political game untouched and inviolable by ideas. This activity of Arnold's we must regret; it might perhaps have been carried on as effectively, if not quite so neatly, by some disciple . . . in an editorial position on a newspaper.

Perhaps Eliot recognized the likelihood of his following Arnold's course, for he concluded in a tone at once stern and sympathetic:

Arnold is not to be blamed: he wasted his strength, as men of superior ability sometimes do, because he saw something to be done and no one else to do it. The temptation, to any man who is interested in ideas and primarily in literature, to put literature into the corner until he cleaned up the whole country first, is almost irresistible (xiii).

At first, Eliot's attention to Arnold in these opening pages of *The Sacred Wood* seems a gratuitous digression, but in retrospect it is understandable. Arnold's temptation was Eliot's own, and it was necessary for him at the beginning of this first, major critical performance to deny that temptation publicly.

Foregoing, at least in the essays he included, the lure of "game outside of the literary preserve," Eliot sought to demonstrate his resistance to the temptations to which Arnold had succumbed. In the preface that he added to the 1928 edition he summarized the nature of his enterprise: "The problem appearing in these essays, which gives them what coherence they have, is the problem of the integrity of poetry, with the repeated assertion that when we are considering poetry we must consider it primarily as poetry and not another thing" (viii). Extraliterary concerns were, thus, apparently disallowed, and even Coleridge, whom Eliot at the beginning of his study characterized as "perhaps the greatest of English critics" (1), could not "be estimated as an intelligence completely free. . . ." Coleridge was possessed by a metaphysical interest that was "like most metaphysical interest, an affair of his emotions. But," Eliot urged, "a literary critic should have no emotions except those immediately provoked by a work of art" (12).

The Arts insist that a man shall dispose of all that he has, even of his family tree, and follow art alone. For they require that a man be not a member of a family or of a caste or of a party or of a coterie, but simply and solely himself (32).

There is here a fervent insistence that is almost amusing; but one does not doubt Eliot's earnestness. While apparently addressing his readers, he was also reminding himself of the requirements of what he took to be an acceptable literary criticism.

We are not here interested so much in Eliot's remarks on specific texts as in the standards he proposed and the principles on which they rested. And, as the reviewer in *TLS* remarked, "Tradition and the Individual Talent" is "the central essay of the book, that most concerned with principle."[35] The issues of tradition and individual talent were, of course, hardly new ones for Eliot in 1919 when his essay first appeared in the *Egoist*. Babbitt long before had decried the "pedantry of individualism"; Eliot had pointed to the exaltation of the individual as a leading tendency of Rousseau's romanticism; and both had often insisted on the importance of the traditional as an element in education, literature, religion, and national culture. To

35. *TLS,* 2 December 1920, p. 795.

their credit, neither had seen the issue to be one of tradition *or* the individual talent; and Eliot's essay retains its value for its wise recognition of the necessary wedding of the two.

"No poet, no artist of any art, has his complete meaning alone," he said. It is, rather, his assimilating and "fitting in" to the tradition that gives him significance. The tradition, however, is no static thing. Constantly developing through history, it is nothing if not living and dynamic, and thus a grasp of tradition requires a vital historical sense, "a perception, not only of the pastness of the past, but of its presence, . . . a sense of the timeless as well as of the temporal and of the timeless and of the temporal together . . ." (49). But it is not only historical perspective that is demanded; one must, as well, possess a breadth of culture that makes him aware of "the mind of Europe— the mind of his own country" and makes him recognize that mind "to be much more important than his own private mind" (51). Just as Babbitt had described the ideal critic as one "whose holding of tradition involves a constant process of hard and clear thinking, a constant adjustment, in other words, of the experience of the past to the changing needs of the present," Eliot's ideal poet was one who "must develop or procure the consciousness of the past and . . . continue to develop this consciousness throughout his career. What happens is a continual surrender of himself as he is at the moment to something which is more valuable. The progress of an artist is a continual self-sacrifice, a continual extinction of personality" (52– 53). Eliot's express interest here was poetry. Yet the supraliterary implications of his ideas are easy to see. One recognizes the same attitudes encountered earlier in Babbitt's writing and in Eliot's journalistic essays: the impatience with the excesses of romanticism; the sense of the insufficiency of the autonomous individual; the recognition of the need for discipline, humility, and order; and the certainty that any truly significant modern achievement must build upon what went before.

The two essays on Blake and Dante that concluded *The Sacred Wood* offered concrete applications of the problem Eliot had treated theoretically in "Tradition and the Individual Talent." Published originally as *Athenaeum* reviews of recent books on those poets, these essays stand together at the end of Eliot's first major critical volume to illustrate what can happen, respectively, to a poet who is deprived of and one who enjoys the benefits of tradition.

The first among a number of disapproving essays he would write on various of the English Romantic poets, "Blake" must, of course, be understood in the context of the antiromantic animus that Eliot derived from Babbitt. A year before, Eliot had spoken of "the Romantic Period as a period of intellectual chaos" and remarked that "the period 1788–1832 was a period hungry for novelty; and its hunger exceeded its strength of digestion."[36] Appearing at a time when Blake was begining to emerge from obscurity, this essay is unmistakably polemic. If it is not an entirely balanced critical performance, it is all the more revealing of the feelings he held so strongly at the time.

Largely self-taught, Eliot observed, Blake was not disciplined by a classical educational curriculum; and thus as a young man he had "nothing to distract him from his interests or to corrupt these interests" (152). "He was naked, and saw man naked, and from the centre of his own crystal" (154–55). But, lacking the clothes of traditional culture, he was also exposed to dangers:

His philosophy, like his vision, like his insight, like his technique, was his own. And accordingly he was inclined to attach more importance to it than an artist should; this is what makes him eccentric, and makes him inclined to formlessness (155).

"We have the same respect for Blake's philosophy," Eliot said, "that we have for an ingenious piece of home-made furniture: we admire the man who has put it together out

36. "The Romantic Generation, If It Existed," *Athenaeum*, 18 July 1919, p. 616.

of the odds and ends about the house" (156). However, his objection to Blake was not so much to the heterodoxy of the philosophy as to its unfortunate artistic consequences. For Eliot, the young poet, the great virtue of the traditional was its conduciveness to the creation of great art. Because their author lacked "a respect for impersonal reason, for common sense, for the objectivity of science," Blake's works were marred by "a certain meanness of culture," "crankiness," "eccentricity," and "formlessness."

What his genius required, and what it sadly lacked, was a framework of accepted and traditional ideas which would have prevented him from indulging in a philosophy of his own, and concentrated his attention upon the problems of the poet (157–58).

Eliot was still a number of years from his own religious conversion, but by 1920 he was already acknowledging the attraction of religion—even if more for artistic than properly religious reasons. Toward the end of his essay on Blake he remarked:

We may speculate, for amusement, whether it would not have been beneficial to the north of Europe generally, and to Britain in particular, to have had a more continuous religious history. The local divinities of Italy were not wholly exterminated by Christianity, and they were not reduced to the dwarfish fate which fell upon our trolls and pixies. The latter, with the major Saxon deities, were perhaps no great loss in themselves, but they left an empty place; and perhaps our mythology was further impoverished by the divorce from Rome . . . (157).

"The concentration resulting from a framework of mythology and theology and philosophy," he said, "is one of the reasons why Dante is a classic, and Blake only a poet of genius" (158).

Still the literary rather than the moral critic, Eliot pointed not to the intrinsic spiritual value of Dante's Christian tradition but rather to the poetic "concentration" for which it made. Lacking such a tradition, Blake had both to create his own intellectual system and poetize it. To Eliot's mind, he was bound to have failed; for, as he remarked in his essay on Dante, "Without doubt, the effort of the philosopher proper, the man who is trying to deal with ideas in themselves, and the effort of the poet, who may be trying to *realize* ideas, cannot be carried on at the same time" (162). Philosophical poetry was possible then when poet and reader shared a common philosophy, and such sharing could take place only in a coherent society informed throughout by a vital tradition. The essay on Blake reflected Eliot's estimation of the impossibility of philosophical poetry apart from such a tradition. The essay on Dante that concluded *The Sacred Wood* was more affirmative.

"Dante, more than any other poet," Eliot said, "has succeeded in dealing with his philosophy, not as a theory . . . or as his own comment or reflection, but in terms of something *perceived*" (170–71). Comparing Dante with Lucretius, he remarked that the Italian poet "had the benefit of a mythology and a theology which had undergone a more complete absorption into life . . ." (163). Dante's advantage over Lucretius was also his advantage over Blake: being able to draw upon an established tradition of philosophy, theology, and mythology, he was able to devote his entire energies to the writing of poetry. Thus Eliot could describe the *Divine Comedy* as "the most comprehensive, and the most *ordered* presentation of emotions that has ever been made" (168).

Shortly after his conversion, he would write another, longer essay on Dante. There he would dwell more extensively on the social and religious factors that made possible Dante's achievement. But by 1920 he at least had recognized how vital Dante's access to a coherent intellectual tradition was to his poetic achievement. Eliot's admiration for Dante was, of course, evident in his early verse. If he were to approach Dante's achievement, he would require a culture that, like Dante's, was auspicious for artistic creation. There was no question of returning to the middle ages in 1920; there remained, however, the challenge of shaping a world in which the creation of poetry like Dante's might once again be possible. Eliot recognized the challenge and, by 1922, he had already begun to respond.

1922-1927

2

THE EARLY *CRITERION*

It can justly be said that with the publication of *Ulysses* early in 1922, modern English literature reached maturity. When the *Criterion,* a new quarterly review, appeared in London that fall, many readers doubtless first turned to the end of the issue to read the English text of part of Valery Larbaud's groundbreaking exposition of Joyce's novel. Yet in that first issue of the *Criterion* was also the first great modern English poem. Sandwiched inconspicuously between an essay by T. Sturge Moore and a story by May Sinclair stood T. S. Eliot's *Waste Land*—without epigraph, or dedication, or notes, or any indication that the author of that revolutionary new poem was also editor of the new review.[1] The poem's importance was immediately obvious; the importance of the review, both to its editor and to modern British literature, would soon become clear.

If only as the review in which Eliot first published his poem, the *Criterion* would remain memorable. But its

1. For personal reasons, Eliot was anxious to retain his anonymity; no indication as to the identity of the editor appeared in early issues. Eliot explained his secrecy in a letter to Edmund Wilson, managing editor of *Vanity Fair,* regarding a contribution he was making to the magazine: "There is one favour I wish to ask you, and that is, that in using my picture, or in any other mention of me, you see that I am not referred to as 'editor' of The Criterion. . . . The reason is that I already occupy one 'official' position—in a bank; and it is inconsistent with the obligations of that position to occupy any other, and the continued or conspicuous publication of my name in that capacity might be troublesome for me. My conscience is quite clear, because the one work does not in fact interfere with the other, and furthermore I am not taking any money for The Criterion work" (11 January 1923, Yale University Library). On the cover of the *Criterion,* Eliot was not identified as editor until January 1927.

achievement was, in fact, far greater. In a preface to the collected, reprint edition of the review, Eliot wrote: "I think . . . that the . . . volumes of *The Criterion* constitute a valuable record of the thought of that period between two wars." The impressive group of writers whom Eliot enlisted for his journal confirms that judgment. By the end of its first year of publication the *Criterion* had included contributions from E. M. Forster, Hermann Hesse, Luigi Pirandello, Ezra Pound, Paul Valéry, Virginia Woolf, and W. B. Yeats. During the next four years alone, Eliot published works by Conrad Aiken, Arnold Bennett, Jean Cocteau, Hart Crane, Aldous Huxley, Joyce, D. H. Lawrence, Wyndham Lewis, Archibald MacLeish, Jacques Maritain, Marcel Proust, I. A. Richards, Edith Sitwell, and Gertrude Stein. And before the *Criterion* ceased publication in 1939, these others had also appeared in its pages: W. H. Auden, G. K. Chesterton, Richard Church, William Empson, Robert Graves, Thomas Mann, T. F. Powys, Stephen Spender, Allen Tate, and Dylan Thomas. Several years after the completion of his editorship, Eliot remarked that "good literary editors have an important part to play in a healthy literature."[2] Eliot had played his part estimably.[3]

For our purposes, however, the *Criterion*'s significance is not primarily its contribution to the development of modern literature. It was, more importantly, Eliot's review; his editorship of those eighteen volumes is as much

2. "What is Minor Poetry?" in *On Poetry and Poets* (New York: Farrar, Straus and Cudahy, 1957), p. 35.

3. Despite its considerable importance, the review never enjoyed a wide circulation. "*The Criterion* had, in its palmiest days, some 800 subscriptions," Eliot said. "Beyond the libraries and colleges in Japan, India, Egypt, South America and the United States, and some at home, and the unknown individual subscribers in unknown places, it was surprising to find how few names on the list were those of people whose names were known to the editor" (*Catacomb*, N. S. 1 [1950], 367).

a part of his literary career as any of his volumes of poetry, drama, or criticism. And, taken as a whole, the file of the *Criterion* is perhaps richer than any one of those more famous volumes in the light it casts on Eliot's intellectual development during a period of seventeen years. In his determination of the journal's contents, his own contribution of articles and reviews, and especially his publication of regular "Commentaries," Eliot provided an index to his evolving concerns. By the time he concluded his editorship and the *Criterion* ceased publication in January 1939, his interests had expanded markedly; to an extent largely unrecognized, the pages of his review record that development.[4] The personal imprint of Eliot's editorship is everywhere apparent, and he acknowledged this in the final issue: "I am convinced that [it] is not the kind of review which can be taken up and continued by one editor after another. Another man might make something better of it, but he would have to make something very different."[5]

With the idea of its becoming "a more chic and brilliant Art and Letters, which might have a fashionable vogue

4. Two useful studies of Eliot and the *Criteron* are Herbert Howarth, "The Editor and His Contributors," in *Notes on Some Figures . . .*, p. 250–99; and Delmore Schwartz, "*The Criterion: 1922–1939*," *Kenyon Review* 1 (1939), 437–49. The unsympathetic review in the *Times Literary Supplement* (25 April 1968, p. 430) on the appearance of the reprint edition of the review also deserves consideration.

5. "Last Words," *Criterion* 18 (1939), 269. Eliot set down some of his principles of editorship in a 1961 tribute to Bruce Lyttelton Richmond, editor of the *Times Literary Supplement* from 1902 to 1937. In his direction of the *Criterion*, Eliot said, he followed many of the examples set by Richmond: "I learnt from him that it is the business of an editor to know his contributors personally, to keep in touch with them and to make suggestions to them. I tried to form a nucleus of writers . . . on whom I could depend, differing from each other in many things, but not in love of literature and seriousness of purpose. And I learnt from Richmond that I must read every word of what was to appear in print. . . ." ("Bruce Lyttelton Richmond," *TLS*, 13 January 1961, p. 17).

among a wealthy few,"[6] the *Criterion* was founded under the patronage of Lady Rothermere, wife of the London newspaper magnate. The review began as a quarterly, partly, Eliot explained later, "for reasons of economy, but also because the editor then had so little time to give it."[7] In 1925 Lady Rothermere discontinued her support and the review's continued publication was briefly dependent on the generosity of a number of individuals. That same year Eliot left his job at Lloyds Bank and joined the board of the new publishing firm of Faber and Gwyer— later, Faber and Faber. Consequently, by 1926, the *Criterion* appeared with the Faber imprint, and its survival became more certain.[8]

Under the Faber imprint its name was altered to the *New Criterion: A Quarterly Review*. Beginning in May 1927, however, the magazine began appearing more frequently and assumed a third title, the *Monthly Criterion: A Literary Review*. With increased frequency of publication, Eliot had not foreseen any essential change in the character of the review. Looking back, he explained:

Many persons think, and the editor of this review was for a time among them, that the time for quarterly reviews passed with Victorian leisure; they regard the long established quarterlies

6. Eliot in a letter to Herbert Read, October 1924. Quoted by Read in "T. S. E.—A Memoir," p. 40.

7. "Last Words," p. 270. At the beginning Richard Aldington assisted Eliot in his editorial duties. Even so, the strain of the editorship—like that of his earlier reviewing—combined with his bank job was considerable. In March 1923, he wrote John Quinn, ". . . I wish to heaven that I had never taken up the Criterion. . . . It has been an evergrowing responsibility; It has been a great *expense* to me and I have not got a penny out of it; There is not enough money to run it and pay me too. . . . In order to carry on the Criterion I have had to neglect not only the writing I ought to be doing but my private affairs of every description. . . . I cannot go on" (quoted in Gallup, "T. S. Eliot and Ezra Pound," p. 58).

8. The Faber sponsorship of the magazine continued to the end; but Eliot insisted that such support from his employer did not inhibit his "complete editorial freedom" ("Last Words," p. 270).

with indifferent tolerance, as useless survivals; and they allude
to what is popularly called "the general speeding-up of modern
life" as demanding something more frequent and ephemeral. . . .
It was tacitly assumed that the quarterly virtues could be preserved in the monthly form, and that to appear twelve times a
year was enough to placate the acceleration of life.

By June 1928, however, it was apparent that the experiment had failed:

It did not occur to us, in acceding to the supposed demands of
"modern life," that something more was required of the review
than appearing three times as often. . . . *The Monthly Criterion*
was too heavy, and it could not have been made consecutively
lighter without sacrificing much of its quality and many of its
interests—which it was not prepared to do.[9]

Consequently, quarterly publication was resumed; and
until the end, in January 1939, it remained the *Criterion:
A Literary Review*.[10]

The title of the journal is doubly significant. In naming
it "The Criterion," Eliot was announcing his confidence
that standards—even, perhaps *a* standard—could be established to provide a foundation for contemporary literature and thought. Its precise character may not yet have
been clear in 1922, but Eliot as editor committed himself
and his journal to the discovery and articulation of such a
criterion. Though his review offers an extraordinarily val-
able chronicle of Eliot's intellectual development, neither
this fact nor the title should suggest that the review was
primarily philosophical. The subtitle makes a second important point: the *Criterion* was always "a literary review." Over the years, Eliot would have to redefine the
meaning of that phrase to keep pace with the growth of
his interests in fields other than literature; his conception

9. "Commentary," *Criterion* 7 (1928), 289–90.
10. Regardless of the temporary changes of title, I shall refer to
the magazine simply as the *Criterion*.

of a literary review proved sufficiently elastic to contain much of that development. But open as it became to considerations of philosophical, political, or religious issues, Eliot's review never abandoned the fundamentally belletristic orientation with which it began. When the political crises of the late thirties and the prospect of a second world war "induced in [Eliot] a depression of spirits so different from any other experience of fifty years as to be a new emotion," he lost "the enthusiasm necessary to make a literary review what it should be."[11] Lacking that enthusiasm, he terminated publication.

Reflecting its editor's own self-definition, the *Criterion* was continually defining its values and its goals. The first issues, however, curiously lacked any explicit program. On the evidence of its early contents, one might have suspected that the review would be merely another—though unusually distinguished—quarterly of poetry, fiction, and criticism.[12] In fact, it was not until the fourth issue that Eliot announced the principles governing his editorship, and then only in a brief note, signed "T. S. E.," on "The Function of a Literary Review":

On the completion of the first volume of the *Criterion,* it is pertinent to define, and perhaps to defend, the purpose of a literary review. . . . A literary review should maintain the application, in literature, of principles which have their consequences also in politics and in private conduct; and it should maintain them

11. "Last Words," p. 274.
12. In addition to Larbaud's essay on *Ulysses,* May Sinclair's "The Victim," T. Sturge Moore's "Story of Tristram and Isolt in Modern Poetry," and, of course, "The Waste Land," the first number of the *Criterion* contained an essay by George Saintsbury on "Dullness"; somes notes by Dostoevsky collected under the title "Plan of the Novel, 'The Life of a Great Sinner' "; and an essay by Hermann Hesse on "Recent German Poetry." The *Times Literary Supplement* noted, "If we are to judge by its first number, *The Criterion* is not only that rare thing amongst English periodicals, a purely literary review, but it is of a quality not inferior to that of any review published either here or abroad" (26 October 1922, p. 690).

without tolerating any confusion of the purposes of pure literature with the purposes of politics or ethics. . . . To maintain the
autonomy, and the disinterestedness, of every human activity,
and to perceive it in relation to every other, require a considerable discipline. It is the function of a literary review to maintain
the autonomy and disinterestedness of literature, and at the
same time to exhibit the relations of literature—not to "life," as
something contrasted to literature, but to all the other activities,
which, together with literature, are the components of life.[13]

The opacity of this statement doubtless reflected the uncertainty of Eliot's own early aims. As we have seen, he
had been concerned for some years with "principles" that
inevitably bore on literary as well as nonliterary matters.
But he had also been anxious, as in *The Sacred Wood,* to
oppose a poetic and critical legacy that had confused "pure
literature" with "politics and ethics"—to the disadvantage
of both. He would gradually reconcile these conflicting concerns, but in 1923 his dilemma was obviously unresolved.

Perhaps feeling that he had rendered the "Function of a
Literary Review" less than clear in his July note, Eliot inserted in the October number a flyer that outlined more
fully his hopes for the journal.

The whole programme of *The Criterion* could hardly be defined
in advance or executed in a single volume; and the October number will commence a further development and expansion. *The
Criterion* differs from other literary periodicals in that it is not
satisfied to be a fortuitous concourse of compositions of fiction,
verse, and *belles lettres.* Every writer whose work appears in *The
Criterion* is there because that writer represents something which
The Criterion wishes to support; each contributor is a contributor to the formation of a design and the execution of a
purpose. *The Criterion* aims at the examination of first principles
in criticism, at the valuation of the new, and the revaluation of
old works of literature according to principles, and the illustra-
tion of these principles in creative writing. It aims at the affirma-

13. *Criterion* I (1923), 421.

tion and development of tradition. It aims at determining the relation of literature to other humane pursuits. It aims at the assertion of order and discipline, and the maintenance of order and discipline in literary taste. It is published not for any class or coterie, but for those individuals who are in sympathy with its ideas.[14]

With such a statement it became clear that Eliot planned to pursue, in the *Criterion,* many of the same interests that had been apparent in his previous writing. Such familiar phrases as "the examination of first principles," "the affirmation and development of tradition," and "the assertion of order and discipline" link Eliot's initial design for the review with the work of his earlier career. Similarly, the tone of almost belligerent independence—"It is published . . . for those individuls who are in sympathy with its ideas"—echoes the harshness in many earlier essays where he set out "to disturb and alarm the public."

However, the notes of July and October 1923 are misleading if they suggest that the interests of the early *Criterion* were narrowly literary. To be sure, it was several years before social, political, and religious issues figured prominently in its pages. But even from the beginning, arts other than literature received considerable attention; and articles on contemporary art, music, ballet, and theater appeared regularly.[15] Those programmatic notes fail to suggest another quality that distinguished the *Criterion* from the start, its internationalism. Early in 1924 Ford Madox Ford initiated his *Transatlantic Review;* and Eliot, in a letter of encouragement published in the first issue,

14. Though the insert is unsigned, the presumption is compelling that it was the work of Eliot.

15. The early volumes of the *Criterion* also included articles on such diverse topics as Freud, the devil, gambling, Cardinal Newman, the French Revolution, and Sir James Frazer. The book reviews, which Eliot considered one of the most important parts of the journal, treated books on philosophy, politics, psychology, and religion as well as books on artistic subjects.

suggested the attitude that was, in fact, already governing
his own editorship:

The present age, a singularly stupid one, is the age of a mistaken
nationalism and of an equally mistaken and artificial internationalism. . . . If anyone has a genuine nationality, let him assert
it. . . . But the more contact, the more free exchange, there can
be between the small number of intelligent people of every race
or nation, the more likelihood of general contribution to what we
call Literature.[16]

Toward this goal, Eliot frequently published essays by
foreign contributors—often translated expressly for the
Criterion; and beginning in the fourth issue he included
regular reviews of American and European periodicals.[17]
His contributors, he remarked later, shared an assumption that "there existed an international fraternity of men
of letters within Europe: a bond which did not replace, but
was perfectly compatible with, national loyalties, religious
loyalties, and differences of political philosophy."[18] In
"Tradition and the Individual Talent" Eliot had insisted
that the artist must recognize "the mind of Europe" to be
"the mind of his own country," and learn that mind to be
"much more important than his own private mind." As
editor he translated that principle into practice.

II

One of the foreign contributors whose work Eliot selected
to appear in an early issue of the *Criterion* was the con-

16. *Transatlantic Review* 1 (January 1924), 95.

17. In 1929 Eliot announced his journal's participation in a short-
lived plan of five European reviews to award an annual, international
literary prize. He remarked, "We feel some pride in the fact that *The
Criterion* was the first literary review in England to print work by
such writers as Marcel Proust, Paul Valéry, Jacques Rivière, Ramon
Fernandez, Jacques Maritain, Charles Maurras, Henri Massis . . .
and others" ("Commentary," *Criterion* 8 [1929], 577).

18. "The Unity of European Culture," Appendix to *Notes
Towards the Definition of Culture* (London: Faber and Faber, 1948),
p. 118.

temporary French philosopher and novelist, Julien Benda.
Doubtless Eliot had solicited an essay from Benda; one
suspects that he may have been disappointed with what
he received. Benda's contribution, entitled "A Preface,"
was in fact rather slight: a dialogue between the author
and an interlocutor, it dwelt on Benda's conflicting desires
to write fiction and to pursue philosophy. More significant
than the "Preface," though, was the note Eliot appended
to the article in that third issue of his review: "M. Benda's
work, especially his two essays on Bergsonism, and his
Belphégor (one of the most remarkable essays in criticism
of our time) will be the object of study in later numbers
of *The Criterion*."[19] As was often the case when further
discussion of an author's work was promised, the study
never appeared.[20] But Eliot's announcement indicated his
esteem for Benda.

Several years earlier, in his 1920 essay on "Imperfect
Critics" in *The Sacred Wood,* Eliot had pointed to the
"formal beauty" of Benda's criticism and the similarity
of his attitudes to those of such American critics as
Irving Babbitt. Describing Benda as "the ideal scavenger
of the rubbish of our time," he had noted that "much of
his analysis of the decadence of contemporary French society could be applied to London."[21] On two further occasions Eliot suggested the importance of Benda's *Belphégor*.
In January 1926 (in the first issue of the *New Criterion*),
Eliot described the "tendency" of his review as one toward
classicism ("a higher and clearer conception of Reason, and
a more severe and serene control of the emotions by Rea-

19. *Criterion* 1 (1923), 242.

20. In fact, Eliot published only one further article by him, a
closely argued philosophical discussion entitled: "Of the Idea of
Order and the Idea of God: Study for a System of Metaphysics,"
Criterion 10 (1930), 75–94.

21. *The Sacred Wood,* pp. 44–45. He added, "Almost the only
person who has ever figured in England and attempted a task at all
similar to that of M. Benda is Matthew Arnold."

son"). Among the books he cited to exemplify this tendency were Babbitt's recent *Democracy and Leadership* and *Belphégor*.[22] Writing in 1928 of the publication of *Belphégor* a decade before, Eliot said, "Some of us recognized [it] as an almost final statement of the attitude of contemporary society to art and the artist."[23]

As his repeated yoking of Benda and Babbitt suggests, Eliot found in *Belphégor* the same criticism of romanticism —a criticism founded on a belief in classicism—that was of such concern to his Harvard teacher.[24] The criticism and its classical assumptions were both evident throughout the early numbers of the *Criterion*. As a book that Eliot cited to suggest the orientation of his review, *Belphégor* deserves attention here.

Bearing, in its original version, the subtitle "Essai sur l'esthétique de la présente société française," Benda's book was almost entirely diagnostic in its analysis of contemporary French art and thought. That Benda's scrutiny was that of a classicist was always implicit, though rarely explicit, in his bitter attack on the symptoms of romanticism he discerned throughout French life. "It seems to us," he said, "that the aesthetic of contemporary French society— or, to be more exact, its aesthetic demand—can be defined thus: 'Contemporary French Society demands that all works of art shall arouse emotion and sensation: it insists that art shall cease to provide any form of intellectual

22. The other four were: *Réflexions sur la violence* by Georges Sorel; *L'Avenir de l'intelligence* by Charles Maurras; *Speculations* by T. E. Hulme; and *Réflexions sur l'intelligence* by Jacques Maritain ("The Idea of a Literary Review," *Criterion* 4 [1926], 5). Any study of Eliot's intellectual development must take serious notice of this list and the authors represented there.

23. "The Idealism of Julien Benda," *New Republic*, 12 December 1928, p. 105.

24. Babbitt contributed an introduction to the translation of *Belphégor* by S. J. I. Lawson published by Faber and Faber (London: 1929). References to this book will be to this translation; page numbers will be inserted in the text.

pleasure' " (3). From such an aesthetic followed the "cult of the indistinct" and its corollary, a "romantic cult of originality in art." But, Benda continued,

Behind this predilection of our contemporaries for the writer innocent of clear ideas, we must not fail to recognize something which lies much deeper and is evidently usual in most groups of society, namely, that to them, weakness of intellect is attractive and mental power repellent (23).

Benda found contemporary philosophy, like art, governed by the reader's desire for "an opportunity to indulge in the *emotion of sympathy*" (40), and in discussions of politics, art, religion, or love he discovered a "flagrant and incredible confusion of thought and the fundamental incapacity to grasp even the most trite and hackneyed ideas" (25). It was not easy to maintain a vital current of ideas and to create and sustain significant art in such a society.

Benda's description of the contemporary French intellectual milieu was not unlike Eliot's of the English and Babbitt's of the American. It was clear to each of them that the causes were in part educational and sociological. Benda lamented the disappearance "of the influence of theological education and the cult of classic literature. . . . The inter-relation between the dropping of these disciplinary studies (especially Latin) and the disappearance of all intellectual restraint, of all sense of the distinct and sharply-defined, of plastic sensibility, will be admitted even by those who despise these latter qualities" (116–17). Eliot's sense of the unfortunate consequence for literature of the power of the middle class and the decline of "the Civilized Class" was also Benda's:

We would suggest that besides numerous other causes (the development of sport, reading almost entirely limited to newspapers, etc.) the lowered standard of culture may be due to the entrance into French society of people of a different class, whose minds are in a state of nature (parvenus of trade, industry and

44

finance, etc.). It seems to us that generally speaking these sociological changes are not given their due importance in accounting
for the decadence of the taste of society (117).

Eliot himself would become increasingly concerned about
such "sociological changes"; Benda's book may well have
pointed him in that direction.

More a lament over the state of modern culture than a
call for reform, *Belphégor* was largely pessimistic; in fact,
Benda was skeptical at the possibility of any reform. Eliot
could hardly have found there the bracing assertion of
classical principles he might have hoped for; and Benda's
diagnosis of the diseases of modern thought hardly went
beyond Babbitt's. The importance of Benda's presence in
that 1923 issue of the *Criterion* is not that he was a seminal
influence in the development of Eliot's thought, but that
he represents the early antiromantic (and thus, if here only
implicitly, classical) bias of Eliot's review. In light of
Eliot's considerable interest in the French, it is furthermore significant that this first in a series of classicists whom
Eliot would publish in the *Criterion* should be French. Several years before Eliot's 1926 description of the classical
"tendency" of his review, Benda had appeared as a har-
binger of that inclination.

III

The only English author represented in Eliot's 1926 list
of books exemplifying the classicist tendency of the *Criterion* was T. E. Hulme.[25] If the concrete indebtedness of

25. Such critics as Frank Kermode, Murray Krieger, and C. K.
Stead have pointed to the apparent inconsistency between the "classicism" that Eliot, Hulme, and others professed and the "romanticism" implicit in their poetic theories. While not denying the force
of these criticisms, I do not feel they should detain us here. As Eliot
himself observed, the antithesis between "classic" and "romantic"
belongs to "literary politics" ("What is a Classic?" *On Poetry and
Poets,* p. 53). Eliot and many of the other early twentieth-century
classicists were literary politicians, campaigning for their positions;
as such, they naturally made the distinction between their party and

Eliot to Benda is difficult to define, there is no such difficulty with Hulme; in a letter to Allen Tate, Eliot acknowledged that debt unequivocally: "Hulme has influenced
me enormously."[26] Doubtless Hulme's *Speculations* was
foremost in his mind when he made that comment. But he
had expressed interest in Hulme some years before the
book's publication in 1924; his interest was an evolving
one, and the pattern of that evolution provides an epitome
of the development of Eliot's own career. His first published references concerned Hulme's poetry; later, he discussed his critical theory; and finally, after his own
conversion to Anglo-Catholicism, he drew on the theological implications of Hulme's thought.

In reviewing a book about men killed in the First
World War, Eliot in 1919 made his earliest reference to
Hulme. While pointing to other weaknesses in the book,
he called especial attention to the author's having "omitted
one dead soldier who was a real poet—T. E. Hulme. . . ."[27]
The next year, he regretted that reviewers had still not
recognized Hulme's excellence: "Let the public . . . ask itself why it has never heard of the poems of T. E. Hulme
. . . , and why it has heard of the poems of Lady Precocia
Pondoeuf and has seen a photograph of the nursery in
which she wrote them. . . ."[28] Eliot's having spoken as often
even as twice of Hulme as a poet might well seem curious to
one who knows Hulme's scant output of poetry through

the opposition appear sharper than it was. One should no more expect
thorough consistency from a literary politician than from any other,
and to recognize that many of Eliot's statements grew out of a continuing polemic should not be to discount their significance. Seen as
the product of such debate and not as isolated pronouncements of
literary theory, such statements may be more meaningful—if not less
open to such criticisms as have often been made.

26. 22 February 1929, Princeton University Library.
27. "The New Elizabethans and the Old," *Athenaeum*, 4 April
1919, p. 134.
28. "A Brief Treatise on the Criticism of Poetry," *Chapbook* 2
(March 1920), 2.

"The Complete Poetical Works of T. E. Hulme" (five in number!) printed as an appendix to Ezra Pound's *Ripostes* (1912) and who thinks first of the many critical and philosophical essays he published before the war. But his having spoken thus suggests the nature of Hulme's importance for Eliot early in his career.

With the beginning of his editorship and his efforts to reassert classical principles through the *Criterion,* Eliot's attention turned to Hulme's essays. In the issue for July 1925 he included some fragments from Hulme's previously unpublished writings. These "Notes on Language and Style" were edited and introduced by Herbert Read, from the beginning a regular contributor to the *Criterion* and the man who was quite likely responsible for directing Eliot's attention to Hulme's prose. In 1924 Read published a selection of Hulme's writings under the title *Speculations,* and Eliot was apparently impressed by the undertaking. After Eliot's death, Read recalled his desire to form "a party, . . . a 'new front' " through the *Criterion:*

The illusion that I might become one of [his] disciples was fostered for a time by my editing of the posthumous papers of T. E. Hulme. I do not think that Hulme's *Speculations,* when they were published in 1924, made any difference to Eliot's political idealism or philosophical faith, but his convictions were immensely strengthened. As the man who had rescued Hulme from a probable oblivion I had earned Eliot's deep gratitude.[29]

When *Speculations* first appeared, however, Eliot was uncertain that the "rescue" would be successful. "The posthumous volume of *Speculations* of T. E. Hulme . . . appears to have fallen like a stone to the bottom of the sea

29. "T. S. E.—A Memoir," p. 38. Perhaps the most obvious sign of Eliot's feeling for Read was his having assigned him the review of Babbitt's *Democracy and Leadership,* published in 1924. During the run of the *Criterion,* Read contributed five articles, as many poems, a short story, frequent surveys of American periodicals, and reviews of no fewer than sixty-five books.

of print," he wrote. "With its peculiar merits, this book is most unlikely to meet with the slightest comprehension from the usual reviewer." Nonetheless, Eliot insisted, "it is a book of very great significance . . . [in which Hulme] appears as a forerunner of a new attitude of mind, which should be the twentieth-century mind, if the twentieth-century is to have a mind of its own. Hulme is classical, reactionary, and revolutionary; he is the antipodes of the eclectic, tolerant, and democratic mind of the end of the last century."[30]

Like Benda, Hulme was concerned equally with philosophy and art; like Benda, he endeavored to demonstrate the philosophical causes of what he took to be the weakness of much contemporary art; and, like Benda, he found the fault to lie primarily in romanticism. "I object," he said, "to the sloppiness which doesn't consider that a poem is a poem unless it is moaning or whining about something or other. . . . There is a general tendency to think that verse means little else than the expression of unsatisfied emotion. . . . The essence of poetry to most people is that it must lead them to a beyond of some kind."[31] More hope-

30. "Commentary," *Criterion* 2 (1924), 231. This "Commentary" was the first of a series of such articles written by Eliot for nearly every issue of his review. Most were unsigned; some appeared over the initials "T. S. E."; and some—like this one—were signed "Crites." The name "Crites" appears to derive from either a character in Ben Jonson's *Cynthia's Revels* (a man of "straight judgment and strong mind" thought to be Jonson's representation of himself) or from the spokesman for the ancients in Dryden's "Essay of Dramatic Poesy." While the quality and importance of these "Commentaries" vary greatly from quarter to quarter, together they offer a valuable record of Eliot's wide range of interests—some in matters of great moment, others in matters apparently trivial. They provide indispensable material for any study of Eliot's intellectual development during the twenties and thirties.

31. "Romanticism and Classicism," *Speculations: Essays on Humanism and the Philosophy of Art,* ed. Herbert Read (London: Kegan Paul, 1924), pp. 126, 127. Subsequent references, inserted in the text, are to this edition.

fully than Benda, however, Hulme looked toward the future. "After a hundred years of romanticism, we are in for a classical revival. . . . A period of dry, hard, classical verse is coming. . . . The great aim is accurate, precise and definite description" (113, 133, 132).

For Hulme—as for Benda and Babbitt and Eliot—romanticism was not merely a literary phenomenon; it was an entire disposition of mind. Rousseau, again, was seen as its chief prophet: "Here is the root of all romanticism," Hulme said in his essay "Romanticism and Classicism": "that man, the individual, is an infinite reservoir of possibilities; and if you can so rearrange society by the destruction of oppressive order then these possibilities will have a chance and you will get Progress." Against this notion Hulme reaffirmed the classical attitude, "quite clearly . . . the exact opposite. . . . Man is an extraordinarily fixed and limited animal whose nature is absolutely constant. It is only by tradition and organisation that anything decent can be got out of him" (116).

These ideas, however, were hardly new to Eliot in 1924. Doubtless more striking was the essay that Read placed at the beginning of *Speculations*, "Humanism and the Religious Attitude." There Hulme demonstrated how romanticism in literature was bound up with what Hulme spoke of as humanism in ethics; and how classicism, conversely, implied the religious attitude. It may well be that it was in demonstrating the close relationship between classicism (which Eliot for some time now had embraced) and the religious attitude (to which he had not yet passed) that Hulme "influenced [Eliot] enormously." Wyndham Lewis, a close friend of Hulme before his death and of Eliot in the early years of the *Criterion*, remarked—with characteristic flippancy—on the importance of Hulme's religious thought. "Hulme is mainly distinguished as a 'thinker'," Lewis wrote in 1937, "for having heard of the theological doctrine of Original Sin. No one else in England at the time had ever heard of it, or would, I am persuaded, have done so since, had it not been for him."[32]

"The essence of all Romanticism," Hulme held, is the tendency to "place *Perfection* where it should not be—on this human plane . . ." (33). He found such a belief to be central to humanism as well. As a corrective he proposed the religious attitude. Significantly, in describing it he used terms quite similar to those he had used to describe classicism: "Man," he said, "is . . . essentially limited and imperfect." But he went on to add a theological explanation:

He is endowed with Original Sin. While he can occasionally accomplish acts which partake of perfection, he can never himself *be* perfect. . . . As man is essentially bad, he can only accomplish anything of value by discipline—ethical and political. Order is thus not merely negative, but creative and liberating. Institutions are necessary (47).

The realm of human affairs, then, is not the whole of reality, as Hulme found romanticism suggesting. He said that man, fallen as he is, must accept the fact that he lives on only one plane of existence (that of the organic world). Discrete and absolutely discontinuous from the organic world are other regions: the inorganic world of mathematical and physical science, and the world of ethical and religious values (where, alone, perfection is real). Against humanism and romanticism, which had confused these distinctions, Hulme proposed the religious attitude: "There must be an *absolute* division between each of the three regions, a kind of *chasm*. There must be no continuity, no bridge leading from one to the other" (6). Christianity, of course, offers the hope of such "bridges." But Hulme was not an active Christian; nor, in 1924, was Eliot.

It was no doubt their common antipathy to romanticism

32. *Blasting and Bombardiering* (London: Eyre and Spottiswoode, 1937), p. 107.

and tendency toward classicism that first drew Eliot to Hulme and prompted him to recommend *Speculations* when it appeared in 1924, print Hulme's "Notes on Language and Style" in 1925, and include the book in his 1926 list of exemplary *Criterion* texts. But Hulme's demonstration of the kinship between classicism and the religious attitude must also have caught Eliot's attention. Though Eliot was himself still preoccupied with what was essentially a secular, literary form of that attitude, he surely recognized in Hulme's book important implications for his own classicism. "Classicism," Eliot remarked in his 1924 discussion of Hulme, "is in a sense reactionary, but it must be in a profounder sense revolutionary."[33] To Eliot, one imagines, Hulme's discussion of the religious attitude was just that.

Between 1928 and 1930 Eliot made three further references to Hulme. Now a Christian himself, he called upon Hulme neither as a poet nor as a classicist, but, rather, as a religious thinker. He cited Hulme's "theory of gaps" to explain Paul Elmer More's notion of dualism;[34] and both in "Second Thoughts about Humanism" and "Baudelaire" he quoted extensively from Hulme's discussion of original sin in "Humanism and the Religious Attitude." "I agree with what Hulme says," Eliot asserted in 1929. "It is to the immense credit of Hulme that he found out for himself that there is an *absolute* to which Man can *never* attain."[35] Hulme, like Benda, is significant in representing the *Criterion*'s classicism. His further role in leading Eliot beyond

---

33. "Commentary," *Criterion* 2 (1924), 232.

34. "Mr. P. E. More's Essays," *TLS*, 21 February 1929, p. 136.

35. "Second Thoughts about Humanism," in *Selected Essays*, New Edition (New York: Harcourt, Brace, 1950), p. 437. Eliot's continued interest in Hulme is suggested by his publication in the April 1932 *Criterion* of Michael Roberts's essay on "The Categories of T. E. Hulme." Many *Criterion* contributors were also publishing with Faber and Faber; several years later, Roberts published his study of Hulme with Eliot's firm.

that classicism to Christianity was, in the precise sense of the word, incalculable.

Eliot's special notice of the work of Benda and Hulme was indicative of the classical tendency of the *Criterion* and its editor. Classical education, he said there, was not only "necessary or desirable for the acquisition of a good English style," but essential because *"all* European civilizations are . . . dependent upon Greece and Rome—so far as they are civilizations at all."[36] And in an early "Commentary" Eliot remarked that "the study of Greek is a part of the study of our own mind. Our categories of thought are largely the outcome of Greek thought; our categories of emotion are largely the outcome of Greek literature. . . . Neglect of Greek means for a Europe *a relapse into unconsciousness.*"[37] But the *Criterion*'s classicism was more than the concern for a certain educational curriculum, just as it was less than a religious creed. "There was never any age or group of people who professed 'classicism' in the sense in which St. Thomas and his followers professed 'Thomism'," Eliot pointed out.[38] It was, as he said, a "tendency," a set of attitudes, a frame of mind.

IV

Eliot recognized the protean character of the term *classicism* and said he used it "with hesitation, for it is hardly more than analogical."[39] But the *Criterion*'s tendency in that direction achieved clearer definition when the review's classicism was contrasted with its opposite, romanticism. One of the distinctive excellences of Eliot's editorship was his willingness to open the pages of his review to authors

36. "Books of the Quarter," *Criterion* 5 (1927), 121; "The Classics in France—and in England," *Criterion* 2 (1923), 104.
37. "Commentary," *Criterion* 3 (1925), 342.
38. "Commentary," *Criterion* 6 (1927), 193.
39. "The Idea of a Literary Review," p. 5.

with attitudes different from his own and to allow the *Criterion* to become a forum for intellectual controversy. The first such controversy concerned classicism and romanticism, and in the essays that Eliot selected to represent his own point of view, his classicism found its most explicit expression. A central document in that controversy was "The Function of Criticism," Eliot's first major theoretical essay since "Tradition and the Individual Talent" and a notable statement of modern classical principles.

John Middleton Murry was the instigator—and, during most of the next several years, the focus—of this controversy. Several years before it erupted in 1923, Murry had been impressed with Eliot's *Prufrock and Other Observations;* and in 1919 he had invited the young poet to become a reviewer for the *Athenaeum* (of which Murry had recently become editor). During the next two years Eliot contributed more than thirty reviews, and the two rapidly became friends.[40] Though they developed a respect for one another that they never lost, they were rarely agreed on fundamental issues. "Dear old boy," Murry wrote Eliot in 1923 when he found himself disappointed with what he took to be the decadence of *The Waste Land,* "I don't know what to say to you. I never do. But in my way believe me I love you—I think of you and feel for you continually."[41]

40. Early in their acquaintance, Eliot wrote to Murry: "You must realise that it has been a great event to me to know you, but you do not know yet the full meaning of this phrase as I write it" (29 July 1919, Northwestern University Library). Murry's respect for Eliot is apparent in his having himself reviewed Eliot's *Ara Vos Prec* in the *Athenaeum* and his having assigned to Eliot a review there of his own verse drama, *Cinnamon and Angelica.*

41. Quoted in F. A. Lea, *The Life of John Middleton Murry* (New York: Oxford University Press, 1959), p. 117. Lea offers an admirable, if necessarily brief, treatment of the Eliot-Murry relationship and remarks, ". . . it is a poor tribute to the intellectual vitality of our time that nobody has yet found the forty-years' debate between these two writers worth an extended study" (p. 346).

In 1923 Murry launched his own monthly, the *Adelphi*,[42] and the public Eliot-Murry dialogue began. From the first, the *Adelphi* was defiantly romantic. "This magazine," Murry wrote in his first article (portentously entitled "The Cause of It All"), "is run neither by capital nor by charity nor by advertisement, but by a belief in life. . . ." The *Adelphi*, he said, "is primarily and essentially an assertion of faith . . . that life is important, and that more life should be man's chief endeavour. . . . The endeavour to be true to experience strikes me at this moment as the most precious privilege of all." The editorial policy of the new monthly reflected those principles:

No matter what the subject, or how apparently trivial the occasion, provided [an author] feels strongly about it and manages to communicate the reality of his feeling in his words, his contribution will be regarded. . . . *The Adelphi* wants only those things that you can't help writing, because you will burst if you don't.[43]

The next month Murry addressed himself to critics (like Eliot?) who might question his definition of *life:*

I am not afraid of the man who writes to me, asking "What do you mean by life? Define it." I have no definitions to give. I am tired of definitions, tired of the people who define poetry and cannot feel it, truth, and have not a grain of it in their hearts, love, and have never been touched by it. *The Adelphi* is not meant for them. If they really and truly want to know what I

42. The first issue of Murry's review appeared only a few months after the initial appearance of the *Criterion*. However, each editor was solicitous for the welfare of the other's enterprise. Eliot helped to forestall the threatened collapse of the *Adelphi* in the late twenties by suggesting possible sources of financial support; and, early on, Murry had offered Eliot encouragement regarding the *Criterion*. "Your support will certainly be of the greatest value," Eliot wrote his friend on 13 October 1922. And he added, somewhat too sanguinely, "I think I am safe in believing that you will be in sympathy with the paper's aims" (Northwestern University Library).

43. *Adelphi* 1 (1923), 6, 8, 9, 10–11.

mean by life let them read the paper, and read it again, until they catch with their being the tone that will forever elude their minds.[44]

In August Murry offered a definition of "the truly religious attitude"—almost as if in parodic anticipation of Hulme's discussion published the following year. "It seems to me that the essence of the truly religious attitude is to be serious about life. . . . Let me say, once for all," Murry added humorlessly, "that to be serious is not to be solemn."[45] The following month he "cheerfully" accepted the *New Statesman*'s description of his review "as the last stronghold of romanticism."

In England there has never been any classicism worth talking about: we have had our classics, but no classicism. And all our classics are romantic. . . . The English writer, the English divine, the English statesman, inherit no rules from their forbears: they inherit only this: a sense that in the last resort they must depend upon the inner voice.[46]

Murry's position in the *Adelphi* was, of course, a challenge to Eliot and his *Criterion*. Whether or not Murry's effusions provoked the essay, they did at least forcefully set forth ideas to which Eliot responded in his essay in the October 1923 *Criterion*: "The Function of Criticism." "Most of our critics are occupied in labour of obnubilation; in reconciling, in hushing up, in patting down, in squeezing in, in glozing over, in concocting pleasant sedatives. . . ." He admired Murry for at least not being one of these. Murry, Eliot said, "is aware that there are definite positions to be taken, and that now and then one must actually reject something and select something else."[47]

44. "A Month After," *Adelphi* 1 (1923), 90.
45. "Religion and Faith," *Adelphi* 1 (1923), 179.
46. "On Fear; And on Romanticism," *Adelphi* 1 (1923), 273, 274–75.
47. In *Selected Essays*, pp. 14–15. Subsequent references, inserted in the text, are to the essay as it is reprinted in this volume.

also, as we have seen, was rejecting and se-
he was clearly not favorably disposed to the
e new *Adelphi*. "With Mr. Murry's formu-
ssicism and Romanticism I cannot agree; the
ence seems to me rather the difference between the
complete and the fragmentary, the adult and the immature,
the orderly and the chaotic" (15). To stress the continuity
of his thought over the past several years, Eliot at the beginning of his essay quoted a lengthy passage from "Tradition and the Individual Talent" "on the subject of the
relation of the new to the old in art" (12). Rather than the
authority of the tradition, however, Murry had proposed
the authority of the "inner voice"—the authority, he said,
to which all Englishmen must, in the last resort, appeal.
Eliot countered with the acerbity characteristic of his responses to romanticism:

My belief is that those who possess this inner voice are ready
enough to hearken to it, and will hear no other. The inner voice,
in fact, sounds remarkably like an old principle which has been
formulated by an elder critic in the now familiar phrase of
"doing as one likes." The possessors of the inner voice ride ten
in a compartment to a football match at Swansea, listening to
the inner voice, which breathes the eternal message of vanity,
fear, and lust (16).

Eliot's distrust of "the inner voice" and his belief in the
authority of tradition were, if anything, stronger now than
in 1919. Moreover, his earlier literary traditionalism had
ripened into a general attitude of classicism. He now acknowledged the important nonliterary implications of his
position:

Those of us who find ourselves supporting what Mr. Murry calls
Classicism believe that men cannot get on without giving allegiance to something outside themselves. . . . If . . . a man's interest is political, he must, I presume, profess an allegiance to
principles, or to a form of government, or to a monarch; and if
he is interested in religion, and has one, to a Church (15).

[handwritten: Romanticism V.S. Classicism]

And if he is interested in literary criticism, a man must give himself over to the work he is scrutinizing. In order that his criticism be directed to "something outside" (the work) and not be corrupted by the mutterings of his "inner voice," Eliot insisted that the critic must have "a very highly developed sense of fact," a faculty that is "something very slow to develop, and its complete development means perhaps the very pinnacle of civilisation" (19).

In the original *Criterion* version of the essay, Eliot remarked further:

> So important [the sense of fact] seems to me, that I am inclined to make one distinction between Classicism and Romanticism of this, that the romantic is deficient or undeveloped in his ability to distinguish between fact and fancy, whereas the classicist, or adult mind, is thoroughly realist—without illusions, without day-dreams, without hope, without bitterness, and with an abundant resignation.

[handwritten margin note: Eliot claimed Romanticism too focused on "the inner self" without the "authority of tradition"]

"But," he added, "this would really be a digression."[48] Curiously, Eliot omitted this revealing passage when he reprinted "The Function of Criticism" nine years later in *Selected Essays*. Perhaps the excision of this "digression" in 1932 reflected a lessening of Eliot's interest in the classicism-romanticism dispute; by then he was more concerned with the struggle between Christianity and atheism.[49] But "The Function of Criticism" remains one of Eliot's most important essays—and another clear announcement of the position of Eliot and his review.

Predictably, it did not go unnoticed in the pages of Murry's *Adelphi*. In December Murry wrote "More about Romanticism":

48. "The Function of Criticism," *Criterion* 2 (1923), 39–40.
49. Looking back on his 1923 essay in 1956, Eliot confessed to being "rather bewildered, wondering what all the fuss had been about —though I was glad to find nothing positively to contradict my present opinions." ("The Frontiers of Criticism," in *On Poetry and Poets*, p. 113.)

Those readers of *The Adelphi* who remember a hurried defense of Romanticism that I made in August last will be pleased to learn that I have found a real opponent in Mr. T. S. Eliot, the gifted editor of *The Criterion*. I at least am glad of the encounter. I am not by inclination provocative; and when I wrote on Romanticism I was not engaged in trailing my coat, or asking for a fight for the fun of the thing. . . . The debate, I profoundly believe, is concerned with fundamentals.[50]

At Eliot's invitation, Murry continued the debate in what he spoke of as "the more leisurely and expansive pages of *The Criterion*."[51] The terms of the dispute were clear in the title of his essay, "Romanticism and the Tradition." The tradition, Murry suggested, was bankrupt: "The vital motion of religion becomes petrified into dogmas and ceremonies; the vital motion of literature is ossified into forms and canons" (276). With the Renaissance, in fact, mankind had liberated itself from such constraints:

The Renaissance meant for a moment the end of fear. The individual could stand alone once more. . . . Now, the foundation of the modern consciousness is this, that the individual man takes his stand apart and alone, without the support of any authority. . . . The modern consciousness begins historically with the repudiation of organized Christianity . . . (282, 283).

"The primary fact is man's consciousness of his own existence, his knowledge of himself as free: and that is an irrational knowledge," Murry said (286).

Romanticism, essentially, is a movement of the soul which begins with the assertion of the I Am [the individual soul] against all external spiritual authority, which proceeds from this condition of rebellion and isolation to a new life-adjustment, and goes on towards the ultimate recognition of a new principle of authority in and through the deeper knowledge of the self. Briefly, it may

50. *Adelphi* 1 (1923), 557.
51. "Romanticism and Tradition," *Criterion* 2 (1924), 272. Subsequent references will be inserted in the text.

be called the rediscovery of the greater I AM [God] through the lesser I AM [the soul] (288–89).

There was here, of course, no compromise, no meeting of the minds. If indeed he could fathom Murry's meaning, Eliot must have sensed the futility of any considered reply. There was not even a paragraph concerning Murry's essay in his "Commentary." Instead, as if by way of response to Murry, Eliot published in that issue his notice on the appearance of Hulme's *Speculations*.[52]

During the next two years Murry did not appear in the *Criterion,* and the dispute between classicism and romanticism seemed to have spent its force. However by 1927 the controversy was renewed; once again, Murry was at its center. In June 1926 he published his essay there on "The Romantic Fallacy." The title is startling, but we are not to suppose that he had abandoned his cause. Rather, the article was an analysis of Tolstoy's literary criticism. Murry objected to Tolstoy's acceptance of Christianity as the

52. Other members of the *Criterion* "family" were not so indirect. In the very issue in which Murry's "Romanticism and the Tradition" appeared, Herbert Read commented on a contribution by Murry to the *Yale Review:* "In 'Flaubert and Flaubart' Mr. Middleton Murry returns to Romanticism; and leaves it without making his point of view any clearer" ("Foreign Review," *Criterion* 2 [1924], 367). In that same issue, Mrs. Eliot, writing pseudonymously as "F. M.," exclaimed. " 'Golly!' as Mr. J. Middleton Murry says in his last outcry but one, revealing his 'sensitiveness to the living soul of the language' and revealing to his readers how much better a Professor of Poetry he would make than that poor insensitive Mr. Garrod. Imagine a Professor of Poetry at Oxford writing 'Golly' in his lectures" ("Letters of the Moment," *Criterion* 2 [1924], 362). In the next issue, "F. M." again attacked Murry, this time in a review of his latest novel: "In reading *The Voyage* . . . one has the sensation of having strayed into a little company composed of neurasthenics and imbeciles, who circle painfully around their complexes and neuroses weaving a tangled web from which there is no escape but physical or mental suicide" ("Books of the Quarter," *Criterion* 2 [1924], 484). One doubts that Murry knew the identity of "F. M." In a letter to Ada Leverson at Easter 1925, Eliot identified contributions so signed as those of his wife (Berg Collection, New York Public Library).

criterion for judging the moral excellence of art. To Murry's mind, post-Renaissance literature clearly demonstrated that there were other, equally useful criteria. "Tolstoy denied that the artist, who should elect to remain an artist, could achieve a higher life-conception than that contained in Christianity," he said.[53]

The claim that post-Renaissance art should be judged good or bad by reference to the life-conception inculcated by Christianity is invalidated if it can be met by the counter-claim that not Christianity . . . but post-Renaissance art itself contains and communicates the highest life-conception of which Western humanity has so far proved itself capable (528).

Murry's defiant antitraditionalism had not diminished during the past two years; he continued to insist that Christianity, the very element of the tradition whose overwhelming importance Eliot would soon acknowledge, was an anachronism. But his other objection to Tolstoy seemed to suggest a development in his thought—and perhaps an approach, however slight, to Eliot's position. According to Murry, an "absolute dichotomy" underlies Tolstoy's theory of art: "His fundamental proposition is that art consists in the communication of feelings, as opposed to thoughts" (522). The emotional—hence, antiintellectual —basis of Tolstoy's aesthetic was doubtless what Murry meant by "The Romantic Fallacy." "That art is an affair of mere emotion . . . is manifestly wrong," he said. And, pointing to a passage he had cited earlier in his essay, he added: "The lines from *Lear* . . . do not communicate a mere feeling, any more than they convey a mere thought. What they communicate is something of a third kind, in which feeling and thought are inextricably blended" (531).

53. *Criterion* 4 (1926), 527. Subsequent references will be inserted in the text.

With such an assertion Murry seemed to be approaching a synthesis of elements that had long been opposed in the classicism-romanticism debate. By 1927 such a wedding was his stated intention in another *Criterion* essay, "Towards a Synthesis," an undisguised gesture toward a rapprochement between Eliot's position and his own. It was written, he said, "in the hope that we may advance a step nearer towards a less perplexing and wasteful distribution of intellectual forces. Its purpose is, most emphatically, not polemical."[54]

Murry began by referring to a recent *Criterion* review in which Eliot, discussing a current controversy over *intuition* and *intelligence,* had declared himself "on the side of what we call 'the intelligence'."[55] To illustrate his position, Eliot had cited Saint Thomas; and Murry sensed, in this appeal to Thomas, Eliot's implicit acceptance of the Thomist theory of knowledge. However, Murry objected, Eliot had adopted the Thomistic epistemology without any sign of having also embraced the Thomistic theology. While Thomism was predicated on a marriage of faith and reason, Murry said, Eliot was apparently cultivating the latter without the former.

Eliot's apparent dilemma seemed to Murry the dilemma of modern man generally. "Once the spiritual life of man was deprived of one of its two natural means of expression, namely faith, then the intellectual schematism into which reason had proliferated in the School ceased also to be adequate," he said (299–300). A return to the classical Thomist system of faith and reason was, according to Murry, impossible for modern man "simply because faith does not exist for him" (300). After the Renaissance the elements of the medieval synthesis—faith and reason—

54. *Criterion* 5 (1927), 294. Subsequent references will be inserted in the text.
55. "Books of the Quarter," *Criterion* 4 (1926), 757.

were replaced by art and science, respectively.[56] "The task of creating, or helping to create, a new synthesis is the most urgent business of criticism today," he said (303). Murry then proposed his synthesis:

As a provisional schematism, therefore, I suggest an equivalence of intelligence and intuition, as aspects of the indivisible soul or psychical reality, maintained in a tense and pregnant antinomy. Intuition is the faculty by which the full, concrete reality is . . . prehended, that is to say, encountered and, as it were, absorbed without necessary cognition; intelligence is the faculty of cognition, that operates through concept and abstraction. The constant effort of a living soul is two-fold: to master by cognition the intuitively prehended reality, and to revivify, as it were, by a new injection of the intuitive reality, the conceptual hierarchy into which cognition has frozen it. This equilibrium between intuition and cognition must always be unstable: precisely in this instability lies the reality of the life of the soul . . . (308).

Classicism, he said, may be thought of as the tendency toward cognition; romanticism, the tendency toward the revivification of thought "by immediate and concrete experience. Classicism and Romanticism, in this sense, are

56. In September 1925, Murry had explained his attitude toward organized, Christian religion. "I am fully conscious of the debt that I owe the Church," he said. But he insisted that "the finer conscience of mankind has now passed definitely outside the Church. . . . A drunken tramp who pads the highways unknowing whence his next meal will come is nearer to following Christ than the whole bench of English bishops. . . . This modern world does not believe in God the Father; and the modern Church does not either. It puts its faith in pensions, and endowments, and 5 or 15 percent" ("Christ or Christianity," *Adelphi* 3 [1925], 233, 238). After reading this article, Eliot wrote to Murry: "It seems to me that one must either ignore the Church, or reform it from within, or transcend it,—but never attack it. . . . You see I happened to be brought up in the most 'liberal' of 'Christian' creeds—Unitarianism: I may therefore be excused for seeing the dangers of what you propose, more clearly than I see the vices of what you attack. If one discards dogma, it should be for a more celestial garment, not for nakedness" (29 August 1925, Northwestern University Library).

moments, constantly recurring, in the full soul life of the complete man" (308). With such an understanding of the relation of intuition and intelligence, Murry offered his "synthesis analogous, but not correspondent, to the mediaeval synthesis of Faith and Reason" (309).

With characteristic passion, Murry had endeavored through his essay to achieve some basis for common understanding with his friend Eliot. But in fact "Towards a Synthesis" served only to renew the *Criterion*'s debate over classicism and romanticism. Nonetheless, while renewing it, Murry's essay translated that discussion to a new level as it tried forthrightly to consider the religious implications of the matter. The article, written to end the controversy, itself became an object of controversy.[57] And as the discussion unfolded in the *Criterion*, Eliot's guiding hand was evident. The development of Eliot's own thinking during the past several years was clear in his eagerness to reopen the consideration of classicism and romanticism from the religious perspective suggested by Murry.

Significantly, the first response to Murry that Eliot published was that of a Jesuit, Father M. C. D'Arcy, who would contribute a number of articles to the *Criterion* during the next twelve years. "Those who defend Intelligence these days are aware that they must meet with unpopularity in certain quarters," he said. "The intellect, as we know it, is hard and unyielding, and there is always a tendency away from it. . . ." Through an extensive discussion of Thomistic thought D'Arcy endeavored to demonstrate that "all that . . . Murry includes in his two factors, intuition and reason, fall within the intelligence as understood by St. Thomas. . . . The same problem con-

---

57. Returning a manuscript to Gertrude Stein in September 1927, Eliot wrote: "I have an immense amount of material awaiting publication. . . . The flow of contributions through 'The Criterion' has been lately very much held up by one or two controversies which, like fire engines, must take precedence" (Yale University Library).

fronted the medievals as tortures the modern lover of synthesis. Quality, and value and intuition are no modern discovery, due 'to the enlargement of the faculties', and a careful scrutiny of the philosophy of St. Thomas will prove this. . . ."[58] One might well imagine that Eliot, himself, was then engaged in such scrutiny.[59]

D'Arcy's essay was followed in the same issue by another criticism of Murry's article—this one, by Charles Mauron, translated from the French by Eliot himself. As D'Arcy had attacked Murry's conception of intelligence, Mauron attacked his use of *intuition*. "I consider the abuse of such a word, without precise meaning, to be a real spiritual peril," he said. After discussing the ambiguity of Murry's thought, Mauron concluded: "I am afraid that intuition, far from explaining anything, is nothing but a catchword applied to all the mental phenomena of which we have no clear idea. . . ."[60]

The October *Criterion* carried yet another French attack, also translated by Eliot. Ramon Fernandez, who earlier had contributed an essay on Newman, challenged Murry's distinction between intelligence and intuition. "The only dualism which I observe to-day is a false dualism between a rich, vivid, complex intelligence, still unprovided with a rigorous terminology, and a short-sighted reason, largely verbal, based on a superficial science and inspired chiefly by preoccupations of social hygiene and defence." In conclusion, Fernandez, one of

58. "The Thomistic Synthesis and Intelligence," *Criterion* 6 (1927), 227–28, 215.

59. In October 1927, Eliot wrote: "My knowledge of Aquinas is slight: it is limited to the accounts of Gilson and de Wulf, to two volumes of extracts, one prepared by Professor Gilson and the other by M. Truc, to two or three books by M. Maritain and modern Dominicans, and to the new edition of the *Summa* published by Desclée. Only nine volumes of this edition have yet appeared, and in these nine volumes I have only read here and there" ("Mr. Middleton Murry's Synthesis," *Criterion* 6 [1927], 340).

60. "Concerning 'Intuition'," *Criterion* 6 (1927), 229, 235.

those whom Eliot had characterized as being with him "on the side of . . . 'the intelligence'," offered his judgment "on the quarrel of romanticism and classicism, which is coming to life again":

Romanticism V.S. Classicism (again)

. . . Both starting from the fact that the human world is peopled with ineffables, the romantic spirit and the classic spirit adopt two opposed methods. The romantic spirit attaches itself to the ineffable as such, would have it still more ineffable, but by an illuminating contradiction tries to extract thought from this ineffable. While the classical spirit, by disposing this ineffable in an intelligible perspective, surrounding it with order and light, allows it to exhale all its perfume.[61]

Eliot doubtless took pleasure in translating that passage.

Immediately following the essay by Fernandez, Eliot published his own criticism of "Mr. Middleton Murry's Synthesis": "I can now make a little clearer what . . . I mean by 'being on the side of what we call the intelligence'," Eliot said.

I mean that intuition must have its place in a world of discourse; that there may be room for intuitions both at the top and the bottom, or at the beginning and the end; but that intuition must always be tested, and capable of test, in a whole of experience in which intellect plays a large part.

What was especially significant in Eliot's article, however, was his insistence on the possibility—even in 1927—of believing in a system of intelligence such as Thomas's. It would be another year before he would publicly announce his Anglo-Catholicism. But in this lingering debate over classicism and romanticism there were anticipations of that announcement: "What bothers me especially in Mr. Murry's fluid world is that Truth itself seems to change. . . . That I simply cannot understand. . . . 'We cannot return

61. "A Note on Intelligence and Intuition," *Criterion* 6 (1927), 332, 339.

to St. Thomas,' [Murry] says. I do not see why not. . . ."[62]

The controversy over Murry's article continued with T. Sturge Moore's "Towards Simplicity" in the November *Criterion* and concluded with yet another statement from Murry, "Concerning Intelligence," the following month. But the rapprochement that Murry had desired was never achieved. If anything, the distance between his position and Eliot's had become greater as Eliot increasingly revealed his attraction to Christianity. In September 1927 Murry wrote his friend about "Towards a Synthesis": "All my hopeful feeling when I undertook that frightful essay has evaporated. It seems that there really is some sort of abyss between us—not humanly thank goodness—but in respect of our ideas and convictions."[63]

Though Eliot continued to follow Murry's evolving interests and criticized him when—as was often the case—he found himself in disagreement, the friendship continued until Murry's death in 1957.[64] Eliot regularly called upon Murry for *Criterion* book reviews; and, in fact, he used his offices to secure other reviewing opportunities for his

62. *Criterion* 6 (1927), 342, 346–47. As an epigraph to his essay Eliot printed a sentence from Irving Babbitt's *Democracy and Leadership:* "What is disquieting about the present time is not so much its open and avowed materialism as what it takes to be its spirituality."

63. Quoted in Lea, pp. 151–52.

64. Though Eliot was only an infrequent reviewer in the *Criterion,* he often undertook the notices of Murry's books. In his *Life of Jesus* Eliot detected "the familiar gospel of Rousseau: the denial of Original Sin." Three years later he admitted to his "fundamental difficulty" with Murry's *God: An Introduction to the Science of Metabiology;* but Eliot admired Murry's recognition that one "must either take the whole of revealed religion or none of it" ("Books of the Quarter," *Criterion* 5 [1927], 255; 9 [1930], 336). He was more enthusiastic about Murry's literary criticism. His biography of D. H. Lawrence, Eliot described as "a brilliant book"; and his study, *Shakespeare,* Eliot found "a very good book indeed" ("Books of the Quarter," *Criterion* 10 [1931], 768; 15 [1936], 708). For some of Eliot's more acerbic remarks on Murry's politics in the thirties see his "Commentaries" of April 1933, and April 1935.

friend.[65] In 1953, four years before Murry's death, Eliot wrote: "I value our friendship in the past—all the more valuable because of differences in temperament and points of view, and I should value whatever the future might restore of it."[66] And the following year Murry wrote Eliot:

I *should* like to see you one day, and have a long talk with you. I have an obscure, but persistent and definite feeling, that we have something to say to each other, though I have no idea what it is. I have a hunch . . . that this feeling of mine is connected with my conviction that my strange and weary pilgrimage . . . is over.[67]

Eliot recalled that his last meeting with Murry, in December 1956, "was a particularly happy one."[68]

V

The controversy between Murry and Eliot, carried on in the *Criterion* intermittently for nearly five years, obviously lasted too long; there could be no resolution. But this extended discussion of that dispute should not suggest that the consideration of classicism and romanticism was an obsessive concern of Eliot and his review. In fact, the *Criterion* all the while had remained a literary review, and these philosophical discussions took their place among the poems, stories, and literary essays that always comprised most of the review's contents. The controversy is quite significant, however, in its reflection of the growth of Eliot's interest in theological matters: what had begun as

65. On 3 February 1927, Eliot wrote Marianne Moore, editor of the *Dial*: ". . . I should like to suggest earnestly that you ought to get some reviewing from Middleton Murry. He is certainly as good a reviewer as anybody and his name carries weight. I am sure he would be glad to do it and I think he needs the money. I should be highly delighted myself to see him among your reviewers: it would in fact be a personal favor to myself" (Yale University Library).

66. 31 July 1953, Northwestern University Library.

67. Quoted in Lea, p. 347.

68. "Foreword," *Katherine Mansfield and Other Literary Studies,* by J. Middleton Murry (London: Constable, 1959), p. ix.

a dispute over classicism and romanticism became one over medievalism and modernism. During the early years of his editorship he had come to see further implications of his earlier attitudes.

Of course the poetry of those five years also suggested the development in Eliot's thought: *The Waste Land* was at once a criticism of society, a lament for the loss of faith, and a not-quite-successful attempt to recover such faith. Three years later, in "The Hollow Men," the truncated passages from the Lord's Prayer offered a more concrete sign of the wholeness toward which Eliot was aspiring. By 1927 the Magus in "Journey of the Magi" seemed to have achieved the goal. Passing through his December waste land and accompanied by the hollow men tending his camels, he ultimately reached "a temperate valley,/Wet, below the snow line, smelling of vegetation." The achievement was, one may say, satisfactory.

The announcement of his conversion in 1928 would make explicit what was implicit in the pages of the *Criterion* and in his poetry: that the years between 1922 and 1927 had been a period of intense intellectual and spiritual exploration for Eliot. But the specifically literary criticism of those years is remarkably slight both in volume and in its illumination of the growth of his thought. He continued to write occasional review essays, especially in the *Dial* and in the *Nation and Athenaeum;* and yet, with the exception of "The Function of Criticism" and his review of Joyce's *Ulysses,* none of these is among Eliot's most important. In 1924 he published his second volume of essays, the thin *Homage to John Dryden.* Significantly, the three reviews gathered there from the *Times Literary Supplement*—"John Dryden," "The Metaphysical Poets," and "Andrew Marvell"—all dated from 1921. In hours not spent at his job in the bank or the publishing house, Eliot since 1922 had been directing his literary energies to his poetry—and to the *Criterion.*

1926-1928

3

THE MUTATION OF THE ARTIST

While the protracted *Criterion* controversy with John Middleton Murry was demonstrating the expansion of Eliot's sympathies from classicism to catholicism, other of his interests were also developing. Even as he was publishing the last chapters of that controversy in 1927, he was aware that "the intellectual and artistic output of the previous seven years had been rather the last efforts of an old world, than the first struggles of a new." Though the issue had by then been translated into religious terms, Eliot's concern over classicism and romanticism had remained fundamentally unchanged in the decade since his Oxford Extension Lectures; as he had suggested in those lectures, catholicism represented less a departure from than an extension of the classical tendency. Somewhat belatedly however, "about the year 1926," he said, "the features of the post-war world [began] clearly to emerge."[1] Eliot and his review sought to adapt to that new world.

Since it first appeared in 1922, the *Criterion* had been edited according to principles consistent with those Eliot set down in *The Sacred Wood*. Reflecting the largely literary interests of its editor, the early *Criterion* was largely a literary review. The first volumes gave little cause for suspecting that Eliot would follow the example of Matthew Arnold and pursue—as he had criticized Arnold for pursuing—"game outside of the literary preserve." Even in his 1923 note on "The Function of a Literary Review," however, Eliot had obliquely acknowledged the bearing of social issues upon art. "It is the function of a literary re-

1. "Last Words," *Criterion* 18 (1939), 271.

view," he had said there, "to maintain the autonomy and disinterestedness of literature, and at the same time to exhibit the relations of literature—not to 'life,' as something contrasted to literature, but to all the other activities, which, together with literature, are the components of life."[2] This early, theoretical understanding became increasingly practical during his editorship. With the "emergence" of the postwar world, he was tempering his former criticism of writers such as Arnold with a recognition of the necessity for the artist's venturing beyond his field of recognized competence. The purview of the *Criterion* was also extended as it increasingly concerned itself with matters of religion and politics.

Eliot's effort to adapt to the demands of the new world that he then saw emerging is nowhere so obvious as in his several adjustments of the review's title. Within two years the *Criterion* became the *New Criterion,* then the *Monthly Criterion,* and finally reverted to its original title in June 1928. The changes reflected Eliot's attempt to refashion his journal so that it could participate in the definition of its times. First, however, self-definition was necessary; through these years of adjustment, Eliot was constantly reassessing the function of his review and his responsibilities as a man of letters.

During the late twenties, there were many indications in the *Criterion* of the expansion both of Eliot's interests and the scope of his review. A notable one appeared when he introduced the first issue of the *New Criterion* in January 1926 and explained his new aspirations for the journal. To the regular reader, that 1926 essay—"The Idea of a Literary Review"—must have recalled the earlier "Function of a Literary Review." In a sense, the later statement was a repudiation of the earlier one. "Many readers have criticized *The Criterion* for not being literary enough," Eliot said in 1926.

2. *Criterion* I (1923), 421.

But I have seen the birth and death of several purely literary periodicals; and I say of all of them that in isolating the concept of literature they destroy the life of literature. It is not merely that there is not enough good literature, even good second-rate literature, to fill the pages of *any* review. . . . The profounder objection [to restricting a review to purely literary matters] is the impossibility of defining the frontiers, or limiting the context of "literature." Even the purest literature is alimented from non-literary sources, and has non-literary consequences. Pure literature is a chimera of sensation; admit the vestige of an idea and it is already transformed.

The literary review, he concluded, should be formed "not merely on literature, but on what we may suppose to be the interests of any intelligent person with literary taste."[3]

Though some of the essays and several of Eliot's "Commentaries" touched on a somewhat broader range of topics and the books reviewed included a few in psychology, philosophy, and politics, the first four issues of the *New Criterion* hardly signaled a radical departure in the orientation of the *Criterion*. "A literary review cannot be realised at once," Eliot explained rather apologetically in January 1927—perhaps himself a bit impatient to expand the journal's scope. But the idea of a literary review, articulated a year before, remained his goal:

The New Criterion aims to preserve its continuity, but yet to make a new beginning with every year and with every issue. To be perpetually in change and development, to alter with the alterations of the living minds associated with it and with the phases of the contemporary world for which and in which it lives: on this condition only should a literary review be tolerated.[4]

With the May 1927 issue the *New Criterion* became the

3. *Criterion* 4 (1926), 3–4. It was in this essay that Eliot specified the six books exemplary of the classical "tendency" of the *Criterion*; significantly, all were at least in part works of social criticism (see chap. 2, p. 43).

4. "Commentary," *Criterion* 5 (1927), 1.

Monthly Criterion, and once again Eliot sought to define its character. Though he appeared to be describing principles that had long governed the review, he was in fact describing his aspirations for the future:

It was part of the original programme, in 1922, to revive some of the characteristics of the quarterly reviews of a hundred years ago. . . . With [their] leisure, ripeness and thoroughness . . . , *The Criterion* was to join another of their characteristics, a certain corporate personality which had almost disappeared from quarterly journalism; it was to exhibit, without narrow exclusiveness or sectarian enthusiasm, a common tendency which its contributors should illustrate by conformity or opposition. It was to be up-to-time in its appreciation of modern literature, and in its awareness of contemporary problems; it was to record the development of modern literature and the mutations of modern thought.[5]

However alert it had been to modern literature, the *Criterion* in its first years had hardly shown great concern for "contemporary problems" or "the mutations of modern thought." Increasingly it would.

In the next month's "Commentary" Eliot acknowledged the receipt of a new French review and announced "Politique d'Abord": "It is a trait of the present time that every 'literary' review worth its salt has a political interest; indeed that *only* in the literary reviews, which are not the conscientious organs of superannuated political creeds, are [there] any living political ideas." Eliot's use of inverted commas around *literary* is telling; the meaning of the word was being strained by the new weight it was bearing. But Eliot was not merely following fashion in devoting greater attention to politics; more importantly, he was accepting what he now recognized as an inescapable responsibility of the artist, especially an artist with his principles.

To assume that everything has changed, is changing, and must

5. "Commentary," *Criterion* 5 (1927), 187–88.

change, according to forces which are not human, and that all a person who cares about the future must or can do is to *adapt himself* to the change, is a fatalism which is unacceptable. . . . If we are to be qualified as "neo-classicists," we hope that "neo-classicism" may be allowed to comprise the idea that man is responsible, *morally* responsible, for his present and his immediate future.[6]

One might suspect that Eliot's sense of moral responsibility had prevailed over his sense of responsibility to art; but this would be a serious misunderstanding of the nature of his development. In fact, the two were inextricably related. Eliot in the mid-twenties embraced politics for the reason he said Joyce had embraced myth: to control and order the immense panorama of futility and anarchy that was contemporary history, to make the modern world possible for art.[7]

"The man of letters of to-day is interested in a great many subjects," Eliot explained in his November 1927 "Commentary." "He finds that the study of his own subject leads him irresistibly to the study of the others; and he must study the others if only to disentangle his own, to find out what he is really doing himself." Eliot instanced three events that were claiming the attention of artists: "the Russian revolution (which has also directed our attention to the East), the transformation of Italy (which has directed our attention to our own forms of government), and the condemnation of the *Action Française* by the Vatican." Of course, the movements in Russia, Italy, and France had been of concern to many Englishmen long before 1927; though Eliot's interest was perhaps overdue, he now recognized that "politics has become too serious a matter to be left to politicians."

We are compelled, to the extent of our abilities, to be amateur economists, in an age in which politics and economics can no

6. *Criterion* 5 (1927), 283.
7. "Ulysses, Order, and Myth," *Dial* 75 (1923), 483.

longer be kept wholly apart. Everything is in question. . . . How can we avoid such subjects, even if our only desire is to be able to ignore them? All this, and much more, is happening not because we wish to take up new hobbies, but because we must submit to the pressure of circumstances. We have to adapt our minds to a new age—new certainly to this extent, that the nineteenth century gave us a very inadequate preparation for it.

If this is read, as it should be, as an explicit statement of Eliot's commitment to think and write on nonliterary matters, one should recognize how little enthusiasm Eliot brought to this new calling. Rather than as a development he embraced eagerly, he greeted this expansion of interests almost begrudgingly as a necessary condition of being an artist—indeed, a citizen—in an unsettled world. The words he used to describe the development are revealing: *irresistibly, compelled, must, have to.* "We can only hope," Eliot concluded, "that all this labour will make it possible for us to return more tranquilly to our own business, such as writing a poem, or painting a picture." And then he added: "The considerations above are given a greater precision by the appearance of Mr. Wyndham Lewis's book, *Time and Western Man.* Mr. Lewis is the most remarkable example in England of the actual mutation of the artist into a philosopher of a type hitherto unknown."[8]

II

It was natural, almost inevitable, that Eliot should have cited Lewis to exemplify the mutation of the artist. Lewis had been one of the earliest admirers of his poetry in the London literary world, a personal friend, a *Criterion* contributor whose essays had complemented the editor's own attacks on romanticism, and, according to Eliot, "the most fascinating personality of our time."[9] More importantly,

8. *Criterion* 6 (1927), 386–87.
9. "Tarr," *Egoist* 5 (1918), 106. In July, 1915—a month after the appearance in *Poetry* of "The Love Song of J. Alfred Prufrock" —Lewis published Eliot's "Preludes" and "Rhapsody on a Windy Night" in his short-lived vorticist review, *Blast.*

however, Lewis had progressed from a classicism largely artistic in orientation to a broader concern for the social, political, and philosophical implications of that classicism. Such was Lewis's mutation, and it would soon be Eliot's; the appearance of *The Art of Being Ruled,* the first of Lewis's books in which the mutation was clear, prompted Eliot to remark that "the artist in the modern world . . . is heavily hampered in ways that the public does not understand." He found in Lewis's book much that recalled the work of Benda and Babbitt as well as an indication of the new demands facing the artist in England. Describing the contemporary artist's situation, Eliot wrote:

He finds himself, if he is a man of intellect, unable to realise his art to his own satisfaction, and he may be driven to examining the elements in the situation—political, social, philosophical or religious—which frustrate his labour. In this uncomfortable pursuit he is accused of "neglecting his art." But it is likely that some of the strongest influences on the thought of the next generation may be those of the dispossessed artists.[10]

Lewis, shortly before Eliot, had recognized himself to be such an artist.[11]

Just as Lewis had been quick to appreciate Eliot's early verse when it was sent to him by Ezra Pound, he had from the beginning been sympathetic to Eliot's endeavor in the *Criterion.* Like Eliot, Lewis himself was trying—albeit in a rather different style—to assert principles of artistic order and discipline against the meanness of culture that in all the arts seemed to prevail. Thus when he received the issue of the *Criterion* containing Eliot's essay on "The Function of Criticism," Lewis responded: "Thank you very much for the Criterion. Your article is superb. It is

10. "Commentary," *Criterion* 4 (1926), 420.
11. In *Blasting and Bombardiering,* Lewis explained: "In 1926 I began writing about politics, not because I like politics but everything was getting bogged in them and before you could do anything you had to deal with the politics with which it was encrusted" (London: [Eyre and Spottiswoode, 1937], p. 303).

like a stone in the middle of a lot of shit."[12] Declaring "that every failure of an exceptional attempt like yours with the Criterion means that the chance of establishing some sort of critical standard here is diminished," he offered to contribute anything he had without thought of payment.[13] For his part, Eliot hoped "that there should be a contribution of some kind from [Lewis] in every number of *The Criterion*. . . , more than I care to take from any other contributor."[14] In five consecutive issues, from February 1924 through February 1925, there was.[15] Lewis lamented that the classical ideal of the artist as "the rare man born for that exacting task, and devoting his life unsparingly to it" was being replaced by a widespread notion that anyone who desired to dabble at it could become an artist.[16] Art had become fashionable and popular; democracy prevailed, and standards suffered. "In our civilisation today there is no place for *art-for-art's-sake*," Lewis said, "or, more shortly, for art at all. . . . The public could render the greatest service to art simply *by not encouraging any art at all*."[17] Several years later he made his point more emphatically:

It would not be easy to exaggerate the naïveté with which the average artist or writer to-day, deprived of all central authority, body of knowledge, tradition, or commonly accepted system of nature, accepts what he receives in place of those things.

12. *The Letters of Wyndham Lewis*, ed. W. K. Rose (London: Methuen, 1963), p. 136. The latter reference was obviously to contemporary criticism and not to the other essays in Eliot's review. Lewis went on to remark, "I've not had time to read the rest of the number yet. . . ."
13. Ibid., p. 137.
14. Quoted in *Letters of Lewis*, p. 150.
15. The first two were excerpts from Lewis's novel, *The Apes of God*; the next two, "Art Chronicles." His fifth contribution was a review of three recent books on anthropology.
16. "The Apes of God," *Criterion* 2 (1924), 306.
17. "Art Chronicle," *Criterion* 2 (1924), 478, 480.

Lewis, no less than Eliot, sought to reassert neglected artistic principles and thus to help establish a new classicism. The current cultural milieu, he said, demanded "a new, and if necessary shattering, criticism of 'modernity,' as it stands at present."[18]

In the essays he had written before launching the *Criterion,* Eliot had offered such "criticism of 'modernity'." During the first years of his editorship, however, he had largely avoided these matters—seeing them as inappropriate to a literary review. But by 1926 Eliot recognized the pressing need for social criticism such as Lewis was practicing; and finding a worthy example of such criticism in Lewis's *Art of Being Ruled,* Eliot recommended the book to his *Criterion* readers. Characteristically diffuse, encyclopedic and overwritten, Lewis's book defies concise summary. Leaving the reader with a much greater sense of what Lewis rejected than of what he proposed, the book was in its expansive iconoclasm quite different from Eliot's more austere criticism.[19] But in its concern for the necessity of some men ruling—and others being ruled—it touched a matter long of importance to Eliot. In its bringing that concern to bear on social as well as literary matters, it pointed the way toward the further development of Eliot's long-standing interests.

Insistence on the importance of intelligence and authority in the arts inevitably implied the necessity for similar qualities in society. But Lewis found them everywhere

18. "The Values of the Doctrine Behind 'Subjective' Art," *Criterion* 6 (1927), 9, 11. The following year Eliot echoed Lewis's terms in expressing the *Criterion*'s belief "that Modernism . . . is a mental blight which can afflict the whole of the intelligence of the time . . ." ("Commentary," *Criterion* 8 [1928], 188).

19. In 1928 Eliot remarked, "Mr. Wyndham Lewis is obviously striving courageously toward a positive theory, but in his published work he has not yet reached that point" ("The Humanism of Irving Babbitt," in *Selected Essays,* New Edition [New York: Harcourt, Brace, 1950], p. 419).

absent. Or, more precisely, the appearances of authority and intelligence had been assumed by men and movements with no proper claim to leadership. The arts, Lewis felt, were enfeebled because society was dominated by the pretensions of the bourgeoisie, the tradesmen of the world, whom he spoke of as the "small man."

What is it that has always brought to nothing the work of the creative mind, and made history an interminable obstacle race for the mind which would otherwise be free? Precisely the competitive jealousy of this famous "small man," with his famous "independence"—snobbish, "ambitious," very grasping, considering himself better than the plain workman. . . . He is not only the enemy of a unification of the intelligent forces of the world; he is the symbol of what has always held back our race. . . .[20]

While Lewis felt the "small man" should be ruled in matters of art by the superior intelligence of the creative mind, he found him in fact dictating artistic standards through his financial power. For the artist forced to pander to such patrons Lewis offered a golden rule: *"You cannot aim too low*. The story you present cannot be too stupid. It is not only impossible to exaggerate—it in itself requires a trained publicist to form any idea of—the idiocy of the Public" (91).

The power of the "small man" was only one among many symptoms in which Lewis discerned the usurpation of authority by the unworthy. A vigorous reassertion of the art of being ruled—of the proper subservience of the intellectually weak to the intellectually strong—was demanded; artists, rather than pander to the "small man," should insist upon their just authority. "There is virtually no intellectual Opposition in Europe," Lewis lamented. "Julian [*sic*] Benda, for instance, is a very marked exception. Similarly, there is no real *criticism* of existing

20. *The Art of Being Ruled* (New York: Harper, 1926), p. 112. Subsequent references, inserted in the text, are to this edition.

society. Politics and the highly organized, deeply entrenched, dominant mercantile society has it all its own way" (430). Lewis and Eliot would be united in articulating such a criticism in England. If their criticism were successful they hoped to be able, as Eliot had said, "to return more tranquilly to our own business, such as writing a poem, or painting a picture." In Lewis's words: "The annihilation of industrial competition and the sweeping the board of the Small Man, commercially and socially, should have as its brilliant and beneficent corollary the freeing for its great and difficult tasks of intelligence of the first order" (449–50).

When *The Art of Being Ruled* appeared Eliot took particular note of it in his "Commentary" and suggested that it "might be added to those [six books] mentioned in the January *New Criterion* as significant of the tendency of contemporary thought."[21] Taking its place, then, alongside the studies of Benda, Hulme, and Babbitt, Lewis's became a canonical *Criterion* book.

As we have seen, the appearance the following year of his *Time and Western Man* also drew special notice in Eliot's "Commentary."[22] Lengthy beyond need, imprecise in its argument, and constantly digressing to examine particular examples of its thesis, *Time and Western Man* is hardly more tractable to summary than its predecessor. More philosophical than sociological, this book sought to demonstrate the substantial influence of romantic notions of time on modern thought. Like Rousseau for Babbitt and Eliot, Bergson—"the perfect philosophic ruffian, of the darkest and most forbidding description"[23]—was the *bête*

---

21. *Criterion* 4 (1926), 419–20.

22. His frequent reference in the "Commentaries" to particular titles, either in praise or criticism, provides a useful catalogue of some of the books Eliot was reading during the period 1924–39.

23. *Time and Western Man* (London: Chatto and Windus, 1927), p. 174. Subsequent references, inserted in the text, are to this edition.

noire here. Under the unfortunate influence of romanticism, thinkers had embraced the romantically unreal time-doctrine of flux and change and had neglected the realist position that insisted that stability rather than change is man's strongest impression of the external world (211–12). Lewis's impatience with the romantic subordination of intelligence to sensation—a characteristic he detected in nearly all modern thought—was intense.

The book was not written, he said, "with a view to promoting any theory of my own" (480–81), but it was unmistakably a document in the controversy between classicism and romanticism. Lewis's preference was clear:

The world of classical "common-sense"—the world of the Greek, the world of the Schoolman—is the world of nature, too, and is a very ancient one. All the health and sanity that we have left belongs to that world, and its forms and impulses. It is such a tremendous power that nothing can ever break it down permanently. But to-day the issue . . . is between that nature . . . and . . . those forces represented by the philosophy of Time. What is suggested here is that, in such a crisis, all the weight of our intelligence should be thrown into the scales representing our deepest instincts (186–87).

Like Hulme and Eliot, Lewis recognized—however tentatively—the affinity between his classical bias and Christian faith.

Looked at from the simplest human level, as a semi-religious faith, the Time-cult seems far less effective, when properly understood, than those cults which posit a Perfection already existing, eternally there, of which we are humble shadows. It would be a very irrational conceit which, if it were given the choice, would decide for the "emergent" Time-god, it seems to me, in place, for instance, of the God of the Roman faith. With the latter you have an achieved co-existent supremacy of perfection, impending over all your life, not part of you in any imperfect physical sense . . . (455).

By 1927 Eliot certainly shared Lewis's feelings. Such a statement is a valuable index to the logic that brought so many literary classicists to the door of—and occasionally into—the Church. But Lewis's still greater significance lay in his exemplification of what Eliot described as the "mutation of the artist into a philosopher of a type hitherto unknown." The mutation was a necessity of the times—not so much an escape from art as a strategic campaign for the order, discipline, and intelligence needed so that genuine art, rather than the sham artifacts produced for the "small man," might prevail. However far they appeared to venture from properly artistic matters, Eliot and Lewis remained artists in their motivation. However certain they appeared to be in their pronouncements, they remained amateurs exploring—often clumsily and wrongheadedly—unfamiliar fields. Both a friend and a valued contributor to the *Criterion* before his mutation, Lewis—one might fairly speculate—gave Eliot heart to embark more deliberately on such explorations himself.

III

The first three issues of the *New Criterion* contained a few articles suggesting the broader range of interests Eliot was bringing to his review. In "Aristotle on Democracy and Socialism," H. G. Dalway Turnbull briefly examined Aristotle's views on government and speculated as to "what would be his attitude, if he were alive to-day, towards modern socialist or communistic schemes."[24] He would, Turnbull concluded, be critical. In the two following issues Henri Massis argued rather hysterically for the "Defence of the West" against the peril he discerned in Asiaticism. "The future of western civilisation, indeed the future of mankind, is to-day in jeopardy," he began.

It is the soul of the West that the East wishes to attack, that

24. *Criterion* 4 (1926), 11.

soul, divided, uncertain of its principles, confusedly eager for spiritual liberation, and all the more ready to destroy itself, to allow itself to be broken up by Oriental anarchy, because it has of itself departed from its historical civilising order and its tradition.[25]

After those three essays, however (and perhaps in part because of responses to Massis's) the *Criterion* appeared to be reverting to its belletristic beginnings. Eliot's "Commentaries" were an important exception. Though in some ways the review seemed to be the *Criterion* of old, the editor was addressing himself to topics that he had not previously discussed in those pages. To be sure, his interest in such issues as the preservation of church buildings was not recent. As early as 1921, we will recall, he had regretted plans to demolish City churches that "gave to the business quarter . . . a beauty which its hideous banks and commercial houses have not quite defaced." The following year, in the note to the Magnus Martyr passage in *The Waste Land,* he had volunteered that the interior of that church "is to my mind one of the finest among Wren's interiors"; he used the occasion to draw his readers' attention to a recent pamphlet on *The Proposed Demolition of Nineteen City Churches.* However, when in 1926 and 1927 he again objected to such plans, he brought that concern directly to the pages of the *Criterion*—and argued now from a concern not for the beauty of London, but for *"the beauty of holiness."* Reacting to a measure passed by the National Assembly of the Church of England to facilitate the demolition of "superfluous" church buildings, Eliot renounced "any attempt to appeal to our Shepherds on the argument for Art, or the beauty of London." He now saw another,

25. *Criterion* 4 (1926), 224, 231. The following year Massis published his book, *Defense of the West,* with Faber and Gwyer. For some time he had been closely associated with Charles Maurras in the reactionary Action Française.

more compelling, argument for the preservation of those structures:

We would remind [the Assembly] . . . that if the church invisible is in decay, it is hardly likely, in the long run, to be restored by the destruction of visible churches. A visible church, whether it assembles five hundred worshippers or only one passing penitent who has saved a few minutes from his lunch hour, is still a church. . . . The destruction of a church which has the added consecration of antiquity and even a little beauty, is a movement towards the destruction of *the* Church, with Disestablishment on the way. . . .

"We shall cease to appeal in the name of Christopher Wren and his school," Eliot concluded, recalling his earlier notice, "and appeal in the name of Laud and the *beauty of holiness*."[26]

In January 1927 he reiterated his argument of the previous October against "the shame and error" of destroying the churches. And the following year he ruefully directed the attention of his readers to proposals for alterations to Westminster Abbey.[27] If only as monuments of English culture Eliot felt such churches warranted preservation; more important to him now, however, was their significance as monuments in England's religious tradition—a tradition whose claim upon himself he felt increasingly, whose current position he recognized to be precarious, and whose cause he was beginning publicly to plead.

Himself a craftsman in words and not stone, Eliot was hardly less distressed by the peril to language than to buildings. Often in his "Commentaries" he pointed accusingly to "alarming signs of rot in the language"; in one he observed, "Language can only be maintained if it is the vehicle for thinking; and recent events seem to indicate

26. "Commentary," *Criterion* 4 (1926), 629.
27. "Commentary," *Criterion* 5 (1927), 4–5; 7 (1928), 1–4.

that language is more and more used for every other purpose except thought."[28] Eliot could hardly have been wanting for material with which to illustrate the decay of
language; thus it is revealing that in a 1927 "Commentary" he should have singled out the recent revision of the
Book of Common Prayer. Again, his concern for the
Church was apparent. Just as he found the authorities
ready to dispense with old church buildings that had fallen
into disuse, Eliot found in the revision of the Prayer Book
a similar attitude toward language. "The Preface," he
said, "reads like a rather embarrassed apology for change:
everything is changing, so the Prayer Book must change."
In particular, Eliot objected to the substitution of *infinite* for *incomprehensible,* and *eternal* for *everlasting*.
"Whether the words were supposed to clarify theology
or not," he said, "they make the English language
vaguer. . . ."

The editors [say]: "in religion as in all else truth is not prized
less highly because it is no longer fenced on any side." But when
fences are down the cattle will roam, including two vagrant
beasts named *infinite* and *eternal,* words which will wander so
far, the fence of meaning being down, that they will cease to
belong anywhere.[29]

Eliot had long used his "Commentaries" as a forum for
his opinions, but his use of those pages to remark on religious matters was a new departure. The idea of a literary
review was evolving considerably in order to contain its
editor's interests. By June 1928 Eliot announced somewhat
expansively:

The Criterion is concerned with everything that can be examined in a critical spirit. . . . [It] wishes to keep its readers in
touch with the most significant thought of to-day and to-

28. *Criterion* 6 (1927), 481.
29. *Criterion* 5 (1927), 190.

morrow; and will continue to invite the most important representatives in every country, of philosophic, religious and political theory, to express their views.[30]

Like Wyndham Lewis, Eliot and his review were experiencing a mutation.

In part, of course, Eliot's interest in politics was that of any conscientious citizen, just as his concern over the demolition of the churches and the revision of the Prayer Book was a function of his increasing commitment to the English Church. And his concern for both matters reflected his desire to affirm the tradition in whatever quarter it might be threatened. It is impossible to determine precisely the relative importance of the considerations that bore on Eliot's mutation. Even with the fullest of biographical information, intellectual and spiritual conversions such as Eliot's defy simple explanation; with Eliot, we do not yet have even that material. What is clear, however, is that Eliot increasingly came to recognize that the monuments of the tradition included churches and Prayer Books and systems of government as well as poems and plays, and that a concern for the tradition inevitably implied a concern for religious and political—as well as literary—matters. An incident in 1928 dramatically pointed up the way in which literature bore on politics; politics, on religion; and the tradition, equally, on them all.

IV

When Eliot published in the *Criterion* in 1928 a two-part translation of Charles Maurras's "Prologue to an Essay on Criticism," the author's name was doubtless familiar to most readers of the review. If they did not know him as a poet, critic, and writer of philosophical fiction, they would at least have recognized him as leader of the controversial French political movement, the Action Française. They might well also have recalled Eliot's inclusion of Maurras's

30. "Commentary," *Criterion* 7 (1928), 291–92.

L'Avenir de l'Intelligence two years earlier in his catalogue of books reflecting the classical tendency of the *Criterion*. Published in 1905, Maurras's book antedated the other five Eliot had cited; its thesis, however, was quite similar.[31]

According to Maurras, France was faced with a conflict between the established, hereditary traditions (*le sang*) and the insurrectionary forces of mercantilism (*l'or*). "The two are vying with each other," he said. "Reason has the power of choosing between them, of calling one the more worthy and making it victorious."[32] "Nothing is possible without the intellectual reform of some of us" (18). Like most literary classicists, Maurras looked first to men of letters for a sign of such reform. But, he concluded, "The influence of the writer is lost" (87).

In face of the grim prospects of the future, the intellectual leaders of the nation must ally themselves with those who are trying to create something beautiful before we founder. In the name of reason and nature, in conformity with the ancient laws of the universe, for the continuance of order, for the survival and the future welfare of a threatened civilization, all hope rests with a counter-revolution (96).

Though more narrowly literary than the book, Maurras's "Prologue" breathed the same classical spirit. His argument was familiar. "In a few words, man is a reasoning animal. This old definition seems to me the only satisfactory one. . . . Barbarism begins, in fact, when the

31. Some years later Eliot recalled that he had purchased his copy of Maurras's *L'Avenir de l'Intelligence* when he was studying in Paris in 1911. He felt certain that it was Babbitt who had first directed his attention to Maurras. And though he did not doubt that Babbitt was critical of certain aspects of Maurras's career, Eliot remarked that the two were similar in their inability to accept Christianity ("Hommage à Charles Maurras," *Aspects de la France et du Monde,* 25 April 1948, p. 6).

32. *L'Avenir de l'Intelligence* (Paris: Flammarion, 1927), p. 16. Subsequent references, inserted in the text, are to this edition. My translation.

sensitive animal, preferring itself to the rational, asserts its right to choose its own paths." Classicism, of course, was the force that, preferring reason to sensation, stood to advance literature and preserve civilization:

If we lose the classical feeling, we lose everything. For it is at once the tradition of the human race and of our ethnic group in particular. On the contrary, if we return to it we gain everything, and we are in a position to add something to the riches of the common treasury.[33]

Throughout, Maurras's "Prologue to an Essay on Criticism" reads as though it might have been the work of Eliot a few years before. It was fitting that Eliot should have translated the essay himself.

Just as he was publishing his translation of Maurras's "Prologue," Leo Ward's highly critical book on Maurras, *The Condemnation of the "Action Française,"* appeared. Distressed by Ward's attack on "the morality and moral influence of a contributor to . . . the *Criterion,*" Eliot felt compelled to consider Maurras's politics.[34] Thus, in the issue of the *Criterion* that contained the second part of the "Prologue," Eliot published his own consideration of "The *Action Française,* M. Maurras and Mr. Ward." The very fact that Eliot felt it necessary to defend the political activity of one of his contributors suggests the way in which he now saw politics and literary theory as impinging on each other. Though Maurras's *Criterion* essay had concerned itself only with literary criticism, Eliot could not disregard Ward's attack on the politics of his author. Moreover, at this point when Maurras was being widely criticized, it seemed especially important for him to acknowledge his considerable debt to Maurras. In his intellectual development, Maurras had been influential—no

33. *Criterion* 7 (1928), 205, 216, 217.
34. "The *Action Française,* M. Maurras and Mr. Ward," *Criterion* 7 (1928), 196.

less by his negative than by his positive example. Eliot's response to Ward's book and his continued defense during the brief controversy that ensued offered an opportunity to acknowledge that debt.

Long an admirer of Greek and French classicism, a vigorous opponent of romanticism, an anti-Semite from the age of seventeen, and a monarchist before thirty, Charles Maurras first became prominent when the Dreyfus affair struck France toward the end of the 1890s. The case of Alfred Dreyfus provided an ideal focus for opponents of the bourgeois-democratic government of the Third Republic; and in May 1899 Maurras joined others of a like mind to create the Action Française Society and publish the *Bulletin de l'Action Française,* the organ of their movement. Begun as a philosophical rather than a political movement, the Action Française at first worked to point out the danger they saw posed to French society by the increasing influence of Jews, the spread of democracy, and the absence of a monarch, which they thought experience had shown France required. Initially, at least, Maurras's concern for such issues was—like Eliot's, later—artistic. As Edward R. Tannenbaum points out, the origins of his movement were in a real sense suprapolitical:

Although Maurras and his colleagues were ostensibly working for a restoration of the monarchy, what they really wanted was a world in which they could write their poems and essays without having to worry about where they would get money to live. Their sensitive natures revolted against the mercenary spirit of modern society. In order to earn a living they had to appeal to the general public. Since they could not satisfy its tastes, they also expressed their longing for a return to the Old Regime in their literary criticism.[35]

35. *The Action Française: Die-hard Reactionaries in Twentieth-Century France* (New York: Wiley, 1962), p. 60. Information about Maurras and the Action has been drawn primarily from this book and: Michael Curtis, *Three against the Third Republic: Sorel, Barrès and Maurras* (Princeton: Princeton University Press, 1959); Ernest

Very quickly, however, the movement took on an increasingly active political character and by the mid-1920s its membership numbered between thirty and forty thousand—mostly from the upper-middle and middle classes. A large source of its support came from Catholic intellectuals and clerics to whom Maurras had appealed through his repeated suggestions that the Roman Catholic Church could play a vital role in realizing the new society he desired. However, as Michael Curtis says, Maurras himself was only "a cerebral Christian." For him,

Catholicism conserved and perfected all his favorite ideas: order, tradition, discipline, hierarchy, authority, continuity, unity, work, family, corporation, decentralization, autonomy, working-class organization. Religious life had become a matter of tradition more than of faith. . . . The virtue of the Church was that it had organized the idea of God.[36]

Maurras's attitude toward the Church is clear in a passage of his book *L'Action Française et la Religion Catholique:*

Whether we are believers or nonbelievers, how can we fail to recognize that France is the daughter of her bishops and monks. When all else has been forgotten, their names will remain inscribed on the land they have shaped. . . . That religion to which we owe the formation and the preservation of the country remains the firmest center of resistance to the varied forces of anarchy and revolution which have been subverting the nation for a hundred years.[37]

Though sympathetic to the antimodernism of the Action Française, the Church hierarchy in the early twenties be-

---

Nolte, *Three Faces of Fascism,* tr. Leila Vennewitz (New York: Holt, Rinehart and Winston, 1965); and Eugen Weber, *Action Française: Royalism and Reaction in Twentieth-Century France* (Stanford University Press, 1962). I am especially grateful to Professor Weber for his personal assistance as I was preparing this discussion.

36. Curtis, pp. 224, 225.

37. (Paris: Nouvelle librairie nationale, 1913), p. 69. My translation.

came increasingly uneasy over the use of the Church by the nonbeliever who directed the movement. Their concern was aggravated by the allegedly amoral behavior of some of the Action's leaders and by apprehension of the consequences of the Church's involvement in Maurras's neomonarchist politics. Many prominent Catholic lay figures were also anxious over the relation of the movement to the Church. Among them was Jacques Maritain, a member of Maurras's movement; the author of *Réflexions sur l'intelligence,* which Eliot in 1926 had listed among those books illustrative of the *Criterion*'s classical tendency; the contributor of an essay on "Poetry and Religion" in the January 1927 *Criterion*; and a man Eliot described as "the most conspicuous figure, and probably the most powerful force, in contemporary French philosophy."[38] In September 1926, Maritain published *Une Opinion sur Charles Maurras et le Devoir des Catholiques.* There he proposed that the youth movement of the Action Française be replaced by a group of Catholic clubs led by priests who would work to see that spiritual values were not neglected. Though Maurras was willing for such a compromise, the Church was not.

In the fall of 1926 Cardinal Andrieu, Archbishop of Bordeaux, took the first step toward a formal condemnation of Maurras's movement. He wrote to the youth of his diocese: "Catholics by calculation, not by conviction, the men who lead the Action Française use the church, or hope at least to use it; but they do not serve it, since they reject the divine message which it is the church's mission to propagate." And in December of that year the Vatican issued the Church's formal condemnation: "Catholics are not permitted to adhere to the school of those who place the interests of parties above religion and make religion the servant of those interests."[39] Seven books by Maurras

38. "Commentary," *Criterion* 5 (1927), 3.
39. Quoted in Nolte, pp. 76, 77.

—including *L'Avenir de l'Intelligence*—and the newspaper *Action Française* were placed on the Index. Laymen who disobeyed the prohibition would be denied the sacraments; seminary students would be dismissed from school; and people in holy orders would be deprived of their titles if they defied the Holy Office.

Inevitably, Maurras and his movement lost the public favor of much of their French Catholic following. Supporting the actions of the Vatican, Maritain wrote an essay on "Le Sens de la Condemnation" that insisted that the Church's action was directed at the Action Française as a school of thought rather than as a political party. "The Catholics of the Action Française are political disciples of an agnostic leader," he said. "It is not, primarily, because of its nationalism that the Action Française has been condemned. Rather, it is primarily because of its naturalism, and because of the blemish left on its nationalism by this mistake."[40]

It was against this background that Leo Ward's book *The Condemnation of the Action Française* appeared in 1928 and Eliot published his essay "The *Action Française,* M. Maurras and Mr. Ward." Eliot's readiness to defend —even to extol—Maurras was much more than an editor's solicitude for the reputation of a contributor. In November of the previous year, he had instanced "the condemnation of the *Action Française* by the Vatican" as one among several recent events that were leading literary men to an increased interest in politics.[41] And in his 1928 essay, Eliot demonstrated his remarkably thorough knowledge of Maurras and his movement. Much of his article was given over to refutation of Ward's specific criticisms of the Frenchman. But Eliot's essay is more notable for its revelation of his great esteem for his contributor. "The work

40. In P. Doncoeur et al., *Pourquoi Rome a Parlé* (Paris: n. p., 1927), pp. 353, 379. My translation.
41. See chap. 3, p. 75.

of M. Maurras is little known in England," he observed. "The fact that he is . . . an important literary critic, and has written as fine prose as any French author living, makes no difference to his reputation. But if anything, in another generation or so, is to preserve us from a sentimental Anglo-Fascism," he predicted, "it will be some system of ideas which will have gained much from the study of Maurras."[42]

As Eliot was himself undergoing a similar mutation, he was no doubt impressed by Maurras's earlier recognition that the contemporary artist must take an active interest in his society in order to make the modern world possible for art. But what to Eliot's mind was most remarkable about Maurras's achievement was his having further sensed the need for the sanction of some traditional institution for the society he desired, and his having then brought his essentially nonreligious nature to see that the Roman Catholic Church offered what he sought. Eliot described Maurras's development sympathetically:

His attitude is that of an unbeliever who cannot believe, and who is too honest to pretend to himself or to others that he does believe; if others can believe, so much the better not only for them but for the world at large. The peculiarity of Maurras's agnosticism (or atheism if you like) is that he recognises that he has much more in common, in the temporal sphere, with Catholics than with Protestants or atheists (197).

What struck Eliot as most unjust in the current controversy was the charge that Maurras had been a pernicious influence on the spirituality of French youth. Acknowledging his reluctance to enter into the quarrels of the Roman Church, Eliot said: "What decided me was [the] suggestion that the influence of Maurras, indeed the intention of Maurras, is to pervert his disciples and students away

42. "The *Action Française,* M. Maurras and Mr. Ward," *Criterion* 7 (1928), 196–97. Subsequent references are inserted in the text.

from Christianity. I have been a reader of the work of Maurras for eighteen years," he continued.

Upon me he has had exactly the opposite effect. . . . I should myself consider it preposterous to suppose that the study of the work of Maurras or of the files of the *Action Française* could by itself make a Christian of anybody. But where genuinely religious influences are at work also, or where there is any religious potency in the individual soul, they will be powerfully advanced (202, 198).

A few months later, in a rejoinder to Leo Ward's response to his essay, Eliot reiterated his statement to make his meaning unmistakable: "I say . . . that if anyone is attracted by Maurras' political theory, and if that person has as well any tendency towards *interior* Christianity, that tendency will be quickened by finding that a political and a religious view can be harmonious."[43]

In 1948, Eliot again wrote of the Frenchman's influence upon him:

For some of us, Maurras was a kind of Virgil who led us to the doors of the temple. The forces are numerous which tear a man away from agnosticism and denial and drive him to the extremity, to the inevitable step. Among the positive forces which oblige the reason to respond to the call of Faith—forces which one must distinguish from those which are merely seductive— one discerns the influences of other men who themselves have escaped neither from servitude nor unbelief. From the Christian point of view, the influence of these men must be counted as a merit.[44]

Eliot was not one to squander his expressions of personal indebtedness. His several tributes to Maurras deserve serious consideration.

In a study such as this, there is profound temptation to credit various thinkers with responsibility for specific

43. "A Reply to Mr. Ward," *Criterion* 7 (1928), 375.
44. "Hommage à Charles Maurras," p. 6. My translation.

stages of Eliot's intellectual development. Both Eliot's own acknowledgment of his debt to Maurras and the fact that his defense of the Frenchman preceded by only a few months the public announcement of his conversion to Anglo-Catholicism could suggest that Maurras had a central role in that conversion.[45] However, striking as it would be to explain Eliot's conversion so neatly, the evidence is insufficient. First, the circumstances of Eliot's statements suggest that in writing of Maurras he was involved in special pleading rather than disinterested analysis. In 1930 the American review, the *Bookman,* criticized him for having expressed in his writings an admiration for Maurras and a lack of respect for Irving Babbitt. Eliot wrote the editor:

Your critic quite overlooks the circumstances. . . . When I have spoken of Maurras it has been to defend him against what I believed to be injustice, whilst Mr. Babbitt, I am very glad to say, needs no such defence. . . . I should be the first to admit that there are far grosser positive errors and far greater dangers in the doctrine of Maurras than in that of Babbitt.[46]

Only a few months after his *Criterion* defense of Maurras, Eliot spoke of the philosopher's "extravagances."[47] And in 1940 he reviewed in detail the affair of the Action Française. "The attitude of Maurras towards the Church was simple," he said. "He made no pretence of Christian

45. Paul Elmer More, who, as we shall see, would have had reason to know, wrote: "Some time between *The Waste Land* and *For Lancelot Andrewes* [Eliot] underwent a kind of conversion, due largely I believe to the influence of Maurras and the Action Française." Letter to Austin Warren, 11 August 1929, quoted in Arthur Hazard Dakin, *Paul Elmer More* (Princeton: Princeton University Press, 1960), p. 269n.

46. 31 March 1930. The text is taken from a carbon copy of the letter sent by Eliot to Paul Elmer More and now in the Princeton University Library. Since the *Bookman* published no letters, Eliot's never appeared.

47. "The Humanism of Irving Babbitt," in *Selected Essays,* p. 427.

belief, but supported the Church as a social institution making for stability. . . . I defended the *Action Française* when it was put on the Index," Eliot recalled. "My *particular* defence may or may not stand; but I believe now that the Pope understood its tendencies better."[48]

It could be, in fact, that Maurras was important in Eliot's intellectual development more as a negative example—as a figure from whose mistakes he learned—than as a model whom he uncritically followed. In the career of Maurras and the ill-fortunes of the Action Française, Eliot no doubt found two lessons of abiding importance. The first concerned the necessity of recognizing the difference between the literary man as a theorist in political and religious matters—a role Eliot was increasingly willing to grant the writer—and as an active leader of political or religious movements. Maurras was an example of a poet and critic who became a political activist. In doing so, he attempted something beyond his power and province, and he failed. Eliot in 1955 spoke to this very point at "a Literary Luncheon organized by the London Conservative Union."

It is . . . everyone's concern to find out what he ought to meddle with and what he ought to leave alone. On this last point, I think of a man whom I held in respect and admiration, although some of his views were exasperating and some deplorable—but a great writer, a genuine lover of his country, and a man who deserved a better fate than that which he had in the end to meet. . . . I have sometimes thought that if Charles Maurras had confined himself to literature, and to the literature of political theory, and had never attempted to found a political party, a *movement* . . . then those of his ideas which were sound and strong might have spread more widely, and penetrated more deeply, and affected more sensibly the contemporary mind.[49]

48. *Christian News-Letter*, 28 August 1940, n. pag.
49. "The Literature of Politics," in *To Criticize the Critic and Other Writings* (New York: Farrar, Straus and Giroux, 1965), pp. 142–43.

This statement is especially significant since Eliot never tried to translate into practice his own rather singular social and political theories. That he should have written a book about the *idea* of a Christian society, rather than have tried to organize one, may have been due partly to the lesson of Maurras.

Moreover, it may be that Maurras's (negative) example was valuable in a second, no less important, way: the Action Française had been condemned by the Church for depending on the strength and order and organization of the Church without subscribing to the supporting dogmas; to the Vatican's mind, Maurras had been trying to use the Church without in fact believing in it. Like Maurras, Eliot had long been attracted by the intellectual and artistic tradition of the Church; and like Maurras, he recognized that in Western civilization Catholicism represented the most complete realization and perhaps the foundation of the values in which he believed. One might speculate that Eliot in 1926 discerned the way in which the Vatican's condemnation of Maurras's movement implied a condemnation of his own position. Though he had tried in the *Criterion* to defend Maurras against some of the more invidious charges made against him, Eliot never quarreled with the logic of the Vatican's position. Perhaps, then, the example of Maurras led Eliot to take the step his French counterpart could not take, and follow his secular classicism to its religious conclusion in Catholicism. In such a case, Paul Elmer More may have been correct in suggesting the large part that Maurras played in Eliot's conversion.

V

Maurras's career bore striking witness to the fact that, for the modern writer, interests in literature, politics, and religion were not distinct from each other, but followed in an almost inevitable sequence. Maurras's classicism had led him to royalism and ultimately to his curious association with Catholicism. Eliot's literary classicism, like Maurras's, implied the need for a corresponding organization of society; doubtless to some extent because of the literature of the Action Française, Eliot recognized the attraction of royalism. But the example—the negative example—of Maurras also demonstrated to Eliot the need for founding that reorganized society on a faith in a coherent system of beliefs. Perhaps Eliot had the controversy over Maurras in mind when he looked back on his editorship and remarked that, "A right political philosophy came more and more to imply a right theology."[50] That Eliot had in fact gone beyond Maurras's agnosticism was evident when *For Lancelot Andrewes* appeared in November 1928, and Eliot announced his "general point of view" as "classicist in literature, royalist in politics, and anglo-catholic in religion."[51]

This famous statement is a remarkably clear—perhaps even too clear—account of the stage that Eliot's thinking had reached by 1928. Another document from that year also reflected Eliot's redefinition of the province proper to the man of letters: it was his review of *The Treason of the Intellectuals* by the former *Criterion* contributor, Julien Benda. The "treason" Benda was concerned with was the involvement of intellectuals in practical, worldly affairs. "Until our own days the men of thought or the honest men remained strangers to political passions," he said.[52]

The value of the artist, the thing which makes him the world's high ornament, is that he *plays* human passions instead of living

50. "Last Words," p. 272.
51. "Preface," in *For Lancelot Andrewes: Essays on Style and Order* (London: Faber and Gwyer, 1928), p. ix. Curiously, Eliot did not capitalize "anglo-catholic" here.
52. *The Treason of the Intellectuals*, tr. Richard Aldington (New York: Morrow, 1928), p. 46. Subsequent references, inserted in the text, are to this edition.

them, and that he discovers in this "play" emotion the same source of desires, joys and sufferings as ordinary men find in the pursuit of real things (71).

In 1928, however, Benda saw in the careers of such men as Maurras evidence that "the 'clerks' [intellectuals] have become as much laymen as the laymen themselves" (140). In his apostasy, Benda felt, the intellectual was betraying the ideal that declared "that his kingdom is not of this world, that *the grandeur of his teaching lies precisely in this absence of practical value, and that the right morality for the prosperity of the kingdoms which are of this world, is not his, but Caesar's*" (191).

In 1920, we will recall, Eliot himself had accused Matthew Arnold of a similar treason: Arnold had succumbed to the "almost irresistible temptation . . . to put literature into the corner until he cleaned up the whole country first"; he had gone "for game outside of the literary preserve altogether"; and in his attention to politics and religion Arnold had "wasted his strength, as men of superior ability sometimes do, because he saw something to be done and no one else to do it." However, during the eight years between those remarks on Arnold and his review of Benda, Eliot had experienced a mutation and his ideas were markedly different. The ideal that Benda held up for the contemporary man of letters seemed to Eliot "infected with romance." Criticizing Benda's book, Eliot said:

You cannot lay down any hard and fast rule of what interests the *clerc,* the intellectual, should or should not have. All you can have is a standard of intellect, reason, and critical ability which is applicable to the whole of a writer's work.

And then Eliot suggested a criterion by which to judge the adequacy of such departures by literary men into non-literary fields:

The surest way, perhaps, of judging the work of an author who ventures into a new field, whether it be that of political controversy or some other, is to trace if we can the growth of his interests and their relations among each other. . . . A man may be led, by the connections of things themselves, far from his starting point. . . . Where there is no vital connection, the man may be a brilliant virtuoso, but is probably nothing more.[53]

The vital connections for Eliot were, by 1928, quite clear.

53. "The Idealism of Julien Benda," *New Republic*, 12 December 1928, p. 107.

1928-1930

4

SECOND THOUGHTS

When Eliot selected the essays for his 1924 collection, *Homage to John Dryden,* he had few to choose from. His job in Lloyds Bank, his poetry, and above all his editorship of the new quarterly, the *Criterion,* left him little time for the varied literary endeavors he had pursued before the initiation of his review. By 1928, however, he had quit the bank to join the Faber publishing house; the *Criterion,* then in its sixth year, was well established; and he was once again regularly contributing to other journals. In fact, between 1926 and 1928 he had written nearly fifty review-essays, more than half of them for the *Times Literary Supplement.* When, in 1928, he selected essays for a new volume of prose he had a wealth of material at hand.

But selection was, if anything, rendered more difficult by the abundance of his recent writings. In choosing among them, Eliot sought to compile more than a miscellaneous collection; as he announced in the preface to *For Lancelot Andrewes,* he wished "to indicate certain lines of development, and to disassociate myself from certain conclusions which have been drawn from my volume of essays, *The Sacred Wood.*"[1] A few months before, he had been prepar-

1. "Preface," in *For Lancelot Andrewes* (London: Faber and Gwyer, 1928), p. ix. All subsequent references, inserted in the text, will be to this edition. On the front of the book's dust jacket was the following statement: "This is Mr. Eliot's first volume of collected essays since his *Homage to John Dryden* (1924), and he considers it his most important prose since *The Sacred Wood* (1920). *For Lancelot Andrewes* consists of seven essays which are selected from Mr. Eliot's work of the last two or three years, and which he believes show some consistency. The subjects cover a wide range of literature, theology and philosophy; but taken together they have a unity of their own."

ing a new edition of that, his first book of essays. "I had intended," he said in his preface to the 1928 edition of *The Sacred Wood,* "when the time came to prepare a second edition of this book, to revise some of the essays." However, he had found the task "impossible, and perhaps even undesirable. For I discovered that what had happened in my own mind, in eight years, was not so much a change or reversal of opinions, as an expansion or development of interests."[2] Eliot sought to make that development clear to his readers. Consequently, the essays in *The Sacred Wood* were reprinted unrevised, as if a monument to his earlier attitudes and interests. And *For Lancelot Andrewes* appeared several months later, declaring the author's new position.

The declaration was, of course, explicit in what Eliot several years later[3] referred to as his "too easily quotable" announcement in the preface that his "general point of view" was "classicist in literature, royalist in politics, and anglo-catholic in religion." His *Criterion* editorship had long before demonstrated his classicism; his defense of Charles Maurras had recently suggested his sympathy for royalism; but his Anglo-Catholicism was the least clearly anticipated of the three. As we have seen, Eliot's interest in religion might easily have been inferred by an alert reader of his review. But such evidence as was provided by the early volumes of the *Criterion* would hardly have led one to conclude that his interests were more than theoretical—that in fact he had in 1927 passed beyond his long-standing intellectual interest in theology to active membership in the Church of England.[4]

2. "Preface to the 1928 Edition," in *The Sacred Wood,* 2d ed. (London: Methuen, 1928), p. vii.

3. "Catholicism and International Order," in *Essays Ancient and Modern* (New York: Harcourt, Brace, 1936), p. 135.

4. Eliot's baptism and confirmation apparently occurred sometime between 10 May and 1 July 1927. Early that year he had written to his friend William Force Stead—an Anglican clergyman and

Just as the *Criterion* had offered hints of Eliot's conversion, so too were there indications in essays he published outside his review. But these other essays were hardly more explicit in announcing his development to his contemporaries than was his journal; a number of the most revealing of those essays had appeared as unsigned reviews in the *Times Literary Supplement*. Consequently, Eliot brought together some of those writings for his 1928 volume and, by acknowledging his authorship of several essays not previously attributed to him, demonstrated the antecedents to the explicit announcement of his conversion that opened the book.

Eliot's decision to join the church obviously did not admit of simple explanations; properly, he did not attempt any in his preface. Several years later, when he did discuss some of the forces that had borne on his conversion, he spoke of it as a process that occurred "perhaps insensibly, over a long period of time."

---

man of letters—to make preliminary inquiry about the procedure for entering the Church of England. By May he was settling final arrangements, and in July he wrote Stead with gratitude for his management of the matter. Since he disliked flamboyant conversions, Eliot from the beginning had insisted on secrecy. According to Stead, who himself performed the baptism, the front door of the small church at Finstock, near Oxford, was locked and a guard was posted in the vestry while Eliot stood at the baptismal font. Eliot's godfathers, apparently enlisted by Stead, were Vere Somerset and Canon B. H. Streeter, both Oxford dons. In his correspondence with Stead Eliot declared his certainty that he had as an infant been baptized in a Unitarian rite. Apparently, though, he had no documentary evidence of that event; and he must, moreover, have had misgivings about the efficacy of a baptism not explicitly Trinitarian. The morning after his baptism, he was confirmed by the Bishop of Oxford—again, privately. Stead recalls his relations with Eliot in "Mr. Stead Presents an Old Friend," *Alumnae Journal of Trinity College* (Washington, D. C.) 38 (1965), 59–66. Eliot's letters to Stead are now in the Osborn Collection, Yale University Library. I am indebted to Professor Albert R. Braunmuller for having provided me a typescript of much of this material.

Towards any profound conviction one is borne . . . by what Newman called "powerful and concurrent reasons." . . . In my own case, I believe that one of the reasons was that the Christian scheme seemed to me the only one which would work. . . . The Christian scheme seemed the only possible scheme which found a place for values which I must maintain or perish . . . , the belief, for instance, in holy living and holy dying, in sanctity, chastity, humility, austerity.[5]

But no such explanation appeared in his 1928 book; the essays were left to provide their own testimony as to the impulses behind his conversion.

Since the book was actually dedicated to Eliot's mother, the title "For Lancelot Andrewes" is perhaps puzzling. But in fact that title is apt enough. The essay on Bishop Andrewes that opened the volume broadly indicated at least one of the forces that brought Eliot to the English Church, its intellectual achievement. Several months before the publication of his 1928 collection, he had remarked that "we demand of religion some kind of *intellectual* satisfaction—both private and social—or we do not want it at all."[6] In his essay on Andrewes, first published in 1926, it was clear that he discovered such satisfaction in the writings of that seventeenth-century divine. "The achievement of . . . Andrewes was to make the English church more worthy of intellectual assent," he said (17). This first of Eliot's books published after his conversion sought to further that achievement.

As his subsequent career demonstrated, Eliot's religion was no mere aesthetic Christianity. Yet he was a poet, and though the aesthetic and intellectual appeal of the Church was not in itself sufficient to attract him to its fold, he clearly could never give himself over to a faith that did not value those enterprises in which he had been—and was still

5. "Christianity and Communism," *Listener*, 16 March 1932, p. 383.
6. "An Emotional Unity," *Dial* 84 (1928), 112.

—engaged. "A Church is to be judged by its intellectual fruits," he insisted, "by its influence on the sensibility of the most sensitive and on the intellect of the most intelligent, and it must be made real to the eye by monuments of artistic merit" (15–16). To Eliot's eye, the sermons of Bishop Andrewes were such a monument:

The English Church has no literary monument equal to that of Dante, no intellectual monument equal to that of St. Thomas, no devotional monument equal to that of St. John of the Cross, no building so beautiful as the Cathedral of Modena or the basilica of St. Zeno in Verona. But there are those for whom the City churches are as precious as any of the four hundred odd churches in Rome which are in no danger of demolition, and for whom St. Paul's, in comparison with St. Peter's, is not lacking in decency; and the English devotional verse of the seventeenth century . . . finer than that of any other country or religion at the time (16).

"The intellectual achievement and the prose style of Hooker and Andrewes," he said, "came to complete the structure of the English Church as the philosophy of the thirteenth century crowns the Catholic Church" (16). If only as a predecessor who was at once an artist and a Christian—"the first great preacher of the English Catholic Church" (18)—Andrewes commanded Eliot's recognition. But Andrewes had a personal as well as an historical importance for Eliot. His familiarity with the bishop's writings was not recent; as early as 1920 he had appropriated a passage from one of his sermons in "Gerontion."[7] Andrewes, Eliot said, was "one of the community of the born spiritual"; a man with the *"goût pour la vie spirituelle";* a writer whose "examination of words" in his

7. "The word within a word, unable to speak a word." As if to point up his debt, Eliot quoted this phrase in his essay on Andrewes. Such phrases, he said, "do not desert us." He also cited the passage that a year later he would use at the beginning of "Journey of the Magi."

sermons leads the reader to "the ecstasy of assent" (20, 30, 24). As an unsigned review in *TLS,* the personal dimension of Eliot's tribute was not apparent. As the initial essay in a volume that announced his conversion, "Lancelot Andrewes" bore witness both to Eliot's debt to the bishop and to his intention to carry on Andrewes's work.

If few of the other essays in *For Lancelot Andrewes* were so implicitly confessional as that title piece, most of them in some measure demonstrated Eliot's growing interest in the history of the English Church and his keener concern for moral and religious issues. The second essay, "John Bramhall," was, like the one that preceded it, an appreciation of a leading figure in the early history of the English Church. The next five essays—on Machiavelli, F. H. Bradley, Baudelaire, Middleton, and Crashaw—all recalled former interests of Eliot: Middleton and Machiavelli, his interest in Renaissance English drama; Baudelaire, his debt to French symbolist poetry; Bradley, his doctoral dissertation; and Crashaw, his enthusiasm for the metaphysical poets. But now in discussing these writers Eliot complemented his earlier literary interest with at least some reference to the religious significance of their work.

Perhaps because it was so obvious, Eliot touched only briefly on the religious dimensions of Crashaw's poetry.[8] However, it may not have been so obvious that Middleton's drama was rich in moral significance, and Eliot hastened to urge that it was. *The Changeling,* he said, is "an eternal tragedy, as permanent as *Oedipus* or *Antony and Cleopatra."*

8. In fact, in his "Note on Richard Crashaw" Eliot seemed more anxious to insist on Crashaw's superiority to the romantic poets. Disputing an unfavorable comparison of Crashaw to Shelley and Keats, Eliot wrote: "Crashaw is, I believe, a much greater poet than he is usually supposed to be; Keats and Shelley are, in their actual accomplishment, not nearly such great poets as they are supposed to be" (120).

It is the tragedy of the not naturally bad but irresponsible and undeveloped nature, caught in the consequences of its own action. In every age and in every civilization there are instances of the same thing: the unmoral nature, suddenly trapped in the inexorable toils of morality. . . . Our conventions are not the same as those which Middleton assumed for his play. But the possibility of that frightful discovery of morality remains permanent (104–5).

As in Middleton, so in Machiavelli, Eliot discovered a writer with profound spiritual insight. "His message has been falsified by persistent romanticism ever since his death. To the humbug of every century Machiavelli has contributed. And yet no great man has been so completely misunderstood" (50).

He merely told the truth about humanity. The world of human motives which he depicts is true—that is to say, it is humanity without the addition of superhuman Grace. It is therefore tolerable only to persons who have also a definite religious belief. . . . What Machiavelli did not see about human nature is the myth of human goodness which for liberal thought replaces the belief in Divine Grace (63–64).

"The utility of Machiavelli," Eliot said, "is his perpetual summons to examination of the weakness and impurity of the soul" (66).

Baudelaire was another writer in whom he discerned the recognition of human depravity. He was "essentially a Christian, born out of his due time" (97).

And being the kind of Christian that he was, born when he was, he had to discover Christianity for himself. In this pursuit he was alone in the solitude which is only known to saints. To him the notion of Original Sin came spontaneously, and the need for prayer (98).

"Baudelaire came to attain the greatest, the most difficult, of the Christian virtues," Eliot concluded, "the virtue of humility" (99).

The essay on Bradley set out to consider "the nature of Bradley's influence and why his writings and his personality fascinate those whom they do fascinate" (69). Eliot had once been so fascinated as to write a dissertation on that philosopher's work; and in the context of *For Lancelot Andrewes*—even if not in the anonymous pages of *TLS* where this review of Bradley's *Ethical Studies* first appeared—it was clear that Eliot was at least in part assessing the nature of Bradley's impact upon himself. As a philosopher who deliberately "wished . . . to determine how much of morality could be founded securely without entering into the religious questions at all" (83), Bradley was unlikely to have exercised a direct religious influence. But "of wisdom," Eliot said, "Bradley had a large share."

Wisdom consists largely of scepticism and uncynical disillusion; and of these Bradley had a large share. And scepticism and disillusion are a useful equipment for religious understanding; and of that Bradley had a share too (76).

That Eliot had imbibed Bradley's skepticism and disillusion was clear in his early poetry and prose; that he was now employing to his own ends that "useful equipment for religious understanding" was evident throughout *For Lancelot Andrewes*.

II

In the Bradley essay Eliot, quite in passing, referred to Irving Babbitt as "one of the most remarkable of our critics, one who is fundamentally on most questions in the right, and very often right quite alone" (79–80). Seven months later he wrote further about his Harvard teacher; and as the most recent of the essays reprinted in his 1928 collection, it appeared at the end of the volume. In a book that sought "to indicate certain lines of [the author's] development," this concluding essay was the most significant. As in many of the previous essays, Eliot here returned to examine a matter of long-standing interest from his new perspective as a Christian. In the earlier essays his Christianity had been implicit; in "The Humanism of Irving Babbitt" it became explicit. His reconsideration of Babbitt and of the intellectual movement in America for which he was largely responsible offered Eliot an opportunity to expose some of the weaknesses that he, as a Christian, now found in Babbitt's thought. But what is more, in discussing his sense of the insufficiency of Babbitt's humanism, Eliot suggested something of the logic that had recently brought him to Anglo-Catholicism.

It was, in fact, none other than Babbitt himself who had urged Eliot to make a public declaration of his Christianity. With unusual autobiographical detail, Eliot recorded the circumstances of the challenge that "provoked" the famous preface to *For Lancelot Andrewes*. In 1928 Babbitt and his wife passed through London on their way home from France. While in London they dined with Eliot; and the conversation turned upon the increasingly religious orientation of the writing of Paul Elmer More, a dear friend of Babbitt's and a man closely associated with him in the American humanist movement. Eliot recalled the conversation:

Anxious though I was to avoid such a painful subject, I found myself obliged to expose and briefly to account for my own position. I imagine that, in view of some of my previous eccentricities in print, this was only a minor shock to him. He took the matter seriously, however, and managed to convince me that it was my duty, in his own words, to "come out into the open." I had not been conscious of skulking, having been more concerned with making up my own mind than with making any public use of it when made. But Babbitt's words gnawed on my conscience, and provoked, for my next volume of essays, a preface that perhaps went to the opposite extreme from that of which I had felt myself accused.[9]

9. In *Irving Babbitt: Man and Teacher,* ed. Frederick Manchester and Odell Shepard (New York: Putnam's, 1941), p. 103. For another account of this conversation see "To Criticize the Critic" in *To Criticize the Critic and Other Writings* (New York: Farrar, Straus and Giroux, 1965), p. 15.

That such a preface was necessary indicated the distance Eliot had traveled in his intellectual development during the previous several years. "The Humanism of Irving Babbitt" offered further indication.

Though Eliot's essay is perhaps most memorable for its criticism, it is important to recognize that he approached this reassessment of Babbitt's thought with no less admiration for his teacher than he had carried away with him from Harvard. Over the years, Eliot had often written in praise of Babbitt. In July 1922, for example, he had recommended that Babbitt be appointed to fill the vacant Professorship of Poetry at Oxford.[10] In January 1926, he had cited his *Democracy and Leadership* as one of the books exemplary of the *Criterion*'s classicism. Six months later he published in his review an essay by one of his American enthusiasts, Gorham B. Munson, on "The Socratic Virtues of Irving Babbitt."[11] And, of course, in the essay on Bradley, Eliot had digressed briefly to praise Babbitt. Eliot, then, had often expressed his esteem for his former teacher. And in his 1928 discussion of "The Humanism of Irving Babbitt," as in the controversy over humanism that ensued, Eliot's approach was constructive. As he said at the beginning of the essay, he did not desire to attack his master's thought so much as to contribute to a critical appreciation of his achievement:

I believe that it is better to recognize the weaknesses of humanism at once, and allow for them, so that the structure may not crash beneath an excessive weight; and so that we may arrive at an enduring recognition of its value for us, and of our obligation to its author (143).

By 1928 Eliot had not, of course, outgrown his conviction as to the importance of such humanist principles as order, discipline, and tradition. He had, however, come to feel that those values were, fundamentally, religious.

10. "London Letter," *Dial* 73 (1922), 96.
11. *Criterion* 4 (1926), 494–503.

To Eliot it was evident that "the problem of humanism is undoubtedly related to the problem of religion"; yet Eliot found Babbitt insisting throughout his most recent book, *Democracy and Leadership,* "that he is unable to take the religious view—that is to say that he cannot accept any dogma or revelation; and that humanism is the *alternative* to religion" (128). To Eliot, however, it was clear that humanism could not exist apart from religion. He asked rhetorically:

Is it, in the end, a view of life that will work by itself, or is it a derivative of religion which will work only for a short time in history, and only for a few highly cultivated persons like Mr. Babbitt—whose ancestral traditions, furthermore, are Christian, and who is, like many people, at the distance of a generation or so from definite Christian belief? Is it, in other words, durable beyond one or two generations? (128)

Eliot believed that humanism, to exist at all, must be "dependent upon some other attitude, for it is essentially critical—I would even say parasitical" (130); and the attitude on which he found it most dependent was, of course, the Christian.

Eliot objected to Babbitt's having appropriated the ethical principles of religion without having accepted the dogmas from which those principles grew. His humanism, Eliot said, is "alarmingly like very liberal Protestant theology of the nineteenth century: it is, in fact, a product—a by-product—of Protestant theology in its last agonies" (133). Ironically, he discerned a certain romanticism in Babbitt's confidence that "the 'outer' restraints of an orthodox religion, as they weaken, can be supplied by the inner restraint of the individual over himself. . . . If you distinguish so sharply between 'outer' and 'inner' checks as Mr. Babbitt does, then there is nothing left for the individual to check himself by but his own private notions and his judgment, which is pretty precarious" (135). Religion, Eliot insisted, offered not only a more substantial ethical authority but also a coherent program of the goals in whose service that authority would be exercised. He shared Babbitt's aspiration that "civilization" be nurtured; but Eliot felt that the church was indispensable in attaining that goal:

Unless by civilization you mean material progress, cleanliness, etc.—which is not what Mr. Babbitt means; if you mean a spiritual and intellectual co-ordination on a high level, then it is doubtful whether civilization can endure without religion, and religion without a church (140).

As at the beginning, so at the end of his essay Eliot insisted that his intention was fundamentally constructive. "My purpose has been, not to predict a bad end for Mr. Babbitt's philosophy, but to point out the direction which I think it should follow if the obscurities of 'humanism' were cleared up. It should lead, I think, to the conclusion that the humanistic point of view is auxiliary to and dependent upon the religious point of view." Eliot, of course, had come to that conclusion himself. Significantly shifting to the first-person plural pronoun, he declared: "For us, religion is of course Christianity; and Christianity implies, I think, the conception of the Church" (141–42).

More clearly than in any of the other essays in *For Lancelot Andrewes*, more clearly even than in the preface, Eliot here announced his new religious position. The significance of this final essay was not lost on contemporary readers. To the reviewer for the *TLS* Eliot's development was nothing less than a betrayal:

By accepting a higher spiritual authority based not upon the deepest personal experience (for that we must still turn to the poems), but upon the anterior and exterior authority of revealed religion, he has abdicated from his high position. Specifically he rejects modernism for medievalism.[12]

12. "Mr. Eliot's New Essays," *TLS*, 6 December 1928, p. 953 Eliot remarked on this "flattering obituary notice" in "Thoughts after Lambeth," in *Selected Essays*, New Edition (New York: Harcourt, Brace, 1950), p. 325.

On the other side of the Atlantic, Edmund Wilson recognized in Eliot's religious position "a point of view which is by way of becoming fashionable among certain sorts of literary people."

It seems to me that the objection to Eliot's position is simply that the Church is now practically impossible as a solution to our present difficulties because it is so difficult to get educated people to believe in its fundamental doctrines . . . I agree that, without a church, you cannot have anything properly describable as religion; and I sympathize with Mr. Eliot's criticism of certain substitute religions. . . . You cannot have real Christianity without a cult of Christ as the son of God. But since it is plainly becoming more and more difficult to accept Christ in this role, it seems that we must do without both the Church and religion. . . . Nothing seems to me more sadly symptomatic of the feeble condition of modern literary people, of their unwillingness or incapacity to confront the realities about them, than the movement back to Thomas Aquinas—or, as in Eliot's case, back to Bishop Andrewes.[13]

It need hardly be added that the remarks of Wilson and of the *TLS* reviewer were among the first expressions of a persistent critical uneasiness with Eliot's Anglo-Catholicism.[14]

III

The essay that especially brought on that criticism, "The Humanism of Irving Babbitt," was the only essay in *For Lancelot Andrewes* that had originally been published in

13. "T. S. Eliot and the Church of England," *The New Republic,* 24 April 1929, p. 283.

14. Babbitt was also quick to react. In a Letter to the Editor of the *Forum,* he wrote: "As an exposition and critique of the position I am attempting to develop, Mr. Eliot's article, 'The Humanism of Irving Babbitt,' strikes me as confused and sophistical and in certain important respects positively inaccurate. It is not without interest, however, for the light it throws on Eliot's own perplexities and also no doubt on those of a portion at least of his numerous following of young intellectuals in England and America" (*Forum* 80 [1928], 638).

an American review. The fact is significant, for Eliot's reconsideration of Babbitt's thought coincided with a considerable interest in the United States during the late twenties in the ideas of the American humanists.[15] Eliot's essay first appeared in the *Forum,* a monthly that had long been distinguished for its symposia on currently controversial issues.[16] In the months before the appearance of the essay in July 1928, the *Forum* had published articles by both Babbitt and Paul Elmer More.

The essays in that review doubtless played some part in the renewed interest in humanism; and the concurrent appearance of a new book by Norman Foerster, one of Babbitt's most devoted disciples, brought still more attention to the movement. Foerster's *American Criticism: A Study of Literary Theory from Poe to the Present* was hardly likely to stir great controversy in its survey of the theories of Poe, Emerson, Lowell, and Whitman. If his perspective was moral rather than literary, such was to be expected of the humanist critics. His final chapter, however, was another matter; in "The Twentieth Century: Conclusion" Foerster proposed a criticism he thought appropriate to his age, and so doing he attempted a comprehensive definition of what had come to be known as the "New Humanism." In asserting the "doctrine" and "discipline" of humanism, Foerster endeavored to systematize the precepts that his master, Babbitt, had left implicit in his own writing. Both because Foerster's summary is a useful

15. The most complete contemporary account of the three-year debate over the New Humanism is Seward Collins's brilliant, though biased essay, "Criticism in America," which appeared in three parts in his pro-humanist review, the *Bookman:* 71 (1930), 241–56, 353–64; 71 (1930), 400–415; 72 (1930), 145–64, 209–28.

16. At the beginning of each issue there appeared a description of the *Forum* as "A non-partisan magazine of free discussion. It aims to interpret the new America that is attaining consciousness in this decade. The *Forum* gives both sides. Whatever is attacked by contributors this month may be praised in later issues."

compendium of what soon became an aggressively self-conscious movement and because it was often cited during the next two years in the controversies over the New Humanism, it deserves to be quoted in some detail.

1. An adequate human standard calls for *completeness;* it demands the cultivation of every part of human nature. . . . It suppresses nothing.

2. But it also calls for *proportion:* it demands the harmony of the parts with the whole. Instead of "accepting life" indiscriminately, it imposes a scale of values.

3. This complete, proportionate standard may be said to consist of the *normally or typically human.* . . .

4. Although such an ethos has never existed, it has been approximated in the great ages of *the past,* to which humanism accordingly looks for guidance. It looks chiefly toward Greece, where it still finds the best examples. . . .

5. Unlike romanticism, which in its quest of a natural ethos repudiated the logical faculty, humanism is always true to its Hellenic origin in its faith in *reason.* . . .

6. Unlike the conceptions of life that grow out of science, humanism seeks to press beyond reason by the use of *intuition* or *imagination.* . . .

7. The ultimate ethical principle is that of *restraint* or *control.* . . .

8. This center to which humanism refers everything, this centripetal energy which counteracts the multifarious centrifugal impulses, this magnetic will which draws the flux of our sensations toward it while itself remaining at rest, is the reality that gives rise to religion. Pure humanism is content to describe it thus in physical terms . . . ; it hesitates to pass beyond its experimental knowledge to the dogmatic affirmations of any of the great religions. It cannot bring itself to accept a formal theology . . . that has been set up in defiance of reason. . . .[17]

Foerster's final point was clearly unacceptable to Eliot. But, more generally, Eliot was troubled to see the attitudes

17. *American Criticism* (Boston: Houghton Mifflin, 1928), pp. 241–45.

of Babbitt (many of which he still shared) codified into a creed (to which he obviously could not subscribe).

Distressed that the New Humanism should be taking the form of a movement with pretensions even to being a religion, Eliot directed the attention of the *Criterion* to the recent developments in America.[18] When he was invited at the end of 1928 to contribute an article about Henry James to *Hound and Horn,* Eliot declined and explained, "Having a busy life, I find I can only accomplish anything by fitting in the subjects I write about to some scheme of my own. At the moment, I am more interested in the New Humanism, and Babbitt and his disciples."[19] In December 1928, the first in a series of articles on the New Humanism appeared in the *Criterion.* As always, the review was reflecting Eliot's interests; as editor, he was adapting the *Criterion* to a scheme of his own.

The first of the essays on the New Humanism, Herbert Read's "Humanism and the Absolute: The Texts of a Debate," anticipated in its subtitle the extended discussion that ensued. Quoting extensively from Foerster's *American Criticism* and from a recent essay by Julien Benda, Read attempted to demonstrate the inadequacy of the American critic by comparison with his French counterpart. "Mr. Foerster, on behalf of the New Humanists," Read said, "nowhere makes it clear that he accepts [the] absolute severance of things divine and things human." And the recent editor of *Speculations* concluded: "With T. E.

18. Several years later, in a notice on Babbitt's death, Eliot wrote: "Any attempt to present his works as a body of canonical writings must end in failure, and worse. I have in mind the attempt, a few years ago, by a number of his devoted pupils to present 'humanism' as almost a proprietary medicine recommended for those who cannot 'believe' yet who abominate the radical materialism which is offered as an alternative" ("Commentary," *Criterion* 13 [1933], 118).

19. Letter to Lincoln Kirstein, 16 November 1928, Yale University Library. Several months later Eliot wrote Allen Tate, "I am trying to work up Humanism in the *Criterion*" (11 February 1929, Princeton University Library).

Hulme, who in this matter is so closely echoed by M. Benda, I hold that most of our errors spring from an attempt on our part to gloze over and disguise a particular discontinuity in the nature of reality."[20] The New Humanists' failure to distinguish clearly between the natural and the supernatural was central to Eliot's objection to the movement.

The first article in the next issue found G. K. Chesterton asking "Is Humanism a Religion?" Foerster's outline of the New Humanism led Chesterton to question "whether Humanism can perform all the functions of religion." Predictably, his conclusion was in the negative:

I do not believe that Humanism can be a complete substitute for Superhumanism. I do not believe it because of a certain truth to me so concrete as to be called a fact. . . . The fact is this: that the modern world, with its modern movements, is living on its Catholic capital. It is using, and using up, the truths that remain to it out of the old treasury of Christendom; including, of course, many truths known to pagan antiquity but crystallized in Christendom. But it is *not* really starting new enthusiasms of its own. The novelty is a matter of names and labels. . . .

The concern that Eliot had broached as a rhetorical question in "The Humanism of Irving Babbitt" was confronted more directly by Chesterton:

. . . I distrust spiritual experiments outside the central spiritual tradition; for the simple reason that I think they do not last, even if they manage to spread. At the most they stand for one generation; at the commonest for one fashion; at the lowest for one clique. I do not think they have the secret of continuity; certainly not of corporate continuity.[21]

The most bitterly critical of the *Criterion*'s essays was Allen Tate's "The Fallacy of Humanism" in the July 1929

20. *Criterion* 8 (1928), 275–76.
21. *Criterion* 8 (1929), 382, 383, 391.

issue. The humanists, he said, lacked any logical foundation for the values upon which they were insisting:

It is this vague understanding on the part of the Humanists of the nature of philosophy, it is their lack of an exact logical and philosophical discipline, which betrays them not only into . . . muddy reasoning . . . ; it leads them to expect to find in literature, ancient or modern, an explicit philosophy sufficient unto itself. . . .

"The Humanists have no technique," he said. "How . . . they intend to validate their values they do not say; they simply urge them."[22] With the sarcasm that characterized much of his attack, Tate remarked that "values are not suspended in the air, to be plucked." In summary he suggested that "Humanism is not enough, and . . . if the values for which the Humanist pleads are to be made rational, even intelligible, the prior condition of an objective religion is necessary. . . . Religion is the sole technique for the validating of values."[23] As might have been expected, Eliot was appreciative of Tate's essay; he acknowledged its receipt with a note saying that he had read it "with the deepest interest"; despite some specific reservations, he characterized it as "a brilliant article."[24]

Thus far, the *Criterion*'s treatment of the New Humanism had been quite one-sided, and Eliot was perhaps uneasy that his interest in correcting the excesses of the movement should have become an apparent effort toward destruction. Thus, with the hospitality to spokesmen for

22. *Criterion* 8 (1929), 667, 662.
23. Ibid., pp. 661, 678.
24. 5 March 1929, Princeton University Library. Shortly after the appearance of Tate's essay, he wrote to Paul Elmer More whom Tate had criticized severely. Eliot indicated his interest in following the course of Tate's career—a career he felt was as promising as that of anyone in Tate's generation (30 December 1929, Princeton University Library). A few months later, however, More described Tate's essay as an "ignorant and conceited outburst" ("A Revival of Humanism," *Bookman* 71 [1930], 7).

opposing points of view that had marked his considerations of romanticism and of the Action Française, he opened the pages of his review to advocates of the humanist position. The next two issues contained essays more favorable to the movement; the first was by Norman Foerster himself.

Foerster addressed himself to the problem that had been of greatest concern to Eliot and the *Criterion* critics, "Humanism and Religion." Though his essay offered little to bridge the intellectual gulf between him and his critics, Foerster hoped at least to clarify the issues that separated them. He denied the repeated assertion that humanism grew from Christianity and insisted, instead, that its "foundation . . . is Classical, is Greek, is pre-Christian." Moreover, he denied that humanism was—or pretended to be—a religion at all:

Humanism is not a religion but a working philosophy, having for its object as a philosophy the clarification of human values, and for its object as a mode of working the realization of human values. Operating in the critical rather than the dogmatic spirit, it conceives that the old religious solutions are inadequate, and it at the same time fears the delusions into which men so easily plunge when seeking to pass, without a via media, from the natural to the superhuman level.

But if humanism were not a religion it could, Foerster suggested, be imagined to be an alternative to religion; in fact, he insisted that it lacked none of the elements essential to religion:

In its insistence on conversion (by right habit), on the exertion of the ethical will (to which, not to reason, it finally assigns supremacy), on the high function of imagination, on the need of meditation, on the need, above all, of humility, and in its offering of substantial happiness (at its best, an exalted peace) as the fruit of right living, humanism would seem to include all that is essential in religion.

"The final effort of the modern or critical spirit," he announced, "must be to render clear and commanding an inner authority competent to take the place of outer authority."[25] Foerster's statement might well have been John Middleton Murry's several years before; as in Murry's "Romanticism and the Tradition," so in Foerster's "Humanism and Religion," there was little comfort for the editor of the *Criterion* or those of his mind.

More than a year after the beginning of the *Criterion*'s consideration of the New Humanism, the final essay on the subject appeared there. The author, Ramon Fernandez, was familiar to the pages of the review; a man whom Eliot had characterized as being with himself "on the side of 'the intelligence'," Fernandez had been one of the critics of Murry's romanticism three years earlier. Now, in an essay translated by Eliot himself, Fernandez defended humanism:

The opponents of humanism have it all their own way. They judge and condemn a doctrine which is not yet self-conscious, or conscious of its tendency or of its exact place in the universe of discourse. They make haste to stifle an embryo of thought, the future of which is still unpredictable. . . . The American humanists, with whom *The Criterion* has lately concerned itself, are essayists rather than philosophers. They do not seem to have tested their notions by a rigorous critique, and are easily entrapped in their own pretensions.

Fernandez then proposed "A Humanist Theory of Value" that might not be so vulnerable. Though aware that it remained philosophically incomplete, Fernandez respected the goals of the movement: "Humanism is in fact man's resumption of possession of that which is his right: that is, the origin, the very foundation of value."[26]

25. *Criterion* 9 (1929), 28, 25–26, 26–27, 31. Foerster's article had appeared a month before in the United States in the *Forum*.

26. *Criterion* 9 (1930), 228, 242. Eliot urged Paul Elmer More to read Fernandez's essay, which he described as impressively—though perhaps sophistically—argued (30 December 1929, Princeton University Library).

Eliot's superintending hand was everywhere apparent in the current symposium on humanism; but since Read, Chesterton, and Tate were arguing his position effectively, he was silent on the issue in the pages of his review. Elsewhere, however, in a 1929 essay in Middleton Murry's *New Adelphi,* he summarized his own—and the *Criterion*'s—point of view. Again Eliot insisted that he sought not to attack humanism but, rather, to help save it. "It can be—and is already—of immense value," he said. "But it must be subjected to criticism while there is still time."[27] In the year since the publication of his earlier essay on "The Humanism of Irving Babbitt," Eliot had grown more uneasy after reading Foerster's *American Criticism.* He found himself increasingly concerned that the New Humanism "may take on more and more the character of a positive philosophy—and any philosophy, in our time, is likely to take on the character of a substitute for religious dogma" (430). Tate's question about the validation of values was Eliot's as well.

Mr. Foerster's Humanism, in fact, is too ethical to be true. Where do all these morals come from? One advantage of an orthodox religion, to my mind, is that it puts morals in their proper place. . . . I cannot understand a system of morals which seems to be founded on nothing but itself—which exists, I suspect, only by illicit relations with either psychology or religion or both . . . (432–33).

To Eliot there was no question that morals properly come from above:

Man is man because he can recognize supernatural realities, not because he can invent them. Either everything in man can be traced as a development from below, or something must come from above. There is no avoiding that dilemma: you must be either a naturalist or a supernaturalist. If you remove from the

27. "Second Thoughts about Humanism," in *Selected Essays,* p. 429. Subsequent references, inserted in the text, will be to the essay as reprinted in this collection.

word "human" all that the belief in the supernatural has given to man, you can view him finally as no more than an extremely clever, adaptable, and mischievous little animal (433).

The latter seemed to Eliot to be the view of the humanists. And their immense faith in man's almost unlimited capacity for self-improvement led him to suspect "that Mr. Foerster and even Mr. Babbitt are nearer to the view of Rousseau than they are to the religious view" (437). For Eliot this was the harshest of comparisons.

Having only recently done so himself, Eliot recognized the difficulty of passing beyond secular humanism to the religious view:

Most people suppose that some people, because they enjoy the luxury of Christian sentiments and the excitement of Christian ritual, swallow or pretend to swallow incredible dogma. For some the process is exactly opposite. Rational assent may arrive late, intellectual conviction may come slowly, but they come inevitably without violence to honesty and nature (438).

It was just such a gradual but inevitable progress toward intellectual conviction that Eliot had been making. "To put the sentiments in order is a later and an immensely difficult task," he added (438). And for a Christian like himself, it was here that humanism was valuable. "Humanism can have no positive theories about philosophy or theology. All that it can ask, in the most tolerant spirit, is: Is this particular philosophy or religion civilized or is it not?" (436) Eliot was aware that religion, institutionalized in the church, stood in constant danger of losing that quality of civilization. Humanism could help ensure that religion not succumb to that danger. "Humanism makes for breadth, tolerance, equilibrium and sanity," he said. "It operates against fanaticism." And thus Eliot welcomed its assistance as "a mediating and corrective ingredient in a positive civilization founded on definite belief" (436).

Though he was uneasy with the secular character of

Babbitt's humanism and was troubled by the ambitions for the movement of such disciples as Foerster, Eliot could never dismiss the New Humanism completely. To disavow Babbitt's philosophy would be at the least disingenuous; he had absorbed his professor's ideas so thoroughly that, by now, there was no recanting. He had, however, gone beyond Babbitt's humanistic traditionalism to religious orthodoxy, and he now felt challenged to bring to bear upon the movement to which he owed so much the insights of his recent development. His approach continued to be that of a sympathetic—indeed, committed—critic.[28]

His willingness to be identified with the New Humanism was evidenced by his appearance in a symposium published in 1930 by Norman Foerster; the contributors, Foerster said in his preface, agreed "in certain broad, fundamental opinions." Among the other contributors to *Humanism and America: Essays on the Outlook of Modern Civilization* were Babbitt, More, and Foerster himself.[29] In such company it was proper that Eliot should insist not so much upon what he took to be the deficiencies of humanism— which he had already made quite clear—as on its positive contribution. A year before, in "Second Thoughts about Humanism," he had suggested the value of the movement as "a mediating and corrective ingredient in a positive civilization founded on definite belief." Now, in "Religion without Humanism," his final essay on the topic, Eliot only incidentally remarked that "humanism is in the end futile

28. His partisanship to the New Humanism was clear in his contribution of two essays within a year to the American review most closely identified with the movement, Seward Collins's *Bookman.* In November 1929, his "Experiment in Criticism" was published there; and the following September, "Arnold and Pater."

29. It is especially significant that Eliot contributed to Foerster's symposium and not another, less sympathetic collection of essays published the same year, C. Hartley Grattan's *Critique of Humanism: A Symposium* (New York: Brewer and Warren, 1930). Among the contributors to that volume were R. P. Blackmur, Kenneth Burke, Malcolm Cowley, Allen Tate, and Yvor Winters.

without religion."[30] Confident that he had already made
that point clearly elsewhere, he went on to "put forward
. . . a view which seems to me equally important, the counterpart of the other, and one which ought to be more wel-
come to humanists. Having called attention to what I
believe to be a danger, I am bound to call attention to the
danger of the other extreme: the danger, a very real one,
of *religion without humanism*" (105).

Humanism can offer neither the intellectual discipline of philosophy or of science . . . , nor the emotional discipline of religion
On the other hand, these other activities depend upon humanism
to preserve their sanity. Without it, religion tends to become
either a sentimental tune, or an emotional debauch; or in theology, a skeleton dance of fleshless dogmas, or in ecclesiasticism,
a soulless political club (110–11).

And then Eliot described the nature of humanism's poten-
tial contribution:

It is the spirit of humanism which has operated to reconcile the
mystic and the ecclesiastic in one church; having done this in
the past, humanism should not set itself up now as another sect,
but strive to continue and enlarge its task, labouring to reconcile
and unite all the parts into a whole (111).

Eliot's extended reconsideration of humanism in the
years immediately following his conversion was in part an
accident of intellectual history: the movement became an
object of lively controversy at nearly the same time that
he was passing through this most dramatic stage of his intellectual development. But his involvement in the controversy also had a personal function. It was proper that Eliot
should reassess in terms of his new, Christian perspective
the philosophy that had, however indirectly, brought him
to that faith. Eliot's own essays and those he solicited for
the *Criterion* are valuable both for their telling criticisms

30. *Humanism and America* (New York: Farrar and Rinehart,
1930), p. 105. Subsequent references are inserted in the text.

and their suggestions of the abiding value of the movement. Still more significant, however, are the implications
throughout Eliot's reconsideration as to some of the forces
bearing on his own conversion. He was at one with the humanists in their uneasiness over the course of modern
civilization; he was united with them in the search, to cite
Babbitt once again, "for standards to oppose to individual
caprice"; and he, hardly less than they, sought discipline,
order, and control in the individual, in society, and ultimately in art. "Humanism," Eliot acknowledged, "has
much to say of Discipline and Order and Control." But
in the end he found its promise unfulfilled. Having been
led by the humanism of Babbitt to a recognition of the
need for these qualities, and having failed to find them
fully realized in any secular system, he had gone beyond
humanism to what he held to be the true source of those
values. "I found no discipline in humanism," Eliot said in
1930, "only a little intellectual discipline from a little study
of philosophy. But the difficult discipline is the discipline
and training of emotion . . . ; and this," he said, "I have
found is only attainable through dogmatic religion" (110).

By the end of 1930, the debate over the New Humanism
had largely exhausted itself in America; and Eliot, too,
had tired of the topic. He wrote to Allen Tate:

I am afraid that, rather like yourself, I am too much of an individualist and too little of a gang-fighter, to win the approval of
any of these contending groups; and I am so sickened by the
kind of publicity which these philosophical discussions have ob-
tained in America, and by the reciprocal violence of vituperation,
that I never want to hear the word *humanism* again.[31]

But Eliot's extensive consideration of the New Humanism
was an important episode in his intellectual development.
As in his earlier considerations of classicism and romanticism and the Action Française, Eliot's own attitudes were

31. 8 August 1930, Princeton University Library.

revealed most clearly in the course of controversy. And it may equally be that the dialectic of such controversy also brought him to a fuller understanding of his own position. Eliot once spoke of Charles Maurras as a kind of Virgil who had led him to the doors of the temple. The same could be said of Babbitt and his humanism.[32] In the controversy over the New Humanists, Eliot announced that he had entered those doors, and why.

IV

The essays in *For Lancelot Andrewes* and his reassessment of humanism both reflected Eliot's interest after his conversion in reconsidering the significance of men and movements with which he had long been concerned. In 1929 he brought this spirit of revaluation to bear upon a poet who had exercised a marked influence on his early verse. Like the essays in *For Lancelot Andrewes,* his small, book-length study of Dante served to "indicate certain lines of development" in Eliot's thought. Because it recalled his study of the same poet nine years earlier, *Dante* demonstrated the expansion of his critical attitudes more clearly than any of his other essays in the late twenties.

The concern with theoretical issues present in so many of the essays in *The Sacred Wood* had been present in the earlier "Dante" essay as well; Eliot had devoted much of his attention there to arguing the possibility of philosophical poetry.[33] "Dante," he had said in 1920, "more than

32. Shortly after Babbitt's death, Eliot wrote: "We must regret deeply that Babbitt's attitude towards Christianity remained, in spite of his sometimes deceptive references to 'religion,' definitely obdurate. Writing so soon after his death, however, we may be permitted to regret, more, that a certain inflexibility, or *raideur,* or almost excessive integrity of doctrine, did not allow him to recognize as disciples some who went too far for him as well as some who did not go far enough, but who acknowledge to him a very great debt and revere his memory in affection, admiration and gratitude" ("Commentary," *Criterion* 13 [1933], 119).

33. See chap. 1, pp. 28–30.

any other poet, . . . succeeded in dealing with his philosophy, not as a theory . . . or as his own comment or reflection, but in terms of something perceived." Though he in the earlier essay had acknowledged that Dante's superiority to such poets as Lucretius was in part due to his having "had the benefit of a mythology and a theology which had undergone a more complete absorption into life," Eliot nowhere there suggested that social and cultural factors might have borne on Dante's achievement; nowhere did he discuss the specifically religious nature of Dante's poem; nowhere, in fact, did the words *Christian* or *Catholic* even appear. In 1920 he was writing the criticism of the workman and was concerned with Dante as a craftsman with words and ideas. When, nine years later, he again wrote on him, Eliot's essay reflected a much enriched understanding of the historical circumstances that had rendered Dante's achievement possible and of the profound religious signficance of his poem.

The later essay was published by Eliot's firm of Faber and Faber as the second of a projected series of small books to appear under the general title, "The Poets on the Poets." An insert distributed with copies of the October 1929 *Criterion* outlined the purpose of the series:

The experiment is especially interesting at a time when, to many, poets seem to be following new and strange tracks. Here, then, is a series of essays by contemporary poets on their predecessors. It is interesting not only for the illumination it throws on the subject it deals with but for the light it reflects on the writers themselves. Those who are unacquainted with contemporary work, or who are puzzled by it, will find in this series a revealing commentary on the tastes of the present time.

It may have been that the writer of that flyer—doubtless Eliot himself—had in mind the light the book on Dante, published the previous month, reflected on its author. In his preface, Eliot insisted on the subjective approach he brought to *Dante:*

A contemporary writer of verse, in writing a pamphlet of this description, is required only to give a faithful account of his acquaintance with the poet of whom he writes. This, and no more, I can do; and this is the only way in which I can treat an author of whom so much has been written, that can make any pretence to novelty.[34]

No longer confining himself to the criticism of the workman, as in *The Sacred Wood,* Eliot would discuss his topic from an unabashedly personal point of view.

Eliot had lost none of his literary acuity since writing the earlier essay; if only because of the greater space now at his disposal, the book was far richer than the essay. In part that richness was a function of the literary maturity achieved during the nine fruitful years of poetizing and criticizing that separated the two works. But in part it was also a function of the added insight he enjoyed as a result of his intellectual development. His 1929 study reflected Eliot's enhanced view of poetry as a function not only of the conjunction of the poet's individual talent and his available tradition, but also of the poet's existence in a specific historical situation. In his own mutation Eliot had come to recognize the manner in which social—and, specifically, political—factors impinge directly upon the work of the artist; in 1929 he took pains to insist that Dante's achievement was in some measure a function of his good fortune in having written at a propitious juncture in the history of Western civilization. Dante's Europe, Eliot said, was not a fragmented collection of distinct nations like his own, or even Shakespeare's. "The culture of Dante was not of one European country but of Europe," he said.[35] "Dante's advantages [over Shakespeare] are not due to greater genius, but to the fact that he wrote when Europe

34. "Preface," in *Dante* (London: Faber and Faber, 1929), p. 11.
35. "Dante," in *Selected Essays,* p. 201. Subsequent references, inserted in the text, will be to the essay as it was reprinted—with little revision—in this collection.

was still more or less one. . . . In Dante's time, Europe, with all its dissensions and dirtiness, was mentally more united than we can now conceive" (203, 202).

Language, of course, is a product of culture; and there, too, Dante was fortunate. In being able to draw upon medieval Italian, Dante became "the most *universal* of poets in the modern languages. . . . The Italian language, and especially the Italian language in Dante's age, gains much by being the product of universal Latin. . . . Medieval Latin tended to concentrate on what men of various races and lands could think together" (200–201). In the context of his other writings in the twenties, it was clear that Eliot's sensitivity to the beneficent influence for poetry of such factors in Dante's society reflected his concern over their absence in his own. He saw modern European nations becoming more and more culturally distinct from one another, and today, he remarked dourly, "mathematics is . . . the only universal language" (201).

Just as Eliot's own social and political concerns were reflected in his attention to the cultural circumstances that had contributed to Dante's achievement, so his own Anglo-Catholicism was reflected in his appreciation of Dante's theology. In 1920 he had been impatient with critics who approached Dante as a "spiritual leader." By 1929, however, Eliot was himself writing in such a vein. The *Inferno*, he said, "reminds us that Hell is not a place but a *state*; that man is damned or blessed in the creatures of his imagination as well as in men who have actually lived; . . . and that the resurrection of the body has perhaps a deeper meaning than we understand" (211–12). Eliot recognized that the profoundly religious character of Dante's *Comedy* posed special problems for the modern reader. "We have (whether we know it or not) a prejudice against beatitude as material for poetry" (225). But to Eliot's mind the very passage in Dante's poem where beatitude was most sublime was also the poem's greatest: "The last canto of the *Para-*

diso . . . is to my thinking the highest point that poetry has ever reached or ever can reach" (212). In part, his little book was written to help readers overcome that prejudice so that they could share his appreciation of *The Divine Comedy*. He specified one of the necessary conditions of such appreciation:

In reading Dante you must enter the world of thirteenth-century Catholicism. . . . You are not called upon to believe what Dante believed . . . ; but you are called upon more and more to understand it. If you can read poetry as poetry, you will "believe" in Dante's theology exactly as you believe in the physical reality of his journey; that is, you suspend both belief and disbelief (219).

By 1929 Eliot hardly needed inverted commas to qualify his own belief in that theology.

In the middle of this Dante essay he remarked, "The majority of poems one outgrows or outlives; Dante's is one of those which one can only just hope to grow up to at the end of life" (212). From the epigraph of "The Love Song of J. Alfred Prufrock" to the modified terza rima passage in "Little Gidding," Dante's impact on Eliot was pronounced. Dante's poetry, Eliot said in 1950, was "the most persistent and deepest influence upon my own verse." But, though he was willing to discuss Dante's role in his poetic development, Eliot was reluctant to speak "of any debt which one may owe to the thought of Dante, to his view of life, or to the philosophy and theology which give shape and content to the Divine Comedy."[36] Despite (and perhaps because of) Eliot's characteristic reserve, one suspects that his intellectual—and, more specifically, religious —debt to Dante was no less great than his poetic debt. Eliot's intense appreciation of Dante's poetry doubtless led in time to a similar appreciation of his theology; in "grow-

36. "What Dante Means to Me," in *To Criticize the Critic*, pp. 125, 132.

ing up to" Dante's poem, Eliot had also "grown up to" his faith.

When it awarded him the 1948 Nobel Prize in Literature, the Swedish Academy described Eliot as "one of Dante's latest born successors. . . . Nor is it due only to chance," they said, "that he has written one of the finest studies of Dante's work and personality."[37] The thin 1929 book to which the academy referred is notable in its reflection of the broader social and religious perspective that Eliot was bringing to literary criticism. Moreover, the very fact that Eliot chose to write on him then suggests that Dante had played a major role in Eliot's religious development during the previous few years. Once again, however, the temptation of attributing Eliot's conversion to any single force must be resisted. As if to remind his readers of the multiplicity of influences working on him in the twenties, Eliot dedicated the *Dante* volume to Charles Maurras.

V

If Dante and Maurras were indeed as influential in Eliot's religious development as the evidence suggests, one might reasonably question why Eliot joined the Anglican rather than the Roman Catholic Church. One explanation recalls an earlier concern of this chapter: humanism. Though Eliot's conversion led him to be increasingly critical of humanism, the very character of that conversion partook of its mediating spirit. His contribution to Norman Foerster's *Humanism and America* expressed his fear of a "Religion without Humanism"; in part, his reluctance to join the Roman Catholic Church reflected his feeling that Roman Catholicism was such a religion. His attitude was clearly implied by his enthusiastic publication during the *Criterion*'s symposium on humanism of Paul Elmer More's essay on "An Absolute and an Authoritative Church." While Chesterton and Tate had seemed to be proposing

37. *Les Prix Nobel En 1948* (Stockholm: Norstedt, 1949), p. 51.

Catholicism as a preferable alternative to humanism, More directly attacked the Church of Rome whose doctrine of papal infallibility he found no less intellectually suspect than the fundamentalist Protestant notion of scriptural infallibility. In an extensive argument More insisted that neither the Bible nor the Pope could logically be held an *absolute* guide in spiritual matters:

The *a priori* arguments for an absolute Church simply fall to pieces the moment one sees that belief in any kind of absolute inspiration is incompatible with the character of the *depositum fidei* as given in the Bible; historically, the evidence, carefully weighed, is against such a theory. But the most serious objection is pragmatic rather than theoretic or historical. The presumption of infallibility has committed Rome, has committed her *irrevocably,* to a series of dogmas . . . which are already a grave embarrassment to the faithful and in the end must cause a complete rupture between a religion so committed and any reasonable philosophy of life.

Instead of an absolute Church, then, More proposed a church in which a believer would be guided by the authority of the church's formulated tradition yet still be free to reject parts of that tradition that in conscience he could not accept. "No doubt there is something unsatisfactory in such a position," More wryly acknowledged; "it demands the constant exercise of our will and intelligence in making an adjustment never quite final, whereas the Roman position, after the first plunge of abnegation, relieves us of all the anxieties of decision."[38] To More, however, it was clear that the position of the authoritative church was the only truly tenable one. And Eliot, as he revealed in a letter to his contributor, shared More's position:

Your essay had the very great value for me of stating what can be taken as the Criterion position on the question. Had I tried to say the same things myself, I not only should have said them

38. *Criterion* 8 (1929), 625, 633–34.

far less well, but a paper under my own name would have given too distinct a theological cast to the *Criterion* itself.[39]

Social, as well as theological, considerations also held Eliot back from joining the Roman Church. In the same year that Eliot entered the Church of England, he had also become a British subject. His preference for the Anglican communion was closely related to that fact. "The great majority of English speaking people, or at least the vast majority of persons of British descent . . . are outside of the Roman communion," he said in 1930.

The Roman Church has lost some organic parts of the body of modern civilisation. It is a recognition of this fact which makes some persons of British extraction hesitate to embrace the Roman communion; and which makes them feel that those of their race who have embraced it have done so only by the surrender of some essential part of their inheritance and by cutting themselves off from their family.[40]

The following year Eliot remarked that "If England is ever to be in any appreciable degree converted to Christianity, it can only be through the Church of England."[41] As a member of that Church—and more specifically of its high, Catholic wing—Eliot dedicated himself to doing his part toward that national conversion.

39. 30 December 1929, Princeton University Library.
40. "Religion without Humanism," p. 107.
41. "Thoughts after Lambeth," in *Selected Essays,* p. 338.

1930-1934

5

REDEEMING THE TIME

Like his prose of the late twenties, Eliot's poetry of those years was intensely personal in its reflections of his movement toward faith. It is difficult not to see something of Eliot in the speaker of his "Song for Simeon," who struggles to accommodate himself to the Christian dispensation. So, too, the purgatorial drama and ultimate spiritual achievement of "Ash Wednesday" could not but suggest the recent experiences of its author. His new faith informed all of Eliot's activities; and just as his Christianity wrought changes in his poetry and criticism, it soon would be leading him to nonliterary writing of a kind previously foreign to him.

A distinctive quality of his career during these years was Eliot's openness—indeed, his eagerness—in following out the consequences of his religious conversion. But, as some of the early reactions to the 1928 announcement of that conversion suggested, his new life as a Christian might well have been a lonely one in the largely secular literary world of the thirties. His disputes with Babbitt and his disciples could only have aggravated his sense of intellectual loneliness. And thus it was especially fortunate that, at the same time he was reacting against the agnosticism of the New Humanism, he was also beginning an immensely fruitful friendship with Paul Elmer More—a humanist who some years earlier had gone beyond the secularism of his colleagues to a religious position similar to that which Eliot himself had recently embraced.

Many years before, while Babbitt's student at Harvard, Eliot had first encountered the writing of More. "More's work was forced on my attention," he recalled, "for one of the obligations of any pupil of Babbitt was to learn a proper respect for 'my friend More.' But while one was directly exposed to so powerful an influence as Babbitt's, everything that one read was merely a supplement to Babbitt." It was only after his conversion led him to question the implications of his teacher's thought that Eliot came to appreciate the independent importance of More's work:

I came to find an auxiliary to my own progress of thought, which no English theologian at the time could have given me. . . . It was of the greatest importance . . . to have at hand the work of a man who had come by somewhat the same route, to almost the same conclusions, at almost the same time: with a maturity, a weight of scholarship, a discipline of thinking, which I did not, and never shall, possess.[1]

Paul Elmer More was such a man; and Eliot's relations with More in the years following his conversion suggest Eliot's endeavor to reconcile the humanism that had been so formative of his earlier attitudes with the Christianity he had just embraced.

More's own career qualified him ideally to assist Eliot in his spiritual development. As literary editor of the *New York Evening Post* and, later, editor of the *Nation*, More had been engaged in a critical enterprise far more voluminous than Babbitt's but, in its philosophical assumptions, hardly dissimilar. His eleven volumes of *Shelburne Essays*, written between 1904 and 1921, were the fruit of a more graceful, more extensive application in practical criticism of many of the humanistic principles also fundamental to Babbitt's thought. Unlike Eliot's teacher, however, More was constantly searching for a faith—in fact, a religion—to replace the Calvinism in which he had been reared and

1. "Paul Elmer More," *Princeton Alumni Weekly*, 5 February 1937, p. 373. Eliot's essay was written at the request of the *Alumni Weekly*. For many years More had been a resident of Princeton and lecturer in Greek philosophy and the history of Christianity at the university.

that he had rejected. His interests turned increasingly from literary and social criticism to philosophy; and his 1917 study of *Platonism* was followed by the five volumes of *The Greek Tradition* where he sought to expound the relation between Greek philosophy and Christian theology. In such books as *The Christ of the New Testament* (1924), *Christ the Word* (1927), and *The Catholic Faith* (1931), More demonstrated an appreciative openness to religious orthodoxy far greater than that of Babbitt. "I still consider *The Greek Tradition* More's greatest work," Eliot said.

There are theological points which will always be matters of contention, but I do not know of any book which gives such a masterly treatment of the process through which Greek thought influenced Christianity. And what will keep the work permanently alive . . . is that nowhere is it a mere exercise of intellect, intelligence, and erudition, or the mere demonstration of a thesis held by the mind. I dislike to use the worn and soiled phrase "spiritual pilgrimage," but More's works are, in the deepest sense, his autobiography. One is always aware of the sincerity, and in the later works the Christian humility . . . of the concentrated mind seeking God.[2]

"More wrote a number of books of great importance," Eliot said in *TLS* shortly after his death.

But what is of the *first* importance is not any particular book or books, but the witness of the whole life-work of a great and good man—a testimony of a different nature from that of his intimate friend Irving Babbitt. During the greater part of his life his name was bracketed with Babbitt's. . . . But in later years, when Babbitt had become famous and the disciples of "Humanism" had gone out from Harvard to spread the gospel in other universities, it was More who appeared the lonelier figure. For he had turned to a still more solitary road, that of Anglican orthodoxy.[3]

2. Ibid.
3. "An Anglican Platonist: The Conversion of Elmer More," *TLS*, 30 October 1937, p. 792.

It was on that road of Anglican orthodoxy that Eliot and More met in London in 1928.[4] In fact, they had first made each other's acquaintance nearly two decades earlier at a reception given by Babbitt; but, as Eliot later recalled, More's writings had then seemed quite remote from the needs of the young Harvard poet.[5] By 1928, however, Eliot and More were brought together by the recognition not only that they shared Babbitt's friendship but also that together they were in some measure alienated from the New Humanism by the Christian faith they held in common.

Having heard from Babbitt "a rumor that T. S. Eliot is going over to Rome," More was doubtless curious to see Eliot when he visited England later in 1928.[6] The appearance of "The Humanism of Irving Babbitt" in the summer of that year could have served only to increase More's eagerness for such a meeting. On 11 July 1928, he wrote Percy H. Houston:

I agree quite heartily with T. S. Eliot in believing (a belief to which I have come slowly and almost reluctantly) that hu-

4. For a fuller discussion of the relationship of More and Eliot see Arthur Hazard Dakin, *Paul Elmer More* (Princeton: Princeton University Press, 1960).

5. See "Commentary," *Criterion* 16 (1937), 666–69. Eliot's early published remarks on More were hardly enthusiastic. In *The Sacred Wood* Eliot had placed More among his "Imperfect Critics," and said: "Mr. Paul More is the author of a number of volumes which he perhaps hopes will break the record of mass established by the complete works of Sainte-Beuve." But Eliot found More to have been "led astray . . . by his guide Sainte-Beuve. . . . Neither Mr. More nor Sainte-Beuve is primarily interested in art" (pp. 38–39, 40). The previous year he had pointed to More in illustrating his assertion that "an interest in morals will not produce sound criticism of art" ("The Local Flavour," *Athenaeum*, 12 December 1919, p. 1333). By 1936, however, Eliot was referring to More—a bit enthusiastically perhaps —as "the finest literary critic of his time" (review of *Selected Shelburne Essays, Criterion* 15 [1936], 363).

6. Letter to Prosser Hall Frye, 24 March 1928. This letter, like all of the letters to and from More cited in this chapter, is in the Princeton University Library. The dates of the letters will hereafter be inserted in the text.

manism without the divine is like a ship without a rudder. And I also believe that the most practical way today of bringing back humanism is indirectly through a stirring of religious imagination. But all this is awful heresy from the point of view of the great I. B.

Arriving in England early in August, More spent a month touring—including, appropriately, a stop at Little Gidding. By late September he wrote Christian Gauss that he had already dined with Eliot once, and had received Eliot's assurance that he was "a strong High Churchman and an enemy of Rome" (21 September 1928). On 2 October, More was looking forward to another dinner with Eliot and wrote his daughter, Alice:

Eliot, I must say, interests me very much. From his earlier work, I gathered that he was on the wild-goose chase of hunting for some ultimate criterion of art entirely severed from life. . . . But he has now given me the proof of a later volume of his now in the press [*For Lancelot Andrewes*], which shows that he has quite escaped from that slough. I dare say his religion—he is very High Church—has helped him out. One can't admire Lancelot Andrewes and be an addict of pure art.

The most palpable achievement of the first months of their friendship was Eliot's enlistment of More to join the *Criterion*'s symposium on humanism. Even before he had left England, More submitted to Eliot his draft of "An Absolute and Authoritative Church"; Eliot accepted it enthusiastically as a statement of "the Criterion position on the question."[7] Informing another daughter, Darrah, that his essay would appear in Eliot's review, More wrote: "His friendship I count the best result of my journey" (26 October 1928).

More continued to write regularly for the *Criterion;* but the personal correspondence that passed between the two after More's return to America was perhaps even more valuable to Eliot than the book reviews More was

7. See chap. 4, pp. 133–35.

also sending.[8] "Theology," he wrote More, "is the one most exciting and adventurous subject left for a jaded mind" (10 August 1930), and the greater part of their correspondence concerned that subject. In his letters to More, Eliot had the opportunity to explore, with the luxury of a private communication, the implications of his recently announced conversion.

In a letter dated "Shrove Tuesday, 1928 [1929?]," Eliot suggested some of the factors that had led to his own conversion and remarked on his continual amazement at the existence of "certain persons for whom religion is wholly unnecessary. . . . They may be very good, or very happy," he acknowledged; "they simply seem to miss nothing, to be unconscious of any void—the void that I find in the middle of all human happiness and all human relations, and which there is only one thing to fill. I am one whom this sense of void tends to drive towards asceticism or sensuality, and only Christianity helps to reconcile me to life, which is otherwise disgusting. . . ."

Though Eliot added that he did not count Babbitt as one of those utterly lacking the religious sensibility, he had by August 1929 publicly stated his feelings about the insufficiency of the New Humanism. In a letter to More, he elaborated on his attitude toward secular humanism:

I find in Foerster and other disciples of Babbitt a kind of impatience to get quick results, over-night programmes and immediate dogmas. Foerster thinks that he and his fellows are the saving remnant, but they seem to me a bargain sale remnant, shopworn. What I should like to see is the creation of a new type of intellectual, combining the intellectual and the devotional— a new species which cannot be created hurriedly. I don't like either the purely intellectual Christian or the purely emotional

8. Between December 1928 and April 1934, More contributed reviews of seven books on philosophy and religion. An essay by Philip S. Richards on "The Religious Philosophy of Paul Elmer More" also appeared in the *Criterion* 16 (1937), 205–19.

Christian—both forms of snobism. The co-ordination of thought and feeling—without either debauchery or repression—seems to me what is needed (3 August 1929).

Eliot was attracted to More because he saw in him a model of this "new type of intellectual."[9]

To embrace any form of Christianity in the modern world, however, was to defy an increasingly prevalent secularism; the reviews of *For Lancelot Andrewes*, Eliot felt, reflected a general misunderstanding of the nature of his conversion:

Most critics appear to think that my catholicism is merely an escape or an evasion, certainly a defeat. I acknowledge the difficulty of a positive Christianity nowadays; and I can only say that the dangers pointed out, and my own weaknesses, have been apparent to me long before my critics noticed them. But it [is] rather trying to be supposed to have settled oneself in an easy chair, when one has just begun a long journey afoot (3 August 1929).

For Eliot, as for any Christian, his faith held out not only the comforting promise of salvation but also the terrible possibility of damnation. "I am really shocked by your assertion that God did not make Hell," he wrote More, discussing the recent *Dante* volume. "It seems to me that you have lapsed into Humanitarianism. . . . Is your God Santa Claus?" (2 June 1930). As it revealed itself in his letters to More, Eliot's religion was hardly a matter—as his critics had suggested—of settling back in an easy chair:

9. On 31 March 1930, Eliot wrote to the editor of the *Bookman* that his attitudes were nearer to those of More than to Babbitt's: "May I state that for the teaching of Babbitt himself I have the greatest admiration; and to Mr. Babbitt, the deepest gratitude. My own position seems to me to be very close indeed to that of Mr. More. . . . What differences there are between Mr. More and myself are all on our side of the fence, do not concern the general issue of humanism, and would appear to most humanists to be trivial theological details." Eliot sent a carbon copy of the letter to More; the letter was never published in the *Bookman*.

To me, religion has brought at least the perception of something above morals, and therefore extremely terrifying; it has brought me not happiness, but the sense of something above happiness and therefore more terrifying than ordinary pain and misery; the very dark night and the desert. To me, the phrase "to be damned for the glory of God" is sense and not paradox; I had far rather walk, as I do, in daily terror of eternity, than feel that this was only a children's game in which all the contestants would get equally worthless prizes in the end. . . . And I don't know whether this is to be labelled "Classicism" or "Romanticism"; I only think that I have hold of the tip of the tail of something quite real, more real than morals, or than sweetness and light and culture (2 June 1930).

Eliot's correspondence with the man he years later referred to simply as "my old friend in America"[10] was valuable for the opportunity it afforded him to share his thoughts and feelings with another man of letters who was at once sympathetic and constructively critical. His appreciation of More's spiritual fellowship was nowhere so clear as in a letter Eliot wrote on 11 January 1937, as More lay on his deathbed. In November 1936, More had published a number of observations on literature, religion, and life under the title "Marginalia." In some of the most personal of those notes he had described his rejection of the Calvinism in which he had been reared, his subsequent "craving, a kind of necessity laid upon the intellect, to find some formula whether of creed or of worship which should respond to those elusive intimations and, as it were, build a new house for the evicted spirit"; his turning to the Brahmanic theosophy of the Upanishads and the Bhagavad-Gita; and the influences on him of John Henry Newman and Joseph Shorthouse.[11] After reading the article, Eliot wrote More:

10. "To Criticize the Critic," in *To Criticize the Critic and Other Writings* (New York: Farrar, Straus and Giroux, 1965), p. 12.
11. *American Review* 8 (1936), 25–26.

What touches me most closely is the suggestion, here and there, of a spiritual biography which, if I may say so without presumption, is oddly, even grotesquely, more like my own, so far as I can see, than that of any human being I have known. And when you say,

> "I have often wondered what line my experience might have taken had I been brought up in a form of worship from which the office of the imagination and the aesthetic emotions had not been so ruthlessly evicted. . . ."

I have made the same speculation. But I am inclined to think that I know how to value these things better, just for having (being me) to struggle so long, and for so many years so blindly and errantly, towards them.

Having reached the bottom of his page, Eliot appended to his typewritten letter, in ink, "May one say, under the guidance of the Holy Spirit?"

At nearly the same time Eliot was writing that letter, he was completing his essay on More for the *Princeton Alumni Weekly*. In the concluding paragraph of that article, he indicated what was perhaps More's greatest significance for him: his representing an alternative within the humanist tradition to the secular thought of Babbitt and his disciples.

It must remain a matter of regret that in later years More and Babbitt were obliged to diverge. To those who have found it necessary to take the way of the Catholic Church, the regret will be particularly acute. Yet, in such a generous friendship, I am sure that each regarded the other as the greater man. . . . From the point of view of their usefulness to the world, we may regard this divergence itself as capable of a great utility to us, if we can see our way to avail ourselves of it. For it points to the decision that we must all of us, if we follow our thought to the bitter end, find ourselves compelled to make. . . . The diversity of created beings is very great, and one is hardly likely to do justice to all: but these seem to me the two *wisest* men that I have known.[12]

12. "Paul Elmer More," p. 374. In a covering letter with the

After More's death, in March 1937, Eliot wrote a review for *TLS* of his *Pages from an Oxford Diary* in which he reiterated much that he had said in the *Princeton Alumni Weekly;* but he went on to make one important criticism of More's religious life. Though Christian by profession and Anglican by inclination, More even on his deathbed refused to accept formal membership in any church. Eliot was clearly disappointed that More was unwilling (or unable) to fulfill his faith in a communion of fellow believers. To Eliot, More's faith seemed insufficiently communal:

His theological learning, which was great, strikes us as the learning of a lonely man—one who learnt from books and solitary thought, rather than from communication with living theologians. . . . The man who can . . . say "Nor do I personally care to be a partaker in the Communion" has surely some cardinal error fundamental to his whole doctrine of the Eucharistic Sacrifice. And one cannot help feeling that—as is not surprising in a lonely and self-taught theologian—More had an inadequate conception of the divine nature of the Church as the Living Body of Christ.[13]

Eliot, on the other hand, had no such doubt as to the divine nature of the Church.

II

After his conversion, Eliot devoted much of his energy to the work of the Church. This impulse soon became apparent in his editorship of the *Criterion*. It was also present in his writing outside his review. In 1930 the Church of England held one of its decennial Lambeth Conferences, and Eliot's reactions to the report of that meeting of the bishops of the Anglican Communion were published in a

---

manuscript, Eliot wrote to Professor Willard Thorp of Princeton, "He seems to me to be one of very few great men I have known" (14 January 1937). For an account of his relations with Babbitt see More's "Irving Babbitt," *American Review* 3 (1934), 24–40.

13. "An Anglican Platonist," p. 792.

pamphlet, *Thoughts after Lambeth*—his first extensive essay on the Church in the modern world.

Much of Eliot's essay considered specific resolutions of the Lambeth bishops on such topics as "youth and its vocation," science and religion, marriage and birth control, and Christian reunion. Eliot clearly valued the openness of the Church of England, which "washes its dirty linen in public. . . . In contrast to some other institutions both civil and ecclesiastical, the linen does get washed."[14] "To a large degree," he said, "the differences within the Church are healthy differences within a living body" (341). But he regretted that at several points the bishops were vague as to the theological principles that underlay their decisions. "When the episcopal mind sees that something is self-evidently desirable in itself, it seems inclined to turn first to consider the means for bringing it into being, rather than to find the theological grounds upon which it can be justified." He continued,

Possibly theology is what Bradley said philosophy was: "the finding of bad reasons for what we believe upon instinct"; I think it may be the finding of good reasons for what we believe upon instinct; but if the Church of England cannot find these reasons, and make them intelligible to the more philosophically trained among the faithful, what can it do? (333)

Just as he urged that basic theological considerations not be overlooked in a preoccupation with immediate social needs, Eliot hoped that the English Church would not compromise itself "in making Christianity easy and pleasant."

"Youth," or the better part of it, is more likely to come to a difficult religion than to an easy one. For some, the intellectual way of approach must be emphasized; there is need of a more intellectual laity. For them and for others, the way of discipline

14. "Thoughts after Lambeth," in *Selected Essays,* New Edition (New York: Harcourt, Brace, 1950), p. 320. Subsequent references, inserted in the text, are to the essay as it is reprinted in this collection.

and asceticism must be emphasized; for even the humblest Christian layman can and must live what, in the modern world, is comparatively an ascetic life (329).

Clearly Eliot was speaking from his own recent experiences as he described the feelings of the contemporary believer: "Any one who has been moving among intellectual circles and comes to the Church may experience an odd and rather exhilarating feeling of isolation" (325).

But he took this very isolation, this difference in values and principles, to be a major source of the Christian's, and the Church's, strength. "The Universal Church is today . . . more definitely set against the World than at any time since pagan Rome," he said.

I do not mean that our times are particularly corrupt; all times are corrupt. I mean that Christianity, in spite of certain local appearances, is not, and cannot be within measurable time, "official." The World is trying the experiment of attempting to form a civilized but non-Christian mentality. The experiment will fail; but we must be very patient in awaiting its collapse; meanwhile redeeming the time: so that the Faith may be preserved alive through the dark ages before us; to renew and rebuild civilization, and save the World from suicide (342).

Saint Paul had enjoined the Ephesians to "walk circumspectly, not as fools, but as wise, Redeeming the time, because the days are evil" (5:15–16). Eliot, too, was working to redeem the time.

One way of achieving this end was by calling attention to outstanding figures in the Christian tradition. In the same year *Thoughts after Lambeth* appeared, Eliot published his introduction to the Everyman Library edition of Pascal's *Pensées*. Four years earlier, he had remarked in a letter to John Middleton Murry on the importance of such introductory essays. "These 'Everyman' editions are the only form in which a good number of important books reach the large public, and . . . this public may be influenced in reading them by the Introductions."[15] It was doubtless with the hope of exercising such influence that Eliot wrote the essay on Pascal. "I can think of no Christian writer," he said there, "not Newman even, more to be commended than Pascal to those who doubt, but who have the mind to conceive, and the sensibility to feel, the disorder, the futility, the meaninglessness, the mystery of life and suffering, and who can only find peace through a satisfaction of the whole being." He saw Pascal as a model of "the intelligent believer," and he sought in his introduction to explain the logic of Pascal's—and, implicitly, his own—conversion:

The Christian thinker—and I mean the man who is trying consciously and conscientiously to explain to himself the sequence which culminates in faith, rather than the public apologist—proceeds by rejection and elimination. He finds the world to be so and so; he finds its character inexplicable by any non-religious theory: among religions he finds Christianity, and Catholic Christianity, to account most satisfactorily for the world and especially for the moral world within; and thus, by what Newman calls "powerful and concurrent" reasons, he finds himself inexorably committed to the dogma of the Incarnation.[16]

To make credible to the modern world conversions such as Pascal's was part of Eliot's effort to "redeem the time."

A similar impulse led him to publish in the *Criterion* a number of essays on important figures in the history of Christianity. In July 1931, Robert Sencourt wrote on "St. John of the Cross," "the most precise authority on mysticism known to the Church of Christ."[17] The following January an essay by Evelyn Underhill appeared on Friedrich von Hügel, another Christian mystic and, according to Miss Underhill, "the one great modern teacher who has held in equal balance and humble reverence the

15. 30 September 1927, Northwestern University Library.
16. "The 'Pensées' of Pascal," in *Selected Essays*, pp. 368, 360.
17. *Criterion* 10 (1931), 638.

reality of finites, and the Reality of God."[18] And T. O. Beachcroft, who in 1930 had written on "Traherne, and the Doctrine of Felicity," contributed an essay to the October 1932 *Criterion* on "Nicholas Ferrar and George Herbert."[19] Likewise the thirties saw a marked increase in book reviews on religious topics. Through his editorship, Eliot was insisting that theology was a vital part of contemporary thought and an appropriate constituent of a modern literary review.

III

More, however, than by recalling outstanding figures in the Christian tradition, Eliot used his review as an instrument of his Christian witness by diagnosing some of the ways in which, as he remarked in *Thoughts after Lambeth,* "the World is trying the experiment of attempting to form a civilized but non-Christian mentality"; he never doubted that "the experiment will fail." Of course, Eliot's uneasiness with what he spoke of as "modernism" was of long standing; many of his early poems and essays had reflected his distress over contemporary society. But his feelings achieved sharper definition with his conversion to Anglo-Catholicism. Thereafter, his judgments were no longer the mere predilections of the classicist or humanist. He now scrutinized society with the dogmatic convictions of the Christian.

As had been the case earlier in his involvement with

18. "Finite and Infinite," *Criterion* 11 (1932), 197. Miss Underhill, one of the foremost modern writers on mysticism, subsequently contributed five book reviews. Eliot himself, several years earlier, had spoken of von Hügel as "almost a saint, . . . a minor master of the devotional life" ("An Emotional Unity," *Dial* 84 [1928], 112).

19. Though he was primarily concerned with Ferrar's influence on English literature, Beachcroft also discussed Ferrar's decision in mid-life "to abandon every worldly interest for a life of self-effacement, whose sole end was religous devotion" and his establishment of the famous religious community at Little Gidding. (*Criterion* 12 [1932], 26.)

romanticism and the New Humanism, much of Eliot's Christian critique of modernism was conducted indirectly through his selection of essays for the *Criterion*. As early as 1928, Max Scheler was writing prophetically there about "The Future of Man": "We must in thorough fashion formulate afresh *the problem of Man's special metaphysical position within the cosmos,* and how this position relates itself to the World-Source."[20] Several months later, John Gould Fletcher described the more specific concern that would exercise the *Criterion* for some time. "The present moment in the world's history," he said, ". . . has produced the first complete confrontation of East and West."

For the first time since the downfall of the Roman Empire, Europeans . . . began to ask themselves the question whether, after all, European culture, highly specialized and limited as it is, was so vastly superior in outlook, and whether there was not a good deal to be said for the Oriental attitude towards it.

The Russian Revolution was, of course, the single event most responsible for Fletcher's apprehension of the East; that event, he said, clearly demonstrated "that Russia was not racially or socially able to take part in the European tradition, that Russia was not occidental in essence."[21]

During the next several years, Eliot devoted many pages of the *Criterion* to an examination of contemporary ideologies that were attempting to reshape society in new, non-Christian ways. In addition to Soviet communism, various of the other *-isms* of modern thought were scrutinized by *Criterion* contributors. In a four-part symposium on "Bernard Shaw's 'Intelligent Woman's Guide'," Harold J. Laski, Fr. M. C. D'Arcy, A. L. Rowse, and Kenneth Pickthorn considered Shaw's recent exposition of socialism.[22] In that same issue Eliot published his own re-

20. *Criterion* 7 (1928), 119.
21. "East and West," *Criterion* 7 (1928), 306, 307.
22. *Criterion* 8 (1928), 194–214.

view article on "The Literature of Fascism." Here, as throughout the *Criterion*'s consideration of political movements, Eliot was primarily interested in the religious implications of political philosophies. "What I am concerned with," he said, "is . . . the possible influence on the public mind of the *idea,* or rather the vague sentiment of approval excited by the word, of fascism. . . . The human craving to believe in *something,*" he said, "is pathetic, when not tragic. . . ."[23]

The popular result of ignoring religion seems to be merely that the populace transfer their religious emotions to political theories. Few people are sufficiently civilized to afford atheism. . . . So far as bolshevism is a practical way of running Russia— if it is—for the material contentment of Russians, it seems to me worthy of study. So far as it is a kind of supernatural faith it seems to be a humbug. The same is true of fascism. There is a form of faith which is solely appropriate to a religion; it should not be appropriated by politics (283, 282).

"Order and authority are good," Eliot said; "I believe in them as wholeheartedly as I think one should believe in any single idea." But he, of course, found those qualities expressed more adequately by the Church than by any secular, political system. "Behind the increasing popular demand for these things, the parroting of words, I seem to detect a certain spiritual anaemia, a tendency to collapse, the recurring human desire to escape the burden of life and thought" (287–88).

In the next issue, A. L. Rowse wrote more sympathetically about "The Literature of Communism: Its Origin and Theory," and J. S. Barnes responded to Eliot's essay with a defense of "Fascism." As of old, the *Criterion* was becoming controversial; Eliot welcomed his opponents to the pages of his review. But however earnestly he endeav-

23. *Criterion* 8 (1928), 281–82. Subsequent references are inserted in the text.

ored to be fair in presenting both sides of an issue, Eliot was not about to suppress his own opinions on such momentous matters. In the July 1929 issue, he offered his rejoinder to the essays of "Mr. Barnes and Mr. Rowse." "What I find in both fascism and communism," he said, "is a combination of statements with unexamined enthusiasms."

Fascism and communism, as ideas, seem to me to be thoroughly sterilized. A revolutionary idea is one which requires a reorganization of the mind; fascism or communism is now the natural idea for the thoughtless person. . . . Nothing pleases people more than to go on thinking what they have always thought, and at the same time imagine that they are thinking something new and daring: it combines the advantage of security and the delight of adventure.[24]

Among the several other essays on communism that appeared in the *Criterion* during the next few years,[25] one by the Roman Catholic historian Christopher Dawson concisely summarized the editor's concern. Dawson's 1934 "Religion and the Totalitarian State" was one of a number of essays and reviews that he had contributed since 1930; but it was perhaps his most important. "The movement towards state control in every department of life is a universal one," he said;[26] in his essay he directed his attention especially to the dictatorships of fascist and commu-

24. *Criterion* 8 (1929), 687, 683. In the next issue, Barnes and Rowse responded in "Fascism: A Reply" and "Marxism: A Reply." Despite his philosophical differences with him, Eliot welcomed Rowse as a regular contributor. He contributed frequent book reviews and two enthusiastic essays on "The Theory and Practice of Communism," in April 1930 and "An Epic of Revolution: Reflections on Trotsky's History," in April 1933.

25. For example, A. L. Morton, "Poetry and Property in a Communist Society," in October 1932; Joseph Needham, "Laudian Marxism? Thoughts on Science, Religion and Socialism," in October 1932; and John Cournos, "Myth in the Making," in January 1934.

26. *Criterion* 14 (1934), 3. Subsequent references are inserted in the text.

nist states. "What," Dawson asked, "is the position of the religious man and the religious society under these new political circumstances?" (5)

There is an obvious and apparently irreductible opposition between Communism and Christianity. . . . . Communism is not simply a form of political organization; it is an economy, a philosophy and a creed. And its hostility to Christianity is due not to its political form, but to the philosophy that lies behind it. Communism, in fact, challenges Christianity on its own ground by offering mankind a *rival way of salvation* (7).

Dawson was apprehensive not so much of totalitarianism's "violent persecution" of the church as of "the crushing out of religion from modern life by the sheer weight of state-inspired public opinion and by the mass organization of society on a purely secular basis" (12). The proper Christian response, he suggested, was not political resistance, but "the creation of a spiritual centre of resistance, a return to the real sources of spiritual vitality" (13).

The essential duty of the Church towards the State and the world is to bear witness to the truth that is in her. If the light is hidden, we cannot blame the world outside for ignoring it. . . . The Church exists to be the light of the world, and if it fulfills its function, the world is transformed in spite of all the obstacles that human powers place in the way. A secularist culture can only exist, so to speak, in the dark (14, 16).

As a member of the Church—and more immediately as a man of letters—Eliot was seeking to do his part in bearing that witness.

In many of his "Commentaries" during the early thirties, Eliot too was scrutinizing political philosophies according to his Christian standards. Like Dawson, he recognized that communism posed a direct challenge to Christianity in offering an alternative faith to that of the Church; also like Dawson, Eliot thought it a paltry alternative. "The great merit of Communism," he acknowledged, "is the same as one merit of the Catholic Church, that there is something in it which minds on every level can grasp."[27] "Communism . . . has come as a godsend (so to speak) to those young people who would like to grow up and believe in something. My only objection to it is the same as my objection to the cult of the Golden Calf. It is better to worship a golden calf than to worship nothing; but that, after all, is not, in the circumstances, an adequate excuse. My objection is that it just happens to be mistaken."[28] Eliot was further critical that, for the security it offered, communism exacted so high a price in human integrity:

The craving for some passionate *conviction,* and for a living organic society, assumes odd and often extremely dangerous forms. Man must have something to which he is ready to sacrifice himself; he must, if necessary, sacrifice himself, but he must not be sacrificed. I question whether Communism would leave the individual in possession of enough of himself to sacrifice.[29]

"To surrender individual judgment to a Church is a hard thing," Eliot said; "to surrender individual responsibility to a party is, for many men, a pleasant stimulant and sedative." But he objected that the latter surrender—especially in its communist form—did violence both to individual reason and humane values. "Those who have once experienced this sweet intoxication [of subscription to a political party] are not easily brought back to the difficult path of thinking for themselves, and of respecting their own per-

27. "Commentary," *Criterion* 12 (1933), 644.
28. "Commentary," *Criterion* 12 (1933), 472, 473.
29. "Commentary," *Criterion* 11 (1932), 470. Eliot's concern over the loss of individuality in the communist state was in part that of an artist. "One great test of a society," he remarked in this "Commentary," "is the kind of art it produces. Art in its highest development, both in Europe and in Asia, can hardly exist without a sense of individuality, a sense of tragedy, for which Communism does not seem to leave room" (471).

son and that of others."[30] Eliot was more concerned in his "Commentaries" to call attention to ways in which communism resembled a religion than to present direct arguments for the superiority of Christianity. But one could hardly mistake the direction of his sympathies. "The Bolsheviks," he said, "believe in something which has what is equivalent for them to a supernatural sanction; and it is only with a genuine supernatural sanction that we can oppose it."[31]

Though it was clearly the most prominent and perhaps the most threatening of the modern experiments "to form a civilized but non-Christian mentality," communism was not the only manifestation of that tendency. A number of other *Criterion* essays during the early thirties expressed concern over the contemporary neglect of Christian values. The review continued to devote most of its pages to literary and artistic matters; but in the same issue with W. J. Lawrence's study of "The Elizabethan Private Playhouse" and Walter de la Mare's story "The Picnic," Christopher Dawson ominously announced "The End of an Age." In the thirties such warnings increasingly broke in upon the literary calm of the *Criterion*.

The widespread feeling that traditional Western values were now irrelevant signaled "The End of an Age" of which Dawson wrote. Around the turn of the century, he said, it appeared that "the old capital was exhausted and there was nothing to take its place." Increasingly men were pinning their hopes on science, which, in its deterministic mechanism, promised at least some standards by which to organize reality. But, Dawson asserted, the age of science would itself soon end; man, under the authority of science, was coming to feel that he had lost his unique superiority and become a subordinate part of the great mechanical system his genius had perfected. Characteristically, Daw-

30. "Commentary," *Criterion* 13 (1934), 453.
31. "Commentary," *Criterion* 11 (1931), 71.

son called for a renewal of spirituality to revive Western civilization:

The reign of the machine cannot be broken by a mere aspiration towards something different. . . . It can only be conquered by the spiritual power which is the creative element in every culture. This is so even in the case of the humanist culture, in spite of its apparent naturalism. The more one studies the origins of humanism, the more one is brought to recognize the importance of an element which is not only spiritual but definitely Christian.

Dawson's proposal—social and spiritual at once—anticipated in general terms the idea of a Christian society that Eliot would himself describe nearly a decade later:

The return to an organic type of society and the recovery of a spiritual principle in social life need not imply the coming of an age of obscurantism or of material squalor and decay. On the contrary, it may well give a new lease of life to Western civilization and restore the creative power which the secularization of modern culture has destroyed.[32]

In an article published in the *Criterion* three years later, two Frenchmen, Robert Aron and Arnaud Dandieu, located "the root of all our troubles" in "the complete failure to assess concrete personality. To the more or less abstract good of the nation, of the race, of humanity, of prosperity," they said, "we have sacrificed the consciousness of the preeminent attributes of human originality—personality and virility." Their solution echoed Dawson's: "Man needs once more to find his roots—the roots from which spring his specifically human strength and the spirit of locality and family. In these he will find the source of creative risk."[33]

32. *Criterion* 9 (1930), 386, 396, 400–401.
33. "Back to Flesh and Blood: A Political Programme," tr. Helen Grant, *Criterion* 12 (1933), 187–88, 199. Eliot himself had expressed similar sentiments in his remarks on Allen Tate's Agrarian sympo-

Eliot was anxious to stress that his concern was not peculiarly British, that the problem being described in his review was, in fact, a problem of all Western peoples. As Dawson had written from England, and Aron and Dandieu from France, two German writers contributed essays expressing similar anxieties. A 1930 speech delivered in Berlin by Thomas Mann was reprinted in the *Criterion* the following year as "An Appeal to Reason." "Humanity," he said, "seems to have run like boys let out of school away from the humanitarian, idealistic nineteenth century. . . . Everything is possible, everything permitted as a weapon against human decency."[34] Similarly, another contemporary German writer, Hermann Broch, offered two brief sections from his novel, *The Sleepwalkers*. The title of those selections summarized pointedly the concern so apparent in the *Criterion*: "Disintegration of Values." "The Middle Ages," Broch said, "possessed the ideal centre of values . . . , possessed a supreme value to which all other values were subordinated: the belief in the Christian God." But modern man lacked any such center of values:

. . . Man, who was once the image of God, the mirror of a universal value created by himself, man has fallen from his former estate; . . . he is driven out into the horror of the infinite, and, . . . no matter how romantically and sentimentally he may yearn to return to the fold of faith, he is helplessly caught in the

---

sium, *I'll Take My Stand:* "The question of the Good Life is raised; and how far it is possible for mankind to accept industrialization without spiritual harm. . . . The old Southern society, with all its defects, vices and limitations, was still in its way a spiritual entity; and now the organization of society is wholly materialistic" ("Commentary," *Criterion* 10 [1931], 483–84). Several months later he remarked, "Agriculture ought to be saved and revived because agriculture is the foundation of the Good Life in any society; it is in fact the normal life" ("Commentary," *Criterion* 11 [1931], 72). See also his remarks in his lectures at the University of Virginia, *After Strange Gods.*

34. Tr. H. T. Lowe-Porter, *Criterion* 10 (1931), 401.

mechanism of the autonomous value-systems and can do nothing but submit himself to the particular value that has become his profession, he can do nothing but become a function of that value.[35]

Recognizing that the Counter-Reformation had once worked to restore the medieval faith challenged by the Reformation, Broch held the hope, however remote, of a similar renewal of faith for modern man.[36]

The *Criterion*—which had earlier considered classicism and romanticism, the Action Française, and the New Humanism—was now concerned with nothing less than the future of civilization. If its contents in the thirties seemed to belie the *Criterion*'s description of itself as "A Literary Review," Eliot did not seem uneasy over the fact. In 1928 he had declared that his review "is concerned with everything that can be examined in a critical spirit";[37] by 1930 he was exploiting that broader range. Discussions of literary and artistic matters, previously the rule in Eliot's "Commentaries," were now the exception, and he devoted most of his quarterly essays to displaying the perversity of contemporary culture. "What we are concerned with," he said in one of them, "is that Modernism . . . is a mental blight which can afflict the whole of the intelligence of the time. . . . Where you find clear thinking, you usually find that the thinker is either a Christian (if he is a European) or an atheist; where you find muddy thinking you usually find that the thinker is something between the two, and such a person is in essentials a Modernist."[38] In his "Com-

35. Tr. Edwin and Christina Muir, *Criterion* 11 (1932), 665, 667.
36. At the conclusion of his essay on "France's Fight against Americanization," Viscount Léon de Poncins wrote similarly that "it is towards a newer form of [the] spirit of the Middle Ages, that the great minds of the West—those, at least, to whom this modern world is an inacceptable proposition—are slowly yet resolutely beginning to turn" (*Criterion* 12 [1933], 354).
37. "Commentary," *Criterion* 7 (1928), 291.
38. "Commentary," *Criterion* 8 (1928), 188.

mentaries" Eliot sought to point out and criticize instances of that blight.

The General Election of 1929 prompted him to remark on "that waste of time, money, energy and illusion which is called a General Election. . . .

A number of kindly, tired gentlemen with hoarse voices and nothing to say, made speeches; when they found themselves forced to mention each other, their remarks were in the best of taste, if not always in the purest English. It was cricket, and extremely slow cricket. In their broadcast-oratory, they only omitted to do two things: split their infinitives, or produce a new idea.

It was "the brainless election."[39] "The first requisite of any political movement which may hope to influence the future," he felt, "should be *indifference to success* and loyalty to slowly formed conviction."[40] But the politics of Modernism were opportunistic and unprincipled. In part, he blamed the power of the press for the condition of political thought in England.

The reader allows his paper to . . . select what is important and to suppress what is unimportant, to divert his mind with shallow discussions of serious topics, to destroy his wits with murders and weddings and curates' confessions, and to reduce him to a condition in which he is less capable of voting with any discrimination at the smallest municipal election, than if he could neither read nor write.[41]

Eliot detected this intellectual anemia no less in education than in politics. Education, also, was infected with Modernism; it, too, was devoid of principles. Criticizing a sanguine article in the *Times* about popular education, Eliot insisted:

Unless popular education is also moral education, it is merely

39. "Commentary," *Criterion* 8 (1928), 377; 8 (1929), 578.
40. "Commentary," *Criterion* 9 (1929), 5.
41. "Commentary," *Criterion* 9 (1930), 184.

putting firearms into the hands of children. For education in History is vain, unless it teaches us to extract moral and spiritual values from History; and education in Political Economy is vain, . . . so long as it is offered as a pure science unfettered by moral principles.

The problem of education, he said, is "in the long run the most important problem of society."

Education is a training of the mind and of the sensibility, an intellectual and an emotional discipline. In a society in which this discipline is neglected, a society which uses words instead of thoughts and feelings, one may expect any sort of religious, moral, social and political aberration, and eventual decomposition and petrification. And we seem to have little to hope from the official representatives of education.[42]

As Eliot saw it, the weakness in politics, journalism, education, indeed in all of modern life, was that of a neglect of principles. "I believe that the study of ethics has priority over the study of politics," he wrote; "that this priority is something immutable which not famine or war can change; and that, even when a philosopher is expressly 'not directly concerned' with ethics, yet his politics and economics will have some obscure ethical assumption, or the defect of some ethical assumption, by which, if I could find it, I could judge them."[43]

Worst of all, Eliot found the practitioners of the various specialized disciplines of modern society ignorant—and even disdainful—of the one discipline he felt was primary:

42. "Commentary," *Criterion* 10 (1931), 309; 13 (1934), 628. Eliot's most extensive discussion during these years of education was "Modern Education and the Classics," written in 1932 but not published until 1936. At the conclusion of the essay he said: "As the world at large becomes more completely secularized, the need becomes more urgent that professedly Christian people should have a Christian education, which should be an education both for this world and for the life of prayer in this world" (in *Selected Essays*, p. 460).

43. "Commentary," *Criterion* 12 (1933), 643–44.

Theology . . . is conceded to be a science on the same footing as the science of Heraldry—a little lower, that is, than Palmistry and Phrenology. Ethics is a *champ libre* for sentimental essayists, or a *champ clos* for supposedly useless but ornamental university pundits, but has no "scientific" standing whatever. Meanwhile, Political Economy boasts itself as a science as Physics is a science. . . . And in fact Economics *is* a science, in the humane sense; but it will never take its due place until it recognizes the superior "scientific" authority of Ethics.[44]

"It may be," he said, "that the *crise dans l'homme* is all the more serious exactly because we take ourselves, theoretically, too seriously; because we have ignored the supernatural and the eternal."

The notion that a past age or civilization might be great in itself, precious in the eye of God, because it succeeded in adjusting the delicate relation of the Eternal and the Transient, is completely alien to us. No age has been more ego-centric, so to speak, than our own; others have been ego-centric through ignorance, ours through complacent historical knowledge. . . . Thus we take ourselves, and our transient affairs, too seriously.[45]

The same impatience with intellectual parochialism and the same insistence upon the importance of the past that had been basic to earlier, literary essays such as "Tradition and the Individual Talent" remained central concerns for Eliot. Now, however, he urged "the historical sense" not so much for the health of literature as for the survival of civilization. "The historical sense," he had written in 1919, "involves a perception, not only of the pastness of the past, but of its presence." Theologically, such a perception would work toward "adjusting the delicate relation of the Eternal and the Transient." Eliot's concern now was not so much that of a poet or literary critic as that of a moralist or philosopher. "I hold that it is ultimately the moralists and philosophers who must supply the foundations of

44. "Commentary," *Criterion* 10 (1931), 310–11.
45. "Commentary," *Criterion* 12 (1932), 76, 75.

statesmanship, even though they never appear in the forum. We are constantly being told that the economic problem cannot wait. It is equally true that the moral and spiritual problems cannot wait: they have already waited far too long."[46]

In his "Commentaries" as well as in essays he published in the *Criterion,* Eliot sought to raise those problems. That he was doing so as part of his Christian witness was apparent. However, his method was more diagnostic than prescriptive; he was more concerned to raise vexing issues than to offer dogmatic religious solutions. His goal, as in many of his early essays, was "to disturb and alarm the public." Eliot did not pretend to sophisticated theological argument in his essays. He wrote as a Christian layman anxious to share his concerns with readers to whom such insights might be new. His approach, in fact, was much like that which he discerned in Hilaire Belloc's *Essays of a Catholic Layman in England.*

His . . . function is to attack, not arguments, but *prejudices*; and prejudices are attacked, not with arguments, but with *convictions.* Those readers who are in sympathy with him—at least, on what seem to them the vital issues—will not be wholly satisfied. . . . Those who already share Mr. Belloc's apprehensions are prepared for a more advanced discussion. But . . . most of the essays are for the direction of those readers, an important number, who have an open mind, but have not yet begun to think. . . . Mr. Belloc cannot remind us too often that there are older, as well as newer, political philosophies; or that there is a science more fundamental than the sciences of psychology and economics, and without which they are vain: the science of ethics.[47]

Eliot, too, was writing for those of his readers who had an open mind but had not yet begun to think. He recognized that, as a respected poet and critic, he commanded an audi-

46. "Commentary," *Criterion* 12 (1933), 647.
47. *English Review* 53 (1931), 245, 246.

ence whom others in the Church did not reach. It was especially to this audience that he was addressing himself.

IV

Eliot's desire to reach an audience broader even than that of his *Criterion* readership was clear in a series of four broadcast talks he delivered in 1932 over the B.B.C. If such proof were needed, his appearance on the B.B.C. bore witness to the fact that Eliot, by 1932, was a public figure. In fact, he had appeared there as early as 1929 in a series of broadcasts on literary topics. When he spoke three years later, however, it was less as a man of letters than as a man of faith. His four talks were printed in the *Listener* under the rubric "The Modern Dilemma," and not—as before—under "Books and Authors." In those four broadcasts, published serially in the *Listener,* Eliot summarized the concerns that were increasingly governing his editorship of the *Criterion*. These talks, too, were part of his Christian effort to "redeem the time."[48]

"I believe that all our problems turn out ultimately to be a religious problem," Eliot said in his initial lecture; and he reiterated his conviction that "theology is, of course, the one fundamental science" (382). Like a number of his *Criterion* contributors, Eliot noted that "religious faith has altered and weakened since the Middle Ages, until it is no longer the rule and standard of social as well as individual life, but a mere extra, like French and Music, which a minority of people treat themselves to." He said he could describe the religious history of Western man only as "a progressive spiritual deterioration" (429), and in his talks

48. The four talks appeared in the *Listener* as follows: "Christianity and Communism," 16 March 1932, pp. 382–83; "Religion and Science: A Phantom Dilemma," 23 March 1932, pp. 428–29; "The Search for Moral Sanction," 30 March 1932, pp. 445–46, 480; and "Building Up the Christian World," 6 April 1932, pp. 501–2. Since Eliot clearly thought of these broadcasts as parts of a unified whole, I shall treat them thus. Page references are inserted directly in the text.

he devoted special attention to three particular challenges to religious faith: communism, psychology, and science. Echoing his statements in the *Criterion,* he insisted that "Russian communism is a religion, and a religion which is not mine"; and he went on to assert that "you can never fight a religion except with another religion. If we are incapable of a faith at least as strong as that which appears to animate the ruling class of Russia, if we are incapable of dying for a cause, then Western Europe and the Americans might as well be reorganized on the Moscow model at once" (383).

To Eliot's mind, science's threat to religion was not great. "No scientific discovery influences people either for or against revealed religion," he said, "except in so far as there already exists an atmosphere either favourable or unfavourable to religion. . . . It is not science that has destroyed religious belief, but our preference of unbelief that has made illegitimate use of science" (429).[49] In psychology, however, he did see a real threat to religion:

It is only when the psychologists tend to persuade us, first that we are all ill in mind, next that we all need to acquire something of their science in order to understand each other and ourselves, and finally that psychology will supply that guide and rule of conduct which the Christian faith used to give, and still does give to some; it is only when these three assertions appear that the modern dilemma is engaged (445).

"Psychology," he said, "seems to me for the most part to ignore the more intense, profound and satisfying emotions of religion" (446).

If you have not the Christian faith, if you are not prepared to live by it to the best of your ability and to study it thoughout your life, and if you are serious enough minded to want some-

49. Several essays in the *Criterion* considered the relation of science and religion. See especially, Joseph Needham, "Religion and the Scientific Mind," *Criterion* 10 (1931), 233–63.

thing to live by, then you must pin your hopes on psychology (445).[50]

Eliot insisted that, "the last thing I want . . . is to revert to any mediaeval or early Christian society" (501).[51] What he did hope for was " a kind of mass-conversion" in which "you do not hope to convert the world to complete Christianity, but cherish the more modest hope that every individual will be a Christian so far as he is anything" (501). As he promised at the beginning of his B.B.C. talks, he did "not say much directly about Christianity" there. He remained more a social critic with Christian standards than an outright apologist for Christian theology. "My whole purpose," he said in the last of his broadcasts, "has been to stimulate the belief that a Christian organisation of society is possible, that it is perhaps now more than at any prevous time possible; to encourage the search for it and the testing of all offers of reform and revolution by its standards" (502). Like Belloc, Eliot was attacking prejudices, not with arguments, but with convictions.

The following year, in another public address—this time

50. Eliot's attitude toward psychology was, in fact, ambivalent. In this *Listener* talk he acknowledged that psychology could also be an ally of religion; and his publication in the *Criterion* of a number of essays on psychology suggests his interest in the field. Among the more important were: Herbert Read, "The Implications of Behaviorism," 7 (1928), 352–63; Owen Barfield, "Psychology and Reason," 9 (1930), 606–17; and Thomas Mann, "Freud's Position in the History of Modern Thought," 12 (1933), 549–70. Eliot himself reviewed Freud's *Future of an Illusion* and remarked, "This is undoubtedly one of the most curious and interesting books of the season. . . . The book testifies to the fact that the genius of experimental science is not necessarily joined with the genius of logic or the generalizing power" ("Books of the Quarter," *Criterion* 8 [1928], 350).

51. "We are in many ways in a position of advantage over our mediaeval ancestors," he said. "We are more humane, cleaner, and have better table manners; we may be less saintly than some, but we are less beastly than others; we have material comforts, hygiene, machinery and invention, which we do not wish to dispense with but to manipulate wisely" (383).

to the 1933 Anglo-Catholic Summer School of Sociology at Oxford—Eliot reaffirmed his belief, "what in the eyes of the world must be a desperate belief, that a Christian world-order, *the* Christian world-order, is ultimately the only one which, from any point of view, will work."[52] Now addressing a group of fellow-believers rather than a mixed broadcast audience, he urged:

We, as Catholics, cannot simply accept or reject the solutions offered by specialized theorists in the world, according to whether they appear on the surface to admit of a place for us and our faith. We have to criticize the moral assumptions, explicit or implicit, and recognize what are, from our point of view, the limitations and errors of their authors (121–22).

In his 1933 speech Eliot made clear the impulse that led him to contribute to the B.B.C. symposium on "The Modern Dilemma" and to travel to Oxford to address the Anglo-Catholic Summer School. Such activities were, of course, a distraction from his poetry and literary criticism. But they were, more importantly, a necessary part of his new life as a Christian. "It is not, I trust, merely because we happen to be Catholics *and* public-spirited individuals, that we are interested in public and international affairs, but because our Faith is of a kind that compels us to the latter interest" (134). None of Eliot's activities after his conversion was unaffected by the implications of that Faith.

V

In one of his 1932 talks on the B.B.C. Eliot had remarked that "The Christian must try to follow his religion out to the bitter end. . . . I would have the consequences of Christian thinking—thinking by genuine Christians—in the practical departments of life pursued courageously and offered to the public on their merits" (501). Literary criti-

52. "Catholicism and International Order," in *Essays Ancient and Modern* (New York: Harcourt, Brace, 1936), p. 117. Subsequent references are inserted in the text.

cism was of course as much a "practical department of life" as politics or the other matters he was considering at the time; and in his criticism, no less than in his other essays, Eliot in the thirties was "following his religion out to the bitter end." It was natural, then, that around the time of his religious conversion Eliot became increasingly concerned with the relation of poetry and belief. What he several years before had noted as "a growing and alarming tendency in our time for literary criticism to be something else; to be the expression of an attitude 'toward life' or of an attitude toward religion or of an attitude toward society"[53] became, after his conversion, a tendency of Eliot's own criticism. "Poetry," he said in his 1928 preface to *The Sacred Wood,* "certainly has something to do with morals, and with religion, and even with politics perhaps, though we cannot say what."[54] By the thirties he was able to "say what" with much greater certainty.

As early as 1927 Eliot was objecting to I. A. Richards's assertion that he had achieved in *The Waste Land* a complete separation between poetry and belief. Even the doubt and uncertainty so evident in that poem was, Eliot held, "merely a variety of belief." Though he acknowledged that it "will not inevitably be orthodox Christian belief," he said that "I cannot see that poetry can ever be separated from something which I should call belief."[55] Two years later, in a long note on poetry and belief appended to his 1929 essay on Dante, Eliot cautioned that his general theory on the matter was still "embryonic." He promptly denied "that the reader must share the beliefs of the poet in order to enjoy the poetry fully." But he went on to suggest somewhat tentatively the direction in which his ideas were then moving.

Actually, one probably has more pleasure in the poetry when one shares the beliefs of the poet. On the other hand there is a

53. "Commentary," *Criterion* 2 (1924), 373.
54. *The Sacred Wood,* 2d ed. (London: Methuen, 1928), p. x.
55. "A Note on Poetry and Belief," *Enemy* 1 (1927), 16.

distinct pleasure in enjoying poetry as poetry when one does *not* share the beliefs, analogous to the pleasure of "mastering" other men's philosophical systems. It would appear that "literary appreciation" is an abstraction, and pure poetry a phantom; and that both in creation and enjoyment much always enters which is, from the point of view of "Art," irrelevant.[56]

The following year, Eliot returned to the problem and announced that he was "now making a fresh start. . . . No art, and particularly and especially no literary art, can exist in a vacuum," he said.[57]

We do tend, I think, to organize our tastes in various arts into a whole; we aim in the end at a theory of life, or a view of life, and so far as we are conscious, to terminate our enjoyment of the arts in a philosophy, and our philosophy in a religion . . . (599).

He insisted that authors endeavor to win readers to their point of view, and that readers are "powerfully influenced by . . . esthetic sanction"—"that is, the partial justification of . . . views of life by the art to which they give rise" (601). "We aim ideally to come to rest in some poetry which shall realize poetically what we ourselves believe" (602). Though he acknowledged that a great poet could conceivably deal more successfully with an inferior philosophy than an inferior poet with a great philosophy, he could "hardly doubt that the 'truest' philosophy is the best material for the greatest poet; so that the poet must be rated in the end both by the philosophy he realizes in poetry and by the fulness and adequacy of the realization" (601).

The suggestion that a poet should be "rated" for his beliefs was, of course, a radically new one in Eliot's criticism; and it is clear that religious more than literary considerations lay behind that judgment. Several years later,

56. "Dante," in *Selected Essays*, pp. 230, 231.
57. "Poetry and Propaganda," *Bookman* 70 (1930), 598. Subsequent references are inserted in the text.

in an essay published as "Religion and Literature," he developed that thought more fully. Significantly, he did so while addressing a largely Christian audience in an explicitly religious setting. His speech was one of a series on the relation of the Christian faith to contemporary problems and was delivered in the parish hall of the Church of Saint John-the-Divine, Richmond, Surrey. "The author of a work of imagination is trying to affect us wholly, as human beings, whether he knows it or not," Eliot said; "and we are affected by it, as human beings, whether we intend to be or not."[58] As a Christian he was clearly apprehensive of the influence of much contemporary work: "The whole of modern literature is corrupted by what I call Secularism. It is simply unaware of, simply cannot understand the meaning of, the primacy of the supernatural over the natural life: of something which I assume to be our primary concern" (352).

It is our business, as Christians, *as well as* readers of literature, to know what we ought to like. . . . What I believe to be incumbent upon all Christians is the duty of maintaining consciously certain standards and criteria of criticism over and above those supplied by the rest of the world; and that by these criteria and standards everything that we read must be tested (353).

"Literary criticism should be completed by criticism from a definite ethical and theological standpoint," he said. "The 'greatness' of literature cannot be determined solely by literary standards" (343).[59]

In a remarkable series of lectures in the spring of 1933

58. "Religion and Literature," in *Selected Essays,* p. 348. Subsequent references are inserted in the text.

59. Eliot's "Commentaries" and occasional essays in the *Criterion* considered the issue of censorship. See especially "Commentaries," *Criterion* 8 (1928), 1–4; 8 (1928), 185–88; 9 (1929), 1–3; and 9 (1930), 382–85. The case for "a reasonable censorship"—ideally by the Church—was made in two essays: Douglas Jerrold, "Authority, Mind, and Power," *Criterion* 12 (1933), 223–43; and Michael de la Bedoyere, "Censorship: More or Less?" *Criterion* 13 (1934), 252–69.

at the University of Virginia, Eliot himself performed the very kind of criticism for which he called in "Religion and Literature."[60] He had come to the United States during the fall of 1932 as Charles Eliot Norton Professor of Poetry at Harvard University, and his eight lectures under that professorship were published the following year as *The Use of Poetry and the Use of Criticism*. As Eliot himself recognized, those "Studies in the Relation of Criticism to Poetry in England" did not demonstrate any significant development in his critical thinking. "There is nothing new in the book," he wrote to Paul Elmer More on 7 November 1933. "The lectures themselves were prepared not under the most favorable conditions; and my choice of subject was directed by the necessity of finding one which would demand the minimum of new reading and new thinking." However, the three lectures that he delivered in Charlottesville after his series in Cambridge represented a singular turn in his critical practice: In them Eliot set about an uncompromising application of his belief in evaluative criticism based on Christian standards.

Published as *After Strange Gods: A Primer of Modern Heresy*, the Virginia lectures stand as the most curious performance of Eliot's long critical career. Contrasting them with the lectures he had delivered at Harvard, Eliot wrote More: "The field of 'After Strange Gods' was one to which my real interest had turned" (20 June 1934). His approach, as he wrote More, was "fundamentally a criticism of the lack of moral criteria—at bottom of course religious criteria—in the criticism of modern literature" (7 November 1933). In these lectures, more explicitly than anywhere

60. On 27 March 1936 Eliot wrote to More and expressed his gratification that More had enjoyed "Religion and Literature." Eliot acknowledged that many of his readers would take his views there to be so different from his earlier attitudes as to amount to a recantation. However, from his own perspective, Eliot wrote, the difference was the product of a gradual evolution in his ideas, "a readjustment of values through a widening of interests."

else, Eliot was "courageously" pursuing the consequences of Christian thinking in the criticism of modern literature. As he was preparing the lectures for the press, Eliot doubtless himself recognized that his approach there strained—perhaps, in fact, exceeded—the conventional limits of literary criticism; thus, in his preface, he insisted that "The three lectures which follow were not undertaken as exercises in literary criticism." He said he spoke "only in the role of moralist."[61]

After Strange Gods returned to much the same issue that Eliot had treated in his first major essay, "Tradition and the Individual Talent." Both the continuity and the development of his career are apparent when the two studies are compared: the continuity, in Eliot's continued concern for the place of the writer in his tradition; the development, in the religious perspective Eliot now brought to the problem. For the latter work, he redefined *tradition* as "a way of feeling and acting which characterises a group throughout generations" and supplemented it with the concept of *orthodoxy. Tradition,* he said, is largely unconscious; whereas *orthodoxy,* "a consensus between the living and the dead," is a quality whose maintenance "calls for the exercise of all our conscious intelligence" (29, 30). In his lectures he "wished to illustrate . . . the crippling effect upon men of letters, of not having been born and brought up in the environment of a living and central tradition" (49). It seemed obvious to Eliot that the modern artist did not share any such unconscious assumptions, and he noted that "the general effect in literature of the lack of any strong tradition is twofold: extreme individualism in views, and no accepted rules or opinions as to the limitations of the literary job" (32).

Though he acknowledged that "it is too much to expect

61. *After Strange Gods: A Primer of Modern Heresy* (London: Faber and Faber, 1934), pp. 11, 12. Subsequent references are inserted in the text.

any literary artist at the present time to be a model of orthodoxy . . ." (34), Eliot surveyed the writing of a number of contemporary authors according to that criterion. And for him, of course, orthodoxy implied Christianity. "What we can try to do is to develop a more critical spirit, or rather to apply to authors critical standards which are almost in desuetude" (35). He applied those standards ruthlessly. "The chief clue to the understanding of most contemporary . . . literature," he said, "is to be found in the decay of Protestantism. . . . With the disappearance of the idea of Original Sin, with the disappearance of the idea of intense moral struggle, the human beings presented to us both in poetry and in prose fiction to-day . . . tend to become less and less real" (38, 42).

As its subtitle promised, *After Strange Gods* was indeed a primer of modern heresy: he found in Hardy's fiction an "interesting example of a powerful personality uncurbed by institutional attachment or by submission to any objective beliefs" (54). Pound's "powerful and narrow post-Protestant prejudice peeps out from the most unexpected places" (41). "Yeats's 'supernatural world' was the wrong supernatural world. It was not a world of spiritual significance, not a world of real Good and Evil, of holiness or sin" (46). Lawrence, Eliot said, had a vision that was "spiritual, but spiritually sick" (60); he was "an almost perfect example of the heretic" (38). Even Irving Babbitt and Gerard Manley Hopkins were judged and found wanting. Babbitt "seemed to be trying to compensate for the lack of a living tradition by a herculean, but purely intellectual and individual effort" (39–40); and Hopkins failed to present a "real development of thought or feeling" (47). "Hopkins has very little aid to offer us," he said, in "the struggle of our time to concentrate, not to dissipate; to renew our association with traditional wisdom; to re-establish a vital connection between the individual and the race; the struggle, in a word, against Liberalism" (48).

In *After Strange Gods* Eliot was fulfilling what he held to be the duty of the Christian, the testing of literature against standards of orthodoxy. "The number of people in possession of any criteria for discriminating between good and evil is very small," Eliot said at Virginia; "the number of the half-alive hungry for any form of spiritual experience, or what offers itself as spiritual experience, high or low, good or bad, is considerable. My own generation has not served them very well. Never has the printing press been so busy, and never have such varieties of buncombe and false doctrine come from it" (61).

Years before, in his *Sacred Wood* essay on "Blake," Eliot had similarly been distressed by the strangeness— that is, the unorthodoxy—of that poet's gods. But Eliot's primary concern then was for the "formlessness" to which Blake's philosophical eccentricity had rendered him liable. At the end of *After Strange Gods* Eliot suggested the vastly different motives behind his 1933 enquiry. "All that I have been able to do here," he concluded, "is suggest that there are standards of criticism, not ordinarily in use, which we may apply to whatever is offered to us as works of philosophy or of art, which might help to render them safer and more profitable for us" (63). Between his earlier concern for form, and his later concern for moral safety and profit, had come Eliot's dedication to doing his part in "redeeming the time."[62]

62. Predictably, the reviews of *After Strange Gods* were mixed. Eliot wrote to More with obvious disappointment over the reception of the book. With the exception of Edwin Muir's review in the *Spectator*, Eliot said, the notices were favorable or unfavorable according to the religious inclinations of the reviewers. He found the situation "symptomatic of the chasm between the 'literary' reviewers and the 'theological' reviewers in the Anglo-Saxon world" (20 June 1934). Significantly, Eliot never allowed *After Strange Gods* to go beyond its first edition.

1934-1939

6

LAST WORDS

"At the present time," Eliot wrote in 1934, "I am not very much interested in the only subject which I am supposed to be qualified to write about: that is, one kind of literary criticism. I am not very much interested in literature, except dramatic literature; and I am largely interested in subjects which I do not yet know very much about: theology, politics, economics, and education."[1] His lack of enthusiasm for "one kind of literary criticism" had been apparent in his Norton lectures at Harvard. His growing concern for theology, politics, economics, and education had been equally apparent in recent volumes of the *Criterion*. And his failure to publish any major poem between "Ash Wednesday" (1930) and "Burnt Norton" (1936) perhaps suggested his not being "very much interested in literature." During the twenties Eliot's most profound intellectual development occurred; during the thirties the implications of that development were working themselves out in his literary career. The very enterprises through which he had distinguished himself—poetry, criticism, and literary editorship—became secondary to the deep moral concern that impelled him to do his part in redeeming the time.

In the years immediately after his conversion, Eliot had endeavored to place his old gifts in the service of his new calling: his poetry had become increasingly devotional; his literary criticism increasingly moralistic; and his editor-

1. "The Problem of Education," in *Harvard Advocate Centennial Anthology*, ed. Jonathan D. Culler (Cambridge, Mass.: Schenkman, 1966), p. 69. This essay was originally published in the September 1934 issue of the *Harvard Advocate*.

ship increasingly committed to the religious examination of contemporary problems. The effort, however, had been only partially successful: if the poetry had gained force and clarity from the poet's new convictions, the criticism had become eccentric at best, and the editorship distressingly like the work of an enthusiastic amateur.

During the latter half of the thirties, Eliot continued to try to adapt the *Criterion* to the responsibilities he felt as a Christian. Ultimately, however, the effort proved impossible. The urgency of social and religious concern and the certainty of conviction that Eliot now brought to his editorship diverted the *Criterion* from its earlier excellence when his interests were primarily artistic, when he was exploring rather than belaboring nonliterary matters, and when his convictions were still taking shape. Eliot himself recognized that the review was declining in its final years; his decision to end publication in 1939 marked the end of one phase of his career.

But those were also years in which Eliot was making a new beginning. Just as he doubtless intended to shock his readers in 1934 by asserting that he was "not very much interested in literature," Eliot surely wanted them to note the reservation that followed: "except dramatic literature." The same religious impulse that was rendering the *Criterion* an inappropriate enterprise for him was also leading him to the drama. As old interests were passing, new interests were taking their place. And Eliot in the thirties opened an important new chapter in his career as he turned to writing dramatic verse for the stage. Just as his commitment to Christianity had been the central conversion of his intellectual life, his dedication to the stage represented the central conversion in his literary career; by the mid-forties, Eliot would be devoting his poetic energies almost exclusively to the stage. And, characteristically, the two conversions were related: the second was a direct consequence of the first. Like most of the developments in his career, it was one that had been anticipated long before.

Eliot's interest in the drama had been of long standing. His dramatic sense had been apparent from the earliest of his mature poems, "The Love Song of J. Alfred Prufrock." His early criticism also had reflected his concern for the drama. It is hardly necessary to rehearse his contribution to modern criticism of Elizabethan and Jacobean drama. But perhaps less memorable from those essays are the early suggestions of Eliot's own attraction to the possibility of writing for the stage. He himself has reminded us that "the poet, at the back of his mind, if not as his ostensible purpose, is always trying to defend the kind of poetry he is writing, or to formulate the kind that he wants to write."[2] Thus his early criticism of the drama may be seen as expressing his own dramatic aspirations that were eventually to be realized in the thirties.

Given the frequent intersection of his career with that of his friend John Middleton Murry, it is fitting that some of Eliot's earliest remarks on the condition of contemporary drama should have been occasioned by the publication of a play by Murry, *Cinnamon and Angelica*. They were, in fact, written for Murry's own *Athenaeum*. The first sentence of Eliot's review established at once the nature of his interest. "The impotence of contemporary drama is a commonplace riddle of cultured pessimism," he said; verse drama was especially afflicted. Eliot described Murry's play as a "Promethean" effort to revitalize the genre, though an effort not entirely successful. He was sensitive to the many difficulties that aspiring playwrights like Murry confronted, but Eliot did not think the lack of an audience was one of them. Commercially, he felt, the prospects for the theater were heartening.

But what is needed is not sympathy or encouragement or appreciation . . . but a kind of unconscious co-operation. The ideal condition is that under which everything, except what only the individual genius can supply, is provided for the poet. . . . A

2. "The Music of Poetry," in *On Poetry and Poets* (New York: Farrar, Straus, and Cudahy, 1957), p. 17.

dramatic poet needs to have some *kind* of dramatic form given to him as the condition of his time, a form which in itself is neither good nor bad but which permits an artist to fashion it into a work of art. And by a "kind of dramatic form" one means almost the temper of the age . . . ; a preparedness, a habit, on the part of the public to respond in a predictable way, however crudely, to certain stimuli.

"The composition of a poetic drama is in fact the most difficult, the most exhausting task that a poet can set himself," Eliot said; "and—this is the heart of the matter—it is infinitely more difficult for a poet of to-day than it was for a poet of no greater talent three hundred years ago. . . . The poet who now applies himself to the drama will be one with a strong and (we may even say) philosophic conviction in favour of this form."[3] Such were Eliot's convictions when he began writing for the stage a decade later.

Several months after his review of Murry's play Eliot again considered "The Possibility of Poetic Drama." "The majority, perhaps, certainly a large number, of poets hanker for the stage," he said, "and . . . a not negligible public appears to want verse plays. Surely there is some legitimate craving, not restricted to a few persons, which only the verse play can satisfy." Eliot suggested that among the several poetic forms, the drama "is perhaps the most permanent, is capable of greater variation and of expressing more varied types of society, than any other." Though not yet ready to attempt to exploit those possibilities himself, he recognized a promising approach to the revitalization of verse drama:

Possibly the majority of attempts to confect a poetic drama have begun at the wrong end; they have aimed at the small public which wants "poetry." . . . The Elizabethan drama was aimed at a public which wanted *entertainment* of a crude sort, but would *stand* a good deal of poetry; our problem should be to

3. "The Poetic Drama," *Athenaeum*, 14 May 1920, p. 635.

take a form of entertainment, and subject it to the process which would leave it a form of art. Perhaps the music-hall comedian is the best material.[4]

Unlikely as it may have seemed, Eliot's appeal to the music-hall was in earnest; he found there the kind of "unconscious co-operation" lacking in the genteel theater and necessary if poetic drama were to be revived.

The character of his attraction to the music-hall—and, implicitly, his sense of the possibilities of the drama—was clearer in 1923 when, in the second issue of the *Criterion,* he paid tribute to the career of Marie Lloyd. "Marie Lloyd was the greatest music hall artist in England; she was also the most popular. And popularity in her case was not merely evidence of her accomplishment. . . . It is evidence of the extent to which she represented and expressed that part of the English nation which has perhaps the greatest vitality and interest." In her achievement, Marie Lloyd fulfilled what Eliot then held as a distinct virtue of the drama. "No other comedian succeeded so well in giving expression to the life of [an] audience, in raising it to a kind of art."

The working man who went to the music-hall and saw Marie Lloyd and joined in the chorus was himself performing part of the act; he was engaged in that collaboration of the audience with the artist which is necessary in all art and most obviously in dramatic art.[5]

In her music-hall performances, Eliot felt, Marie Lloyd had endowed the lives of her audiences with a virtually ritual shape and order.

In the next issue of the *Criterion,* he memorialized an-

4. In *The Sacred Wood,* 2d ed. (London: Methuen, 1928), pp. 60, 61, 70.

5. "In Memoriam: Marie Lloyd," *Criterion* 1 (1923), 192, 193, 194. See also Eliot's remarks on the music-hall in "Notes on Current Letters," *Tyro* 1 (1921), 4.

other great woman of the stage who had recently died, Sarah Bernhardt. Her death and funeral, Eliot said, marked "the termination of an epoch. . . . Bernhardt represented for the world outside of France, and finally for France itself, the genius of the French stage." By contrast, the contemporary British stage seemed lifeless indeed.

So inchoate is the theatre, which, if realised, would be the theatre of our generation, that we can only guess at the scheme of what we grope for by inference from our perceptions, from observation of any instant on the stage which has aroused an hitherto dormant feeling. . . . The realism of the ordinary stage is something to which we can no longer respond, because to us it is no longer realistic. We know now that the gesture of daily existence is inadequate for the stage; instead of pretending that the stage gesture is a copy of reality, let us adopt a literal untruth, a thorough-going convention, a ritual. For the stage—not only in its remote origins, but always—is a ritual, and the failure of the contemporary stage to satisfy the craving for ritual is one of the reasons why it is not a living art.[6]

Eliot's insistence on the ritual foundation of drama was hardly surprising in 1923; he was clearly familiar with the work of such scholars as Gilbert Murray, Francis Cornford, and Jane Harrison on the origins of Greek drama, and his own criticism and poetry—not least of all *The Waste Land*—evinced his interest in the relation of anthropology to art. But in 1923 his interest in ritual was largely that of an artist; as he grew nearer his personal commitment to Christianity, it also became that of a believer. Eliot quickly came to see the possibilities for drama not only in ritual in general, but, more specifically, in religious liturgy. In 1926 he contributed an introduction to the publication of his mother's dramatic poem *Savonarola* and remarked that "Dramatic form may occur at various

6. "Dramatis Personae," *Criterion* 1 (1923), 303, 305–6. Nearly every one of Eliot's "Commentaries" during the next several years included some notice of the drama or the ballet.

points along a line the termini of which are liturgy and realism. . . . In genuine drama the form is determined by the point on the line at which the tension between liturgy and realism takes place. . . . The play, like a religious service, should be a stimulant to make life more tolerable and augment our ability to live."[7]

In the year that Eliot announced his conversion he also published a "Dialogue on Dramatic Poetry" as a preface to a new edition of Dryden's "Essay of Dramatic Poesy." A central concern there was the relation between liturgy and drama. One may reasonably suspect that the speaker labeled "E" utters Eliot's sentiments; and "E" was obviously pursuing Eliot's earlier interest in the relation between ritual and drama. "I say that the consummation of the drama, the perfect and ideal drama, is to be found in the ceremony of the Mass," he declared.

Drama springs from religious liturgy, and . . . it cannot afford to depart far from religious liturgy. . . . When drama has ranged as far as it has in our own day, is not the only solution to return to religious liturgy? And the only dramatic satisfaction that I find now is in a High Mass well performed. Have you not there everything necessary?

Speaker "D" emended "E's" observation: When one attends Mass, he does so in a spirit of devotion; he becomes a participant in the drama; and his awareness is centered on the religious realities to the exclusion of secular matters. "D" continued:

But we are human beings, and crave representations in which we are conscious, and critical, of these other realities. We cannot be aware solely of divine realities. We must be aware also of human realities. And we crave some liturgy less divine, something in respect of which we shall be more spectators and less

7. "Introduction" to *Savonarola: A Dramatic Poem* by Charlotte Eliot (London: Cobden-Sanderson, 1926), pp. x, xi–xii.

participants. Hence we want the human drama, related to the divine drama, but not the same, as well as the Mass.[8]

"E" concurred.

His conversion to Christianity was doubly responsible for leading Eliot in the thirties to what would be a long and fruitful career of writing for the stage. First, the ritual of the Christian church—and not least of all, of Anglo-Catholicism—suggested a direction that the rejuvenation of the drama might follow. Still more important, his Christianity inspired in him a social—one might even say *missionary*—concern that made him impatient with his limited social impact as a writer of difficult, learned poetry. "Of what use is this experimenting with rhythms and words," he asked, "this effort to find the precise metric and the exact image to set down feelings which, if communicable at all, can be communicated to so few that the result seems insignificant compared to the labour?"[9] A year later, in the last of his Harvard lectures on *The Use of Poetry and the Use of Criticism,* Eliot reiterated his attraction to the drama; it was clear that social, no less than literary, impulses now figured in his thinking:

I believe that the poet naturally prefers to write for as large and miscellaneous an audience as possible. . . . The most useful poetry, socially, would be one which could cut across all the present stratifications of public taste—stratifications which are perhaps a sign of social disintegration. The ideal medium for poetry, to my mind, and the most direct means of social 'usefulness' for poetry, is the theatre. . . . Every poet would like, I fancy, to be able to think that he had some direct social utility. . . . He would like to be something of a popular entertainer, and be able to think his own thoughts behind a tragic or a comic mask. He would like to convey the pleasures of poetry, not only

8. "Dialogue on Dramatic Poetry," in *Selected Essays,* New Edition (New York: Harcourt, Brace, 1950), pp. 35, 36.
9. "Christianity and Communism," *Listener,* 16 March 1932, p. 382.

to a larger audience, but to larger groups of people collectively; and the theatre is the best place in which to do it.

For the dramatic poet, Eliot said, there is at least the partial compensation for his labors of "the satisfaction of having a part to play in society as worthy as that of the music-hall comedian."[10] When he returned to England from his year in America, Eliot found awaiting him an invitation to play that part.

The story of Eliot's career as a writer of verse drama is in large part the story of his relationship with E. Martin Browne, who gave him his first opportunity to write a script for production, worked closely with him in the preparation of all his plays, and directed them in their first productions.[11] Significantly, Browne was not only a man of the theater but also a churchman. As Director of Religious Drama for the Anglican diocese of Chichester, Browne approached Eliot to write the pageant that became *The Rock*; as a writer anxious to make a contribution to his Church no less than as a poet attracted to the stage, Eliot agreed.[12]

In March 1933, Browne had been asked by officials of the Diocese of London to prepare a pageant to assist a major effort to raise funds for the construction of forty-five new churches in the developing suburbs around London. Browne prepared a scenario and proposed that Eliot be invited to write the script. By October 1933 Eliot had accepted the commission, and the pageant was scheduled for production in May of the following year. The circum-

10. *The Use of Poetry and the Use of Criticism* (London: Faber and Faber, 1933), pp. 152–54.
11. It is doubtful that Eliot wrote the fragments of "Sweeney Agonistes" with thought of their subsequent production. When they were staged early in 1934 by the experimental Group Theatre in London, it was apparently without Eliot's active collaboration.
12. Browne describes his long relationship with Eliot in his valuable book, *The Making of T. S. Eliot's Plays* (Cambridge: Cambridge University Press, 1969).

stances were in many ways ideal for Eliot. While he was torn between his concern for art and his concern for the Church, this call of the Church offered him an opportunity to fulfill simultaneously both his long-standing desire to try his hand at the drama as well as his sense of Christian vocation. The collaboration of Browne was further advantageous, for he would be sympathetic to Eliot's religious impulses just as he would be able to offer the benefit of his considerable experience in the theater. Even the imminence of the production was helpful, for it would allow Eliot no procrastination in this new literary endeavor. Some years later, he acknowledged the propitiousness of the enterprise:

Twenty years ago I was commissioned to write a pageant play to be called *The Rock*. The invitation to write the words for this spectacle . . . came at a moment when I seemed to myself to have exhausted my meagre poetic gifts, and to have nothing more to say. To be, at such a moment, commissioned to write something which, good or bad, must be delivered by a certain date, may have the effect that vigorous cranking sometimes has upon a motor car when the battery is run down. The task was clearly laid out: I had only to write the words of prose dialogue for scenes of the usual historical pageant pattern, for which I had been given a scenario. I had also to provide a number of choral passages in verse, the content of which was left to my own devices.[13]

The Rock remains memorable largely for the choruses, which were all that Eliot chose to salvage from the pageant for his *Collected Poems*. Those choruses throughout reflected Eliot's fondness for liturgy, just as the prose dialogue recalled his appreciation for the art of the music-hall.[14] But even those passages of choral verse, themselves

13. "The Three Voices of Poetry," in *On Poetry and Poets*, p. 98.
14. Eliot wrote to Paul Elmer More that the choruses were written under the inspiration of biblical poetry, especially that of Isaiah and Ezekiel (7 November 1933, Princeton University Library).

remarkable achievements, were not fully integrated into the play. And *The Rock*—Eliot's first deliberate effort for the stage and the product of little more than six months' work—remains an apprentice-piece. It is perhaps a commentary on the state of the British theater, however, that contemporary critics were enthusiastic in their reviews of the play. As the *Times* review demonstrated, Eliot's endeavor in *The Rock* was not lost on his audience.

The theatre, that long-lost child of the English Church, made a notable reunion with its parent at Sadler's Wells last night. Mr. Eliot's pageant play looked first to liturgy for its dramatic form, though wisely imitating also the ready and popular stage modes, such as music-hall, ballet, and mime. But, more important still, its source was religious. The play is purposive. . . .[15]

That final adjective is one that—perhaps unjustly—would not likely have been used to describe his earlier poetry; it bespeaks the distinctive impulse behind his commitment to the theater.

Doubtless heartened by the reception of *The Rock,* Eliot agreed to accept another commission secured by Browne for a play to be produced the following summer. Again the occasion for the play was distinctly religious, and Eliot was wedding his aspiration to be a writer of plays to his commitment to contribute to the life of his Church. Beginning in 1928, a series of June "Festivals of Music and Drama" had been sponsored by the Friends of Canterbury Cathedral. The series opened with a production of John Masefield's *The Coming of Christ* and during the next several years included two productions of Tennyson's *Becket.*[16]

15. London *Times*, 29 May 1934, p. 12.
16. Eliot's "Commentary" on the publication of Masefield's play is especially interesting in light of his own contribution to the Canterbury Festival several years later: "Having read the text, . . . we question whether such an entertainment serves any cause of religion or art. . . . The theological orthodoxy is more than doubtful; the literary incompetence is more than certain. . . . We venture to counsel our

Given the obvious connection between Canterbury and Thomas Becket, it was natural that when Eliot was invited to write a play for the 1935 festival he thought first of Becket. The result, of course, was *Murder in the Cathedral*.

As with *The Rock*, the circumstances of this commission were auspicious. To be staged only fifty yards from the place where Becket died, this drama of his last days would be an almost ritual reenactment of the most famous event in the history of the cathedral. The audience, expecting an explicitly religious play, would be prepared to offer the "unconscious co-operation" that Eliot held necessary to the drama. And the possibility of including a sermon (which he acknowledged might bear "a faint reflection" of the prose of Lancelot Andrewes)[17] would offer Eliot an opportunity not only to combine liturgy and drama but also explicitly to deal with religious ideas in his art to an extent previously impossible. The play richly realized its possibilities; and though, as Eliot himself recognized,[18] it was not without faults, *Murder in the Cathedral* remains Eliot's most assured dramatic achievement.

The critical reception of the play was enthusiastic, and its success, just a year after that of *The Rock*, could only have reinforced Eliot's commitment to devote further serious effort to the drama. However, both plays had been written for expressly religious audiences; whatever his impact in such circumstances, neither at the Sadler's Wells benefit pageant nor at the Canterbury festival was Eliot achieving the "social 'usefulness'" he desired in writing for "as large and miscellaneous an audience as possible."

---

spiritual pastors, that they should see to it either that they employ artists who are definite in their theology, or else who are really good artists" (*Criterion*, 7 [1928], 293–94).

17. "To Criticize the Critic," in *To Criticize the Critic and Other Writings* (New York: Farrar, Straus and Giroux, 1965), p. 20.

18. See especially "Poetry and Drama," in *On Poetry and Poets*, pp. 84–87.

Any reservations he may have felt over the limitations of his success at Canterbury, however, were quickly dispelled when *Murder in the Cathedral* moved to a long and successful run in London and then on tour. The enthusiasm for the play among secular audiences outside Canterbury augured well for Eliot's future as a playwright. Four years, in fact, would pass before the production of his next play, *The Family Reunion,* his initial effort for the commercial stage. But the impulse that lay behind his first two religious plays—that of sharing his Christian vision with an audience perhaps not reached by his poetry or prose—would continue to inform Eliot's work in the theater. And that work would engage the greater part of Eliot's creative energies during the last two decades of his career.

II

In the verse of *The Rock* and *Murder in the Cathedral,* Eliot's religious impulses found eloquent expression—and, in fact, provided a direction for his subsequent career. However, those impulses were not similarly fruitful for his literary criticism. The New Critical approach that he had done so much to establish no longer interested him, while the moralistic criticism toward which his convictions led him was obviously suspect in literary circles. Thus, he was unable to find an adequate critical mode for expressing his faith, and his output of literary criticism during the latter half of the thirties was slighter in volume than during any previous five years in his career.

But Eliot had not lapsed into inactivity. He continued to carry on his Christian witness through his writing on nonliterary topics and, above all, through his editorship of the *Criterion.* In his review, Eliot included a number of essays on subjects in which—as he said in 1934—he was interested but largely unschooled, especially economics and politics. Trusting that such specialized topics were being adequately dealt with by his contributors, he devoted most of his own writing there to a more general, wide-ranging social commentary.

In all that he wrote, Eliot's own religious conviction was evident. The firmness of that conviction is suggested by a statement in 1937:

I take for granted that Christian revelation is the only full revelation and that the fullness of Christian revelation resides in the essential fact of the Incarnation, in relation to which all Christian revelation is to be understood. The division between those who accept, and those who deny, Christian revelation I take to be the most profound division between human beings.[19]

But however ready he seemed there to separate the sheep from the goats, Eliot's social commentary was remarkably temperate. To his credit, he avoided the extremes of hortatory writing and spoke, instead, in a tone that might be described as Christian skepticism. "The Church offers today the last asylum for one type of mind which the Middle Ages would hardly have expected to find among the faithful," he said: "that of the sceptic."

Obviously, I mean by the sceptic, the man who suspects the origins of his own beliefs, as well as those of others; who is most suspicious of those which are most passionately held; who is still more relentless towards his own beliefs than towards those of others; who suspects other people's motives because he has learned the deceitfulness of his own.[20]

Eliot was such a man; and his skepticism, founded as it was on his Christian faith, became an instrument of his religious witness. "A task for the Church in our age," he suggested, "is a more profound scrutiny of our society, which shall start from the question: to what depth is the foundation of our society not merely neutral but positively

19. In *Revelation,* ed. John Baillie and Hugh Martin (London: Faber and Faber, 1937), pp. 1–2.

20. "Notes on the Way," *Time and Tide,* 5 January 1935, p. 6.

anti-Christian?"[21] Much of Eliot's writing during the late thirties and especially his *Criterion* "Commentaries" were concerned to pose such a question.

The four essays he contributed in January 1935 to the *Time and Tide* series "Notes on the Way" exemplified his Christian skepticism. In the first he pointed to the controversy over Russia's admission to the League of Nations as "one instance of theological muddleheadedness and the refusal to think things out."

The question raised was whether it was or was not compatible with the Christian principles of the League of Nations to admit Russia; the unexamined assumption was the Christian foundation of the League of Nations. It should have been obvious that the League of Nations never had had any closer relation to the Christian Faith than any other piece of temporal machinery of government; that it was to be judged by Christians like any other such machine, according to its works. . . .[22]

Eliot was constantly pointing out "unexamined assumptions"; and the following week he questioned whether, as he took the popular belief to be, war was in all cases bad and peace good. To Eliot it was not self-evident that the death wrought by war is final, "that the great thing is to go on living," nor that "Peace is a valuable state in itself."

I do not see how you can condemn War in the abstract unless you assert (a) that there is no higher value than Peace; (b) that there is *nothing* worth fighting for; and (c) that a war in which one side is right and the other wrong is inconceivable. I am prepared to admit that any number of particular wars have been unjustifiable by either side but not to admit the foregoing assumptions.[23]

In his third essay Eliot scrutinized the popular faith in

21. "The Church's Message to the World," *Listener,* 17 February 1937, p. 294.
22. "Notes on the Way," *Time and Tide,* 5 January 1935, p. 7.
23. *Time and Tide,* 12 January 1935, p. 34.

the value of freedom and liberty. "What," he asked skeptically, "is the ultimate nature and reason for liberty? To me, the notion of *liberty* is meaningless without the further notion of *liberation*. One lives, not to be free, but to be freed. And to be *freed from* is meaningless unless one has some notion of what one is to be *freed for*."[24] In his final essay Eliot discussed current thinking about the problem of unemployment and about the school-leaving age. As many years before, his purpose was to disturb and alarm the public and to examine ideas in terms of their first principles. "We do need to think a great deal harder and more patiently about the nature of education; as we do also about the nature of work and leisure, war and peace," he concluded. "We need to think about the relation of one thing to another, and to be a little clearer about our 'standards of moral value'."[25]

Eliot's "Notes on the Way"—which he described as his "ten-minute lunch hour sermons"[26]—were written more to generate thought among his readers than to serve as an exposition of his own beliefs. Taken as a series, the "Notes" are somewhat repetitious and disappointingly unconstructive. His quarterly *Criterion* "Commentaries" in the later thirties were often similar. With his sense of Christian skepticism, he examined what he took to be the bankruptcy of principles throughout modern life. The aims and achievements of the English Association were scrutinized and found wanting; the concern expressed by the *Times* over the consequences for a previously unknown Asiatic tribe of their recent "discovery" by anthropologists was seen to reflect a lack of confidence in Western civilization; the drift of people away from the country and into the cities prompted Eliot to regret the increasing "urbanization of mind" among the British; proposals for centralized

24. *Time and Tide*, 19 January 1935, p. 89.
25. *Time and Tide*, 26 January 1935, p. 121.
26. Ibid., p. 119.

coordination of artistic activity raised the specter of government control; the priorities for future development at Oxford suggested the "Americanization" of that university; and, as before, the stupidity of politicians and statesmen, the inadequacy of the press, and the persistent danger of communism exercised Eliot in his late "Commentaries."

Such a catalog can only begin to suggest the range of topics Eliot treated in his quarterly notes during the final years of the *Criterion*. Apparently nothing was irrelevant to his scrutiny of contemporary life. The most incidental pamphlet or newspaper story was sufficient occasion for Eliot's examination in the "Commentaries." While those essays had earlier reflected the development of his ideas, the later ones seemed to suggest that the development had ended and his attitudes were settled; while the earlier "Commentaries" had been especially notable for Eliot's recommendation there of books he had found valuable, later he mentioned titles more often in condemnation than in praise.[27] To the unsympathetic reader, many of those "Commentaries" must have seemed the work of a cranky, querulous man.

The problem of tone in many of the late "Commentaries" was in part a function of Eliot's difficulty in accommodating his review to his sense of Christian duty. Not to remark on contemporary society in his "Commentaries" seemed to him a dereliction of his Christian responsibility. However, to offer the kind of incisive criticism he might have liked would have demanded that he make quite explicit the Christian foundations of his judgments; and

27. The remarks of the *TLS* essayist in reviewing the reprint edition of the *Criterion* are just: "Reading these 'commentaries' straight through, the obsessive strain is very marked. Whatever the topic, however immense or trivial, it tends to get treated in much the same way, and with much the same weight, as grist for Eliot's dark, dogmatic mill" ("The Criterion," *TLS*, 25 April 1968, p. 430).

Eliot clearly did not see the *Criterion* as an appropriate place to insist upon his faith. His dilemma, then, was that he could not remain silent or speak in the fully religious terms that his ideas demanded. Events were occurring rapidly and ominously in the late thirties, and Eliot's Christian concern over those events grew accordingly. That concern, in fact, had grown far beyond what Eliot took to be appropriate to his "Commentaries."

III

Economics and politics were two matters to which Eliot devoted considerable attention in the *Criterion* during the late thirties. In both cases, he himself made general remarks in his "Commentaries," and left to his contributors the discussion of more technical matters. The recent depression had made clear the inadequacy of current economic practice; but there was no consensus as to the nature of the difficulty. "The trouble with the Science of Economics of to-day," he remarked, "is that it appears in a form in which very few people, if any, can understand it."

I am confirmed in my suspicion that conventional economic practice is all wrong, but I can never understand enough to form any opinion as to whether the particular prescription or nostrum proffered is right. I cannot but believe that there are a few simple ideas at bottom, upon which I and the rest of the unlearned are competent to decide according to our several complexions; but I cannot for the life of me ever get to the bottom.[28]

If Eliot was perplexed after several years' experience at Lloyds Bank, he could assume the still greater perplexity of his many readers who lacked even such experience. He endeavored to use the *Criterion* to "get to the bottom" of the current economic morass.

"About certain very serious facts no one can dissent," he said. "The present system does not work properly, and more and more are inclined to believe both that it never

28. "Commentary," *Criterion* 10 (1931), 309.

did and that it never will; and it is obviously neither scientific nor religious."[29] For Eliot, of course, economic issues—like all issues—quickly resolved themselves into religious issues. "I believe that all our problems turn out ultimately to be a religious problem. Its most pressing form, probably, is the economic problem; but economic questions depend finally upon moral questions, as morals depend upon religion."[30] From the religious perspective, the economic problem was a function of sin. "Perhaps the dominant vice of our time, from the point of view of the Church, will be proved to be Avarice," he said. "Surely there is something wrong in our attitude towards money. The acquisitive, rather than the creative and spiritual, instincts are encouraged."[31] Eliot sought a society in which the creative and spiritual instincts would not be subordinated to the acquisitive.

Unlike some of his contributors, he never succumbed to the allurement of a nostalgic medievalism that romanticized the simpler, more spiritual life of centuries past. Rather, he sought a new set of economic and political ideas that, while preserving the traditional values of Christianity, would speak to the realities of modern society. "I do not want to see machinery destroyed," he insisted, "but only to repeat that a machine age requires a fresh economic theory, and a fresh economic theory requires a fresh viewpoint in morals, and a fresh viewpoint in morals must get back to the foundations of morals."[32] The social, political, and economic revolutions of the previous hundred years demanded a correspondent spiritual and intellectual revolution. "It is hardly excessive to say that to-day, everyone

29. "Commentary," *Criterion* 11 (1932), 467.

30. "Christianity and Communism," *Listener,* 16 March 1932, p. 382.

31. "The Church's Message to the World," *Listener,* 17 February 1937, p. 326.

32. "The Search for Moral Sanction," *Listener,* 30 March 1932, p. 480.

who thinks, and everyone who feels, is in some way a 'revolutionist'," he remarked.

Of good revolutionists, there are two kinds, distinguished by the end from which they start. There are those who are impatient with human stupidity; these begin by wanting some kind of monetary reform; their imagination is haunted by the spectre of coffee burnt, wheat dumped into the sea, herrings ploughed into the soil, etc. And there are those who begin from the other end, who talk, in France, of *le spirituel*, or with us (I am sorry to say) of "change of heart."[33]

But between those two kinds of revolutionists, Eliot saw an important difference. "The real issue," he said a year later, "is between the secularists—whatever the political or moral philosophy they support—and the anti-secularists: between those who believe only in values realizable in time and on earth, and those who believe *also* in values realized only out of time. . . ."[34] The word *also* is crucial. The anti-secularists, among whom he clearly numbered himself, sought not to deny material progress but, rather, to complement contemporary worldliness with a renewed sense of the other-worldly.

Eliot was naturally uneasy with the effort of the secularists: "The danger, for those who start from the temporal end," he said, "is Utopianism; settle the problem of distribution—of wheat, coffee, aspirin or wireless sets—and all the problems of evil will disappear." But he was equally aware of the hazards of a narrow antisecularism: "The danger, for those who start from the spiritual end, is Indifferentism; neglect the affairs of the world and save as many souls out of the wreckage as possible." Wisdom mediated between such extremes: "Sudden in this difficulty, and in pity at our distress, appears no one but the divine Sophia. She tells us that we have to begin from both

33. "Commentary," *Criterion* 14 (1935), 262.
34. "Commentary," *Criterion* 16 (1936), 68. Emphasis added.

ends at once."[35] It was in such a spirit that he brought his economic interests to his editorship of the *Criterion*.

While his own remarks there on economics were quite general, he published a number of essays in the thirties that offered more specific discussions. In January and April 1932 the pseudononymous "Gallox" wrote on "Property and Poetry" and adduced arguments from history, theology, and poetry to urge that the institution of private property, while fundamentally just, could be better organized. The famous guild socialist, Arthur J. Penty, appeared several times to denounce the consequences of industrialism and the slighting by modern economic theory of spiritual in favor of material values. "It is to be affirmed," he said, "that a society can only be in stable and healthy condition when its manufactures rest on a foundation of agriculture and home-produced raw material and its commerce on a foundation of native manufactures; and when its people share a common life in the family, the guild and locality."[36]

Like Penty—who in April 1934 had written under the title "Beauty Does Not Look After Herself"—Ezra Pound wrote in the *Criterion* about the effect of capitalism on the arts; his title was "Murder by Capital."[37] In his several *Criterion* essays Pound frequently called attention to the "Social Credit" economics of Major C. H. Douglas ("the first economist to include creative art and writing in an economic scheme")[38] and to one of Douglas's leading pop-

35. "Commentary," *Criterion* 14 (1935), 262. "One difference," he said in this essay, "between the 'economic' and the 'spiritual' revolution is this, that while the spiritual by itself cannot hope to affect directly any but a small spiritual elite, which must be perpetually recruited anew, the economic revolution is certain to affect society very deeply, to affect the relations of man with man. . . . The difficult effort is that to expect neither too much nor too little of the changes which it is possible to operate directly upon society" (263, 264).

36. "Means and Ends," *Criterion* 11 (1931), 4.

37. *Criterion* 12 (1933), 585–92.

38. Ibid., p. 592.

ularizers, A. R. Orage.[39] Though Pound hardly shared
Eliot's own religious concern, his remark in an essay on
the economics of Silvio Gesell aptly summarized the point
Eliot was trying to make through the essays on economics
he published in the *Criterion*. "You can not," Pound said,
"make good economics out of bad ethics."[40]

Several other essays addressed themselves directly to
the ethical implications of the current economic crisis.
Philip Mairet examined "The Moral Dilemma of the Age
of Science" and found it to be the anomaly that while an
industrial society requires less work of fewer people, Western man has continued to hold his "moralistic devotion to
work, to work as duty, as discipline—even as man's highest
function. . . . Modern Society," he said, "can only survive,
to preserve and augment its superb scientific faculties,
upon condition of endowing all its members with sufficient
means, whether their work is required or not."[41] The failure
of the Church of England in influencing the economic life
of the nation was the subject of Henry S. Swabey's "The
English Church and Money." When, in 1611, Lancelot Andrewes was passed over in favor of George Abbot for the
archbishopric of Canterbury, the Church lost its influence
over economics. "Had the tradition Andrewes maintained
prevailed," Swabey said, "Finance would not be in a position to dominate and starve England."

Calvin had a spite against Nature, and his anti-reason, *contra
rationem naturalem,* led the English Church, through Abbot, to
muffle the difference between good and evil regarding money.
Money is necessary for food, and before he can give attention to
God, man must feed himself. The English Church in forgetting
money skipped the first step, and its moralising since has been
in the air. As a result, Moral Laws based on Revelation and on

---

39. "In the Wounds," *Criterion* 14 (1935), 391–407.
40. "The Individual in His Milieu," *Criterion* 15 (1935), 45.
41. *Criterion* 13 (1934), 197, 200.

Nature have been replaced by Economic Laws enunciated in Manchester.[42]

Eliot, we will recall, was "For Lancelot Andrewes." By 1937 his editorship of the *Criterion* suggested that he agreed with F. S. Flint's assertion there that "the proper study of mankind is, for the time being, economics."[43]

The contents of the later volumes of the *Criterion* indicated that politics, no less than economics, was also of intense concern to Eliot. Earlier, of course, he had considered such movements as the Action Française, fascism, and communism in his review. Now, however, he was less concerned with the scrutiny of particular political systems than with the consideration of fundamental political principles—especially the principles of Christian politics. During 1936 and 1937 Eliot was a member of the Archbishops' Committee that prepared the important Conference on Church, Community, and State held during July 1937 in Oxford.[44] The issues considered in that conference —the relations, one with another, of Church, community, and state—were also issues much. deliberated in Eliot's review. "*The Criterion* has never undertaken, but has rather avoided, the discussion of topical political issues, however extensive," he said in January 1936.

There are enough other periodicals, of every shade of opinion, which exist primarily for such discussion: discussion which in any case can be more adequately conducted in journals appear-

42. *Criterion* 16 (1937), 619, 634–35.

43. "The Plain Man and the Economists," *Criterion* 17 (1937), 1. Flint's essay, replete with graphs and mathematical formulas, was the most technical of the *Criterion*'s articles on economics for the "plain man."

44. The daily coverage in the *Times* (9–26 July) attests to the general interest in the conference. Eliot's B.B.C. talk, "The Church's Message to the World," cited above, was presented to generate discussion of issues the conference would be considering several months later. An account of Eliot's own address in Oxford was published in the *Times* on 17 July

ing at more frequent intervals. If—what is often doubted—there remains any place for quarterly reviews in the modern world, their task is surely to concern themselves with political philosophy, rather than with politics, and with the examination of the fundamental ideas of philosophies rather than with the problems of application.[45]

In writing that, Eliot may well have forgotten earlier interests of his review; but now the *Criterion* addressed itself primarily to political theory. The Civil War in Spain and the growth of National Socialism in Germany were recognized only by occasional remarks in essays or in Eliot's "Commentaries." Instead, the *Criterion* confined itself to articles bearing such titles as "Dialectics and Prophecy," "Divine Democracy," "Philosophy and Politics," and "Christian Politics."

The last of those essays, the Reverend Edward Quinn's "Christian Politics," was in many ways typical of the *Criterion*'s excursions into political philosophy. "Christian political theory is not concerned with particular constitutions nor with the justification of any one type of regime," he began.

Rather is it concerned to maintain those fundamental principles which should be fulfilled in every State and at all times; it requires too that the State should take account also of the new situation which arises from the entry of Christianity into the world, creating new and supernatural values and exalting the older, natural ones.

Such an insistence on "fundamental principles" could at worst have seemed quaint to the non-Christian and at best inspiring to the believer. But in 1938 it was perhaps naïve to believe that such theoretical discussions were adequate to contemporary events. The naïveté is apparent in Quinn's discussion of Mussolini, Hitler, and Stalin.

45. "Commentary," *Criterion* 15 (1936), 265.

No matter how their popularity is acquired, no matter what propaganda and censorship is used, the fact is that these leaders really embody in themselves the soul of their people. That is why they have attained the position of leadership, and there is at least this to their credit that, even if they attained it by intrigue, they could not have remained in power as long as they have if they had not sincerely tried to provide for the common welfare and been supported in their efforts by the genuine approval of the mass of the people. . . . No one can deny that both leaders and people in every case have been united in a sincere desire to provide for the commonweal.[46]

To cite such a passage is not to suggest that the *Criterion* was enthusiastic over or even uncritical of events in Germany, Italy, or Russia; when it recognized them, in fact, the contrary was generally the case. But that the theoretical preoccupation of the review with politics in their Christian perspective allowed for such blindness to the harsher, political realities of the late thirties bespeaks the inadequacy of the *Criterion* in its final years.

Events were developing at an alarming rate, and Eliot and his review were simply unable to keep pace. Inspired by his religious concern, Eliot recognized that the times demanded that his review somehow respond to the crises in government and finance. Yet, lacking the expertise of the political scientist or the economist, his attempts to do so had been awkward at best. If there was an exceptional moral passion in the later volumes of the *Criterion,* there was also a certain amateurishness as Eliot and his review ranged into considerations of politics and economics. And, no less distressing, the *Criterion*'s new scope had been achieved at considerable cost to the traditional excellence of the review. When its editor declared himself not very much interested in literature and when contemporary affairs were engaging the attention of most conscientious

46. *Criterion* 17 (1938), 626, 638.

men, *The Criterion: A Literary Review* had outlived its usefulness. In January 1939, in the space normally occupied by his "Commentary," Eliot published instead his "Last Words" and there announced that the current issue of the review was to be the last.

IV

The announcement was sudden and to many, no doubt, unexpected. There had been no explicit indication in the review that its editor was contemplating an end to publication. But Eliot was too shrewd a critic—not least of all of his own work—to have failed to recognize that during its last several years the *Criterion* had lost much of the vitality that had previously distinguished it. He explained in his "Last Words" that during the final years of his editorship "a feeling of staleness has crept over me, and a suspicion that I ought to retire before I was aware that this feeling had communicated itself to the readers."[47] The freshness of the earlier volumes of the *Criterion* had been largely a function of its editor's intellectual curiosity, his willingness to entertain the positions of others, and his eagerness to follow his own attitudes to perhaps unanticipated conclusions. By the mid-thirties, however, his development had been largely achieved. Resting securely on his Christian faith, his attitudes became considerably less flexible; and the vitality of earlier years resolved itself into what was at worst a complacent dogmatism totally uncharacteristic of the tradition of the review.

In a 1946 speech Eliot described the *Criterion* as "a literary review which had clearly failed of its purpose several years before events brought it to an end." It is difficult to quarrel with his judgment. The earlier excellence of the review, he said, had been its "common concern for the highest standards both of thought and of expression," its "common curiosity and openness of mind to new

47. "Last Words," *Criterion* 18 (1939), 269.

ideas." Among the contributors there had been a shared belief "that it was our business not so much to make any particular ideas prevail, as to maintain intellectual activity on the highest level." Eliot went on to describe the later history of the review:

I do not think that *The Criterion*, in its final years, wholly succeeded in living up to this ideal. I think that in the later years it tended to reflect a particular point of view, rather than to illustrate a variety of views on that plane. But I do not think that this was altogether the fault of the editor: I think that it came about partly from the pressure of circumstances.[48]

The "particular point of view" that the *Criterion* reflected in its final years was, of course, its editor's; and that Christian perspective seemed to allow all too little for the curiosity and openness of mind once so distinctive there.

In announcing the termination of the *Criterion*, Eliot pointed out that he had been contemplating such an action for some two years; he had apparently sensed the "staleness" of his review as early as 1937. By 1939, however, his own sense of its literary failings was compounded by his sense of the *Criterion*'s inadequacy to the rapidly deteriorating European situation. Clearly, those circumstances figured centrally in Eliot's decision to draw the review to an end.

In the present state of public affairs—which has induced in myself a depression of spirits so different from any other experience of fifty years as to be a new emotion—I no longer feel the enthusiasm necessary to make a literary review what it should be.

During the autumn of 1938, he remarked, "the prospect of war had involved me in hurried plans for suspending publication; and in the subsequent *détente* I became convinced

48. "The Unity of European Culture," an appendix in *Notes Towards the Definition of Culture* (London: Faber and Faber, 1948), pp. 117, 118.

that my enthusiasm for continuing the editorial work did not exist."[49]

The *Criterion* was in many respects a journal *entre deux guerres*. It began publication after the First World War with the hope that there was place for a distinguished review of international arts and letters in a world that would never be tortured by another war. As his editorship continued, however, Eliot found himself trying to accommodate his review to the religious responsibilities he had by then accepted. The difficulties of that accommodation and the growing pressure of contemporary events increasingly called into question the viability of his enterprise. In his "Last Words" Eliot described the uneasiness he had lately felt as editor:

I have felt obscurely during the last eight years or so—and how obscure and confused my own mind has been, my Commentaries bear painful witness—the grave dangers to this country which might result from the lack of any vital political philosophy, either explicit or implicit. . . . For myself, a right political philosophy came more and more to imply a right theology—and right economics to depend upon right ethics: leading to emphases which somewhat stretched the original framework of a literary review. . . . I have wondered whether it would not have been more profitable, instead of trying to maintain literary standards increasingly repudiated in the modern world, to have endeavoured to rally intellectual effort to affirm those principles of life and policy from the lack of which we are suffering disastrous consequences. But such a task, again, would be outside the scope of *The Criterion,* would require the whole of the editor's time, and probably a more competent editor: this is perhaps another indication that *The Criterion* has served its purpose.[50]

The *Criterion* had, in fact, served at least two purposes. During its seventeen years, it had afforded a regular oppor-

49. "Last Words," pp. 274, 269.
50. Ibid., pp. 272–73.

tunity for contributors and readers to come together and share their common intellectual and literary concerns. In a period marked by many brilliant, but short-lived, reviews, Eliot's achieved a singular distinction coupled with remarkable longevity. But, no less important, the *Criterion* had served an immensely valuable and intensely personal function for its editor. During the period when Eliot's attitudes and interests were developing most rapidly, its regular appearance gave him an opportunity to explore and articulate the implications of that development. Both in his own contributions and in those he solicited from others, the *Criterion* provided a chronicle of Eliot's interests and attitudes. The file of the *Criterion* is, in fact, the closest approximation to an intellectual autobiography that this most reserved of men has left us.

Ultimately, as Eliot recognized, the two purposes came into conflict. His growing concern for religion and contemporary affairs was stretching the original framework of the review; to pursue those concerns as he felt he must was not appropriate to the *Criterion*. In choosing to terminate publication, he was not only bearing witness to the urgency of his religious calling, but also suggesting that he had outgrown the interests with which he had begun his editorship and which for many years had given the review its distinctive character. One may regret that Eliot felt it necessary to make such a choice; but it is equally important fully to recognize—as doubtless Eliot did—the implications of his decision.

In a very real sense, the end of the *Criterion* represented the end of a chapter in Eliot's career. It would, of course, be unreasonable to assert that it marked the end of his commitment to literature. But it did suggest that his future commitment would be different from that in the past—that he would often be writing more as a man of faith than as a man of letters, and that he would seek to reach audiences with whom he could not hope to communicate through the

Criterion. Liberated from the responsibilities of literary editorship, he was now free to pursue more extensively the other interests that he had embraced during the previous seventeen years.[51] As we have seen, one of those interests was the relation of religion and society. Another was the writing of verse drama. As if in testimony to the freedom that Eliot had achieved in January by terminating the *Criterion*, the year 1939 also saw the publication of his first book-length essay on Christian sociology and the production of his first play written expressly for the commercial stage.

51. One need hardly be reminded that Eliot's greatest poem, *The Four Quartets*, was completed during the early forties. The first of the "Quartets" appeared in 1936; the next three in 1940, 1941 and 1942, respectively. These poems, however, were in a sense incidental to Eliot's primary creative interest at the time, the drama. In a 1958 B.B.C. interview published after his death, Eliot explained that "the inspiration" for "Burnt Norton" "was certain lines which were cut out of the beginning of *Murder in the Cathedral*. The lines are not identically reproduced, but essentially they are the same. This was my first actual play, of course, and the producer pointed out to me that the lines were strictly irrelevant to the action and didn't get things forward. Well, those lines led to 'Burnt Norton'." Similarly, Eliot explained that he had wanted to continue writing plays after the production of *The Family Reunion* in 1939. "When I saw it produced I thought there were certain obvious faults of construction and I wanted to sit down and write immediately another play free from those faults. Well, the war came and I had other duties and things to do, and I was here and there, so I turned to writing the other three *Quartets*, and they occupied the war years very well. I was able in the conditions in which I was living to write poems of that type and length. When the war was over I wanted to turn again to write the play which I had planned to write in 1939" ("A Conversation, Recorded in 1958, Between T. S. Eliot and Leslie Paul," *Listener*, 11 September 1969, p. 335).

1939

POSTSCRIPT

THE NEW BEGINNING

Lacking "the enthusiasm necessary to make a literary review what it should be,"[1] Eliot closed down the *Criterion* in 1939. Seventeen years before, when he initiated his review, he had been full of enthusiasm for the enterprise; he had felt that through his editorship he could make an important contribution to that which then mattered most to him, literature. Over the years, however, he discovered that religion mattered more to him than literature and that the *Criterion* was an unsatisfactory medium for the pursuit of his new concern. As his enthusiasm for his review waned, other enthusiasms dawned; and Eliot turned eagerly to writing essays on religion and society and plays for the popular stage. Just as the termination of the *Criterion* in January marked the end of one phase of Eliot's career, the appearance later that year of *The Idea of a Christian Society* and *The Family Reunion* marked the beginning of another.

Like many essays by Eliot published after 1930, *The Idea of a Christian Society* was originally prepared as a series of lectures—in this case for delivery during March 1939 at Corpus Christi College, Cambridge. His use of the lecture platform to announce his convictions was by then hardly remarkable; he had, a number of years earlier, overcome his passion for impersonality in order to reach as broad an audience as possible with his religious message. What is especially noteworthy about *The Idea of a Christian Society,* however, is the care and wide reading he brought to this, his first extended consideration of the relations of religion and society. While most of his earlier

1. "Last Words," *Criterion* 18 (1939), 274.

speeches had been merely published without revision, his Cambridge lectures were substantially revised and amplified by extensive notes before their publication as a book.[2] Liberated now from the burden of putting out the *Criterion*, Eliot was free to lavish considerable attention on matters of more profound urgency to him.

Just as the contemporary political situation had been an important factor in Eliot's decision to terminate the *Criterion*, it also figured centrally in his approach to the Cambridge lectures. "Deeply shaken by the events of September 1938," he said that he had been brought to "a profounder realisation of a general plight."

It was not a disturbance of the understanding: the events themselves were not surprising. Nor, as became increasingly evident, was our distress due merely to disagreement with the policy and behaviour of the moment. The feeling which was new and unexpected was a feeling of humiliation, which seemed to demand an act of personal contrition, of humility, repentance and amendment; what had happened was something in which one was deeply implicated and responsible. It was not, I repeat, a criticism of the government, but a doubt of the validity of a civilisation. We could not match conviction with conviction, we had no ideas with which we could either meet or oppose the ideas opposed to us. Was our society, which had always been so assured of its superiority and rectitude, so confident of its unexamined premisses, assembled round anything more permanent than a

2. The twenty-two pages of notes (following the sixty pages of text) are valuable for their qualifications and elaborations of Eliot's remarks in his lectures. Like the notes to *The Waste Land,* these may have been written to flesh out a thin volume; but, like those to the poem, these notes are useful in suggesting the sources of many of Eliot's ideas. He was candid about the eclecticism of his lectures. "To aim at originality," he wrote in the preface, "would be an impertinence: at most, this essay can be only an original arrangement of ideas which did not belong to me before and which must become the property of whoever can use them." Eliot specifically acknowledged his debt to the writing of four men: V. A. Demant, Christopher Dawson, John Middleton Murry, and Jacques Maritain. All four had been contributors to the *Criterion.*

congeries of banks, insurance companies and industries, and had it any beliefs more essential than a belief in compound interest and the maintenance of dividends? Such thoughts as these formed the starting point, and must remain the excuse, for saying what I have had to say.[3]

Such thoughts had also been increasingly apparent elsewhere in Eliot's recent writing. Crystallized by the general deterioration in international affairs, they led to his melancholy description of the contemporary situation. "The problem of leading a Christian life in a non-Christian society is now very present to us. It is not merely the problem of a minority in a society of *individuals* holding an alien belief. It is the problem constituted by our implication in a network of institutions from which we cannot dissociate ourselves: institutions the operation of which appears no longer neutral, but non-Christian" (22). At the root of the problem lay the bankruptcy of values that Eliot attributed to the liberalism of modern society. Liberalism, he explained, "is a movement not so much defined by its end, as by its starting point; away from, rather than towards, something definite" (15). In terms that recalled his attack on humanism a decade earlier, he described the consequences of the prevailing philosophy:

By destroying traditional social habits of the people, by dissolving their natural collective consciousness into individual constituents, by licensing the opinions of the most foolish, by substituting instruction for education, by encouraging cleverness rather than wisdom, the upstart rather than the qualified, by fostering a notion of *getting on* to which the alternative is a hopeless apathy, Liberalism can prepare the way for that which is its own negation: the artificial, mechanised or brutalised control which is a desperate remedy for its chaos (16).

3. *The Idea of a Christian Society* (London: Faber and Faber, 1939), pp. 63–64. Subsequent references, inserted in the text, will be to this edition.

To Eliot's mind, the alternatives were clear. "The choice before us is between the formation of a new Christian culture, and the acceptance of a pagan one" (13). "It is only by returning to the eternal source of truth that we can hope for any social organisation which will not, to its ultimate destruction, ignore some essential aspect of reality" (63). The reader was hardly surprised to learn that Eliot held Christianity to be that source of truth. But his further description of a society organized on that faith marked a significant extension of the largely diagnostic essays he had published thus far. In his writing in the *Criterion* he felt that he could, at most, offer criticisms of the existing order. In *The Idea of a Christian Society* he went on to suggest the shape of a new and better order, "the only hopeful course for a society which would thrive and continue its creative activity in the arts of civilisation" (24).

Eliot insisted that he was not concerned in his book "with the means by which a Christian society could be brought about" (48). Instead, he confined himself to setting forth the *idea* of such a society, "something that can only be found in an understanding of the end to which a Christian Society, to deserve the name, must be directed" (8).[4] The Christian Society, he said, would be one "in which the natural end of man—virtue and well-being in community—is acknowledged for all, and the supernatural end—beatitude—for those who have the eyes to see it" (34).

Eliot envisaged three elements in his Christian Society: the Christian State, the Christian Community, and the

4. In his notes Eliot said: "In using the term 'Idea' I have of course had in mind the definition given by Coleridge, when he lays down at the beginning of his *Church and State* that: 'By an idea I mean . . . that conception of a thing, which is not abstracted from any particular state, form or mode, in which the thing may happen to exist at this or that time; nor yet generalised from any number or succession of such forms or modes; but which is given by knowledge of its ultimate aim' " (p. 67).

Community of Christians. The first he described as "the Christian Society under the aspect of legislation, public administration, legal tradition, and form" (26). "It is not primarily the Christianity of the statesmen that matters, but their being confined, by the temper and traditions of the people which they rule, to a Christian framework within which to realise their ambitions and advance the prosperity and prestige of their country" (27). The second element, the Christian Community, consists of "the great mass of humanity whose attention is occupied mostly by their direct relation to the soil, or the sea, or the machine, and to a small number of persons, pleasures and duties." Since "their capacity for *thinking* about the objects of faith is small," he suggested that for the Christian Community "their Christianity may be almost wholly realised in behaviour: both in their customary and periodic religious observances, and in a traditional code of behaviour towards their neighbors" (28–29).

It was the third element, however, the Community of Christians, that was central to Eliot's scheme. "These will be consciously and thoughtfully practising Christians, especially those of intellectual and spiritual superiority" (35). It would be they, in fact, who would give the Christian Society its direction:

The Community of Christians is not an organisation, but a body of indefinite outline; composed of both clergy and laity, of the more conscious, more spiritually and intellectually developed of both. It will be their identity of belief and aspiration, their background of a common system of education and a common culture, which will enable them to influence and be influenced by each other, and collectively to form the conscious mind and the conscience of the nation (42).

Had his Christian Society been more than an ideal, Eliot would have been a member of this Community of Christians. But even in the current, secular society he would try to serve a similar function—"to form the conscious mind and the conscience of the nation."

The Idea of a Christian Society is a remarkable summary of the concern for society and religion that Eliot had developed during the previous two decades. It is remarkable, further, for the way in which it points the direction of much of his subsequent prose writing. Yet it is perhaps more notable as a document in the study of Eliot's career than it is as an essay in religious sociology. The sincerity of his concern and the passion of his conviction are apparent throughout the book. But the precise character of his alternative to the "liberalism" of modern thought is not at all certain. "We may say that religion, as distinguished from modern paganism, implies a life in conformity with nature," he explained (61).

We need to know how to see the world as the Christian Fathers saw it; and the purpose of reascending to origins is that we should be able to return, with greater spiritual knowledge, to our own situation. We need to recover the sense of religious fear, so that it may be overcome by religious hope (62).

Such statements, however, are evocative rather than definitive; and the fact that Eliot rarely goes beyond the one to the other points to the fundamental weakness of his socioreligious prose. So far as he saw himself in the orthodox tradition of those Christian Fathers, perhaps he felt it unnecessary to describe more precisely the content of his faith. But so far as he hoped to convert to that faith a world increasingly separated from it, his lack of specificity seriously diminishes the impact of his argument.

Though he had by 1939 written often on such matters, Eliot was not then—nor would he ever become—a scholar of politics, economics, sociology, or theology. "This is a subject," he said at the beginning of his book, "which I could, no doubt, handle much better were I a profound scholar in any of several fields. But," he added, "I am not writing for scholars, but for people like myself" (7). His *Criterion* "Commentaries" and essays, his B.B.C. talks, his addresses to gatherings of the faithful were, likewise, addressed to people like himself—conscientious, concerned people; people uneasy with the course of contemporary society; people willing and perhaps even predisposed to entertain the alternative possibilities of Christian faith.

But there were, additionally, the many for whom Eliot's exposition of Christianity was not so clearly attractive and who were perhaps more amused or irritated than touched by his explicitly religious writing. Naturally, he hoped to reach them too—if not directly through Christian polemics, then indirectly through imaginative literature. The same year that saw the termination of the *Criterion* and the publication of *The Idea of a Christian Society* also saw the production of *The Family Reunion*. In his Cambridge lectures Eliot had been addressing a largely academic audience; in his earlier plays, *The Rock* and *Murder in the Cathedral,* he had written for specifically religious occasions. He had still to reach the "large and miscellaneous" audience that had long attracted him. *The Family Reunion* was the first of four plays he wrote expressly for the commercial stage. Behind all four lay the desire, hardly fulfilled in a Sadler's Wells benefit performance or at the Canterbury Festival, to have "a part to play in society as worthy as that of the music-hall comedian."

In 1926 Eliot had observed that "dramatic form may occur at various points along a line the termini of which are liturgy and realism."[5] His first two efforts at the drama tended toward liturgy, a tendency entirely appropriate for the religious audiences for whom he was then writing. However, the more heterogeneous audience he now sought would be less ready to accept such a liturgical framework; and he recognized the need to join his religious concerns

5. "Introduction," to *Savonarola: A Dramatic Poem* by Charlotte Eliot (London: Cobden-Sanderson, 1926), p. x.

and liturgical forms with the realism generally expected on the modern stage. To aspire to realism, however, did not for Eliot imply the abandoning of verse in his plays. For him, the verse was integral to the religious impact he hoped to achieve; in all of his plays, the moments of profoundest spiritual insight are also the moments of his most intense poetry. His challenge in *The Family Reunion,* then, was to bring together the ritual of religious experience and the poetry of spiritual understanding with the reality of contemporary life. Describing his goals for the play (and, implicitly, for the three plays that followed), he said:

People are prepared to put up with verse from the lips of personages dressed in the fashion of some distant age: therefore they should be made to hear it from people dressed like ourselves, living in houses and apartments like ours, and using telephones and motor cars and radio sets. . . . What we have to do is to bring poetry into the world in which the audience lives and to which it returns when it leaves the theatre; not to transport the audience into some imaginary world totally unlike its own, an unreal world in which poetry is tolerated. What I should hope might be achieved, by a generation of dramatists having the benefit of our experience, is that the audience should find, at the moment of awareness that it is hearing poetry, that it is saying to itself: "*I* could talk in poetry too!" Then we should not be transported into an artificial world; on the contrary, our own sordid, dreary daily world would be suddenly illuminated and transfigured.[6]

Eliot's aspiration to illuminate and transfigure the quotidian world of his audience was fundamentally, of course, a religious goal; he hoped to "convert" his audience so that they would realize not only their capacity for talking in poetry but moreover their ability to perceive ways in which supernatural, spiritual experience informs the natural, secular world.

Though ostensibly the account of a family reunion in an

6. "Poetry and Drama," in *On Poetry and Poets* (New York: Farrar, Straus and Cudahy, 1957), p. 87.

English country home, this 1939 play was, in fact, a drama of spiritual conversion in which a young man gains a new perception of the supernatural and, as a consequence, sets out to follow what he takes to be his new religious vocation. In *Murder in the Cathedral,* of course, Eliot had also written a play of conversion and vocation; the pattern was hardly novel in 1939. What was distinctive about *The Family Reunion* was that Eliot now was seeking to present such experience to secular audiences. In part, his motive was the natural desire of the artist to share his work with as many people as possible. But more importantly his motive was religious, for his commitment to the commercial theater was part of his commitment as a Christian to share his understanding of the spiritual life. "What we have written," a character in *The Family Reunion* says, "is not a story of detection,/Of crime and punishment, but of sin and expiation." Hoping to attract his audiences with the excitement of the former, he presented moreover the edification of the latter. Unlike most of his prose writing, his plays for the commercial stage were rarely explicitly Christion because Eliot realized that his audiences were largely, at best, only nominally so. He was meeting them on their, rather than his, terms; and this development, seventeen years after the publication of *The Waste Land,* bespeaks the effect of Eliot's religious conversion on his literary career.

But the political situation in the late thirties that had contributed to Eliot's decision to terminate the *Criterion* and to the inspiration behind *The Idea of a Christian Society* also had its impact on the play. As the prospect of British involvement in another war became more and more likely, the theater suffered increasingly. After opening in late March 1939 to mixed reviews, *The Family Reunion* was shortly closed—an early casualty of the war that had not yet begun. Nevertheless, its brief appearance on the London stage marked the commencement of a career in popular verse drama to which Eliot devoted most of his imaginative energies for the rest of his life. Like the decision to terminate the *Criterion*, and like the publication of *The Idea of a Christian Society*, the production in 1939 of *The Family Reunion* marked a new beginning for Eliot. Like the central characters of his plays, Eliot was working out his salvation with diligence.

INDEX

Action Française, 75, 87–99.
See also Maurras, Charles
L'Action Française et la Religion Catholique (Maurras), 91
Adelphi, 54–58
Agrarianism, 157–58, 192
Aiken, Conrad, 34
Aldington, Richard, 36n
American Criticism (Foerster), 116–17, 118, 123
Andrewes, Lancelot, 106–8, 188, 198–99
Aquinas, Saint Thomas, 61–66 passim
Arnold, Matthew, 23–24, 42n, 71, 72, 100
Aron, Robert, 157
The Art of Being Ruled (Lewis), 77, 79–81
Athenaeum, 13, 53
Auden, W. H., xiv, 34
L'Avenir de l'intelligence (Maurras), 43, 87–88, 93

Babbitt, Irving, 23, 25, 26, 66n, 77, 88n, 116, 118n, 125, 127, 139, 140, 141, 142, 145; compared to Benda, 42–44; Eliot's criticisms of, 96, 110–14, 128n, 173; on Eliot's criticisms, 115n; Eliot's debt to, 4–6, 9, 14, 16, 19, 111, 127–28, 137–38, 143n; ideas of, 6–9
Barfield, Owen, 166n

Barnes, J. S., 152–53
Baudelaire, Charles, 108–9
B. B. C. (British Broadcasting Corporation), 164–67
Beachcroft, T. O., 150
Belloc, Hilaire, 163, 166
Belphégor (Benda), 42–45
Benda, Julien, 42–45, 48, 77, 80, 99–101, 118
Bennett, Arnold, 34
Bergson, Henri, 81
Bernhardt, Sarah, 182
Blake, William, 27–29
Bookman, 96, 125n
Book of Common Prayer, 86
Bradley, F. H., 14, 108, 110, 147
Bramhall, John, 108
Broch, Hermann, 158
Brooks, Van Wyck, 17–18
Browne, E. Martin, 185–89

Canterbury Festival, 187–89
Catholicism (Roman): Eliot's early appreciation of, 16; Eliot on limitations of, 133–35; Lewis on, 82–83; and Maurras, 91–97; More criticizes, 133–35; related by Eliot to classicism, 12. *See also* Aquinas, Saint Thomas; Religion
Chesterton, G. K., 34, 119
Church, Richard, 34
Church of England: and economics, 198–99; Eliot joins,

219